# SPECULATIVE MARKETS

EXPERIMENTAL FUTURES: *Technological Lives, Scientific Arts, Anthropological Voices*
A series edited by Michael M. J. Fischer and Joseph Dumit

# SPECULATIVE MARKETS

## Drug Circuits and Derivative Life in Nigeria

*Kristin Peterson*

Duke University Press   Durham and London   2014

© 2014 Duke University Press

All rights reserved

Printed and bound by CPI Group (UK) Ltd, Croydon, CR0 4YY

Designed by Courtney Leigh Baker

Typeset in Arno Pro and Univers by Westchester Book Group

Library of Congress Cataloging-in-Publication Data

Peterson, Kristin, 1966–

Speculative markets : drug circuits and derivative life in Nigeria / Kristin Peterson.

pages cm—(Experimental futures : technological lives, scientific arts, anthropological voices)

Includes bibliographical references and index.

ISBN 978-0-8223-5693-6 (cloth : alk. paper)

ISBN 978-0-8223-5702-5 (pbk. : alk. paper)

1. Pharmaceutical industry—Nigeria.   2. Free enterprise—Nigeria.   I. Title.   II. Series: Experimental futures.

HD9673.N5P47 2014

381'.45615109669—dc23

2014000763

Cover art: A pharmacy in Lagos, Nigeria. AP Photo/Sunday Alamba.

# CONTENTS

In the early 1990s, I obtained a bachelor's degree in biology from the University of California, Santa Barbara. The United States was emerging out of the 1980s Reagan era, characterized by late capitalist flexibility and anticommunism, each of which had profoundly different impacts within the country. During the 1980s, manufacturing industries in the Midwest and on the East Coast were steadily going bust as corporations went overseas in search of lower manufacturing and labor costs. The state of California remained afloat partly because of defense industry subsidies that leaked into other areas, including public education. But by the early 1990s a recession had hit California, leaving thousands jobless.

I attempted to get an entry-level research job at the university, but grant money for such positions had evaporated the year I graduated. And so, like other newly graduated biology majors, I joined the migration to Silicon Valley in search of a job in the emerging life-sciences industry, which was flooded with new money from investors. One strategy used by the investment community to seduce these new sources of funds was to generate plenty of hype that guaranteed new breakthrough products; future exorbitant earnings promised a way out of the stagnation that had characterized the industry in the early 1980s.

I got a job in no time, thanks to the temporary work agencies that catered to creating the long-term temporary work force typical of this period. The temp agency made more money per hour for my labor than I did, and I remained a temp throughout my fourteen-month stay. Yet I felt lucky. After searching six months for a job, I had been hired not at one of the biotech start-up companies that no longer exist but rather with a well-established one—Genentech—which is now owned by Roche, and I worked in a quality control microbiology lab. Genentech is well known for being the very first biotechnology company to provide an initial public offering on the stock market: that is, it "went public," in 1980. This was preceded by an important U.S. Supreme Court decision, *Diamond v. Chakrabarty*, which permitted for the first time the patenting of genetically modified organisms. Indeed, the use of patent protection from this point on gave the biotech industry enough stability to jump-start it as well as allowing the drug industry to be completely tied to the speculative marketplace, where the industry's future could be traded on the NASDAQ.

The time I spent working at Genentech and living in San Francisco was full of contradictions. Company lavishness and management hype regarding the high status of Genentech within the biotech world was offset by the relative poverty I would return home to at night in the Mission District of San Francisco. There was a stark contrast between the world of recession and the world of abundant investor money swirling within, yet confined to, a few industries. It was not until the late 1990s when these contradictions would kick in, as property values skyrocketed and many start-up biotech firms went bankrupt. There was a massive remaking of San Francisco during this period. While dot-coms and biotech companies went bust, the city rid itself of its poor and, indeed, many of its middle-class residents. It is remarkable that an entire U.S. city can now welcome only the most affluent.

While I worked at Genentech, my routine was to take BART, the Bay Area's public transportation system, from 24th Street in San Francisco to Glen Park. There I picked up a corporate shuttle that would take workers to different companies in the area. One day on the bus, I sat next to a man who worked at a firm called Shaman Pharmaceuticals, a start-up that relied on the stock market to raise research funds. He was laid back in a way that defied the corporate culture of these places, despite the fact that it entertained plenty of alternative types who seemed to have gotten somewhat lost in the woods. The name "Shaman" caught my attention, and we got to talking. Shaman's methodology was to travel to rain forests, consult with shamans on medicinal plants, collect samples, patent biologically active ingredients, and embark on ambitious research agendas. This was the moment that intellectual property law began to pique my interest, just a few years before the World Trade Organization "harmonized" it across nation-states. I left Genentech and earned a master's degree in women's studies at San Francisco State University, focusing on Shaman—partly in an attempt to get a handle on how to think about science (through a transnational, postcolonial, and feminist lens) instead of doing science and partly to digest more fully what I had experienced in the biotech industry.

A few years later, in the late 1990s, I left San Francisco and began graduate school in anthropology at Rice University. A number of events and circuitous routes led me to the expansive pharmaceutical market in Lagos. My dissertation research focused on AIDS policies at the time. Because of this work, I was hired by the Futures Group, based in Washington, D.C., as a consultant to study access to HIV/AIDS drugs in Nigeria. I conducted this project jointly with Olatubosun "'Tubosun" Obileye, a Lagos-based pharmacist and former staff member of Médecins Sans Frontières (Doctors Without Borders). The focus of the project was almost entirely on AIDS and AIDS-related drugs, which were scarce at the time. When they were available, they mostly circulated within donor programs and not private drug markets. 'Tubosun urged that the project should consider conducting research on the private drug markets in order to see what kind of synergy the two spheres—private drug circulation and drug distribution by the state and nongovernmental organizations—might have on access to HIV/AIDS drugs.

Because I knew next to nothing about pharmaceuticals in the private sector, the first thing I did was to search the stacks in the Lagos medical libraries (specifically, those of the Nigerian Institute of Medical Research and the University of Lagos). I came across shocking research conducted by academic pharmacists, life science researchers, and physicians that revealed the striking levels of disease resistant to the most common and affordable drugs, the high and wildly varying numbers of substandard and fake drugs circulating in unofficial markets, the incredible rates of patients' self-medication, and endless debates about what was consistently referred to as a "chaotic drug distribution system." But I also discovered that the Nigerian pharmaceutical landscape was not always like this, that the drug market was once home to brand-name drug manufacturers that commanded a booming, thriving market. I wanted to know more about how such radical changes within a national market could take place in a mere decade. With each trip to the library, I collected stacks of periodicals several feet high, hoping that the electricity would remain on long enough (or that it would return after a long blackout) so I could get photocopies. When the power was out, an occasional kind librarian would allow me to take as many periodicals as I could carry. I would then flag down an *okada* (motorcycle taxi) and go to a nearby business center, usually a small shop piloted by a generator, where I would have photocopies made.

The vast drug markets I encountered during these library trips did not exist until the 1980s, when Nigeria's economy was being restructured according to the mandates of the International Monetary Fund and was quickly taking a radical turn for the worst. It was hard to imagine what life was like then in formerly noncommercial neighborhoods that are now packed with constantly pumping markets and unceasing commercial activity. These neighborhoods were essentially remade, not in the same way that San Francisco was reconfigured to usher in an almost exclusively wealthy set of residents but to accommodate the country's newly impoverished people after the implementation of a structural adjustment program. My experience made one thing clear: at the same moment I was temping my way through biotech's self-assured and speculative future, the Nigerian brand-name drug market was crashing. How these phenomena were ultimately tied together is a primary subject of this book.

When I arrived at Rice University, I knew I wanted to think about the future of drug development through the lens of political economy. The problem was that I did not really have a framework, much less training, for going about that methodologically. But when I read *Anthropology as Cultural Critique* for the first time, the following passage struck me:

> What we have in mind is a text that takes as its subject not a concentrated group of people in a community affected in one way or another by political economic forces, but "the system" itself—the political and economic processes spanning different locales or even different continents. Ethnographically, these processes are registered in the activities of dispersed groups or individuals whose actions have mutual, often unintended consequences for each other, as they are connected by markets and other major institutions that make the world a system. Pushed by the holism goal of ethnography beyond the conventional community setting of research, these ideal experiments would try to devise texts that combine ethnography and other analytical techniques to grasp whole systems, usually represented in impersonal terms, and the quality of lives caught up in them. These are the truly ambitious experiments in the political-economy vein. (Marcus and Fischer 1986, 91)

Since then George Marcus, Michael Fischer, Kim Fortun, Anna Tsing, Arjun Appardurai, Akhil Gupta, and James Ferguson, among others, have hammered out and refined just how to ethnographically capture "the system itself." With my ethnographic focus on the distribution systems of pharmaceutical markets, the challenge has not been about bridging the often wide gap found between complex and intangible macro economic systems and the quotidian, hidden, and often nuanced things that people do to make markets work. After I had made several trips, it became relatively easy to see the structure of Lagos drug markets as simultaneously urban, regional, and transnational—but only because actors working in or through these markets consistently imagined and described them as such. Although they taught me how things worked and provided very strong opinions about the implications of market dynamics, I still needed to do a great deal of conceptual and analytical work at other scales.

One scaling challenge was to understand how disparate yet simultaneous events could produce unexpected convergences that generate long-term market patterns. For example, speculative practices in the drug industry (such as massive mergers and investing in high-risk biotech companies), as well as lateral arbitrage strategies that speculate on wild currency fluctuations in unofficial Nigerian drug markets, must be understood alongside each other even though they emerge in different contexts. The reason for this is not because they sound like similar practices; rather, it is because they are two reverberations occurring in a volatile transcontinental supply chain.

Beyond event and place as objects to be scaled, it was also important to capture and represent temporal scales. Drug traders, pharmacists, regulators, and industry workers always marked their analyses of drug circulation against very specific historical events dating from the early post-colonial period up to the present. They helped me understand how events occurring at very different times, such as the Nigerian civil war (late 1960s) and brand-name pharmaceutical company divestment out of Nigeria (mid 1990s) converged in ways that materialized in the current dynamics of Nigerian drug markets.

A multi-scalar ethnographic project of this sort does not simply capture how the thing or the idea exists within a larger world system. Rather, objects of study may have disparate multiple lives or expressions. High levels of fake drugs in Nigeria, for example, do not simply reveal a problem with pharmaceutical regulation, which can lead scholars to conclude that the African state is "failed" or "weak." Instead, the making of fake drugs is largely an outcome of drug prices and global market volatility. In this sense, recent and historical propulsions of capital (such as past market dispossession and current downward pricing pressures) largely drive fake drug production, which makes it not that different from regulated drug economies. In order to capture these dynamics methodologically, regulation and its link to the state must be brought into the realm of chemistry, geopolitics, and market logics. My experiment here is to think about how the thing or the idea articulates at scales beyond their linear paths and trajectories of event, place, and time. By exploring anthropological "third spaces" (Fischer, 1–27), I hope to "discover new paths of connection and association by which traditional ethnographic concerns with agency, symbols, and everyday practices can continue to be expressed on a differently configured spatial canvas" (Marcus 1995, 98).

Tracking what happened in San Francisco here in this preface and what happened in Lagos throughout the rest of this book is part of this pursuit. At the same time as the California economy struggled to resurrect itself via an industry that never produced a significant therapeutic revolution, the postcolonial dreams of an equally promising Nigerian pharmaceutical future were sacrificed in the name of speculative pursuits.

# ACKNOWLEDGMENTS

This book emerged during many years of hits and misses, comings and goings. It was not directly funded by any particular organization because the project materialized as a spin-off of other funded research trips to Lagos. I am very thankful to the following institutions for providing research funds to Nigeria since January 2000: the Institute for the Study of World Politics, in Washington, D.C.; the Lodieska Stockbridge Vaughn Dissertation Fellowship at Rice University; the Center for Afroamerican and African Studies at the University of Michigan; the Intramural Research Grants Program at Michigan State University; and the National Science Foundation's Science and Society Program.

*Speculative Markets* exists because many generous people shared their time and intellectual gifts with me. My deepest gratitude goes to Olatubosun Obileye, who introduced me to the world of Nigerian pharmaceuticals. I could not have written this book without his guidance, nor without the company of his wife, Doo, and their three lovely girls. Morenike Ukpong, my long-term research partner based at Obafemi Awolowo University; and Johnson Ekpere, who was my advisor during my first long-term stay in Nigeria, at the University of Ibadan, and his wife, Marie Ekpere, have been sources of intellectual and familial support when I have been far from home.

I am especially grateful to Fola Tayo, who provided great friendship, supported my project, and helped me gain access to the University of Lagos's medical library. Ifeanyi Atueyi, editor in chief of *Pharmanews*, the Nigerian pharmaceutical industry's leading newsmagazine, generously allowed me access to the publication's archives. Kunle Okelola of the Pharmaceutical Manufacturers Group of the Manufacturers Association of Nigeria assisted me in accessing pharmaceutical industrial history. Ahmed T. Mora at the Pharmacists Council of Nigeria helped me with archival research. Charles

Bassey facilitated my access to the library at the Central Bank in Abuja. Eva Edwards at NAFDAC generously facilitated research access. Special appreciation goes to Mr. Bongo Records, which agreed to reprint lyrics from the album *Seun Kuti + Fela's Egypt 80*.

Friends and colleagues in Lagos offered me tremendous insights into the workings of health care systems, economic markets, and the pharmaceutical industry. I especially thank those who let me into their working lives and who took time to explain the dynamics of the pharmaceutical market in Nigeria. I do not name them here in order to protect their confidentiality, but I could not have written this book without their tremendous kindness and patience. I am highly indebted to them.

I am very appreciative of those in Nigeria who have provided friendship and care over the years: Kemi Ailoje, Olayide Akanni, Ibrahim Atta, John Cashin, Wole and Bisi Daini, Fijagbade Onaopepo Damilare, Christy Ekerete-Udofia, Bede Eziefule, Bode-Law Faleyimu, Omololu Falobi, Jane Galton, Stella Iwuagwu, Jerome Mafeni, Tony Marinho, Pat Matemilola, Alex Muoka, Kent Nnadozie, Emeka Nsofor, Luqman Obileye, Odia Ofeimun, Dan Ogwu, Ifeanyi Okekearu, Pat Okekearu, Yemisi Ransome-Kuti, Bankole Sodipo, Peter Ujoma, Jens Wenkel, and Nnamdi Wosu. Special thanks go to Janice Olawoye, Austine Offor, and Uju Ogonu, who gave me tremendous assistance in getting settled in Lagos. Janice Olawoye facilitated my affiliation with the Department of Agricultural Extension and Rural Studies of the University of Ibadan as well as my access to libraries at nearby institutions. My cousin, Father Bill Peterson, always generously provided me a place to stay at his seminary during all my visits to Ibadan. Uju Ogonu and Austine Offor helped me find and set up a home when I first arrived in Lagos. Rolake Odetoyinbo graciously provided camaraderie and a place to stay on subsequent summer visits. I greatly appreciate all of them.

Victoria Bernal, Tom Boellstorff, Sean Brotherton, Jae Chung, Joe Dumit, Michael M. J. Fischer, Kim Fortun, Angela Garcia, Jeremy Greene, Nancy Rose Hunt, Julie Livingston, Lilith Mahmud, George Marcus, Keith Murphy, Vinh-Kim Nguyen, Kaushik Sunder Rajan, and anonymous reviewers at Duke University Press read partial or full drafts of the book. I could not have worked through the rather complex issues discussed here without their very caring guidance and friendship.

I presented parts of this manuscript at several venues, and I am indebted for the feedback I received on those occasions: the Knowledge/Value

Property Workshop at the University of California, Davis (April 2013); the "Speculation" Keywords Roundtable, Women Studies Department at the University of California, Irvine (February 2013); the Medicine, Body and Practice Workshop and the Law, Culture and Society Workshop at the University of Chicago (November 2011); the Publics of Public Health Conference in Kilifi, Kenya (December 2009); and the Authority of Science in Africa Workshop at the Max Planck Institute, in Halle, Germany (June 2009). Special thanks go to Brenna Bhandar, Melinda Cooper, Judy Farquhar, Steve Feierman, Wenzel Geissler, Cori Hayden, Laura Kang, Guillaume Lachenal, Sabina Leonelli, Javier Lezaun, Manjari Mahajan, Clapperton Mavhunga, Meghan Morris, Ruth Prince, Peter Redfield, Justin Richland, Richard Rottenburg, Jeanne Scheper, Jenny Terry, Bertram Turner, and Susan Reynolds White.

This project put down its first roots in graduate school. While I was at San Francisco State University, I switched to a new field and learned a great deal from Inderpal Grewal, Minoo Moallem, Caren Kaplan, Eric Smoodin, and the graduate students in the Department of Women Studies. When I relocated to Rice University, I worked closely with George Marcus, Hannah Landecker, Elias Bongmba, Benjamin Lee, and most especially the very generous Jim Faubion. They were all exceptionally caring and supportive mentors. I am very fortunate that George Marcus is now my good comrade in the Department of Anthropology at the University of California, Irvine. I also benefited from numerous intellectual dialogues that occurred in cafes, enthusiastic writing groups, living rooms late at night, and Houston ice houses with: Michael Adair-Kriz, Jae Chung, Denise Coleman, W. R. Duell, Arial Espino, Andrea Frolic, Jennifer Hamilton, Hank Hancock, Chuck Jackson, Lamia Karim, Chris Kelty, Shannon Leonard, Carolyn Jean McGoran, Nahal Naficy, Valerie Olson, Aimee Placas, Brian Riedel, Pat Seed, Kayte Young.

As a Dubois-Mandela-Rodney postdoctoral fellow at the Department of Afroamerican and African Studies of the University of Michigan, I had fabulous intellectual stimulation: Lori Brooks, David Cohen, Mamadou Diouf, Freida Ekotto, Amal Fadlalla, Kevin Gaines, Francoise Hamlin, Nancy Hunt, Sean Jacobs, Nick King, Elisha Renne, Julius Scott, Howard Stein. At Michigan State University, where I worked in the Department of Anthropology, I gladly thank the following: Nwando Achebe, Sean Brotherton, Laurent DuBois, Kiki Edozie, Mara Leichtman, Sabrina McCormick, Folu Ogundimu, Zakia Salime.

I currently have the great fortune to be part of the vibrant, supportive, and intellectually rich Department of Anthropology at the University of California, Irvine. This project was not possible without the department members' collective will to be deeply invested in each other's work. Thanks to Victoria Bernal, Tom Boellstorff, Leo Chavez, Susan Coutin, Julia Elyachar, Robert Garfias, David Theo Goldberg, Angela Jenks, Karen Leonard, Lilith Mahmud, George Marcus, Bill Maurer, Michael Montoya, Keith Murphy, Valerie Olson, Roxanne Varzi, Mei Zhan, and the many graduate and undergraduate students who have taught me much since my arrival.

There are certainly many other important friendships and sources of intellectual engagement and great support in California and beyond that I have greatly appreciated over the years: Maylei Blackwell, Kevin Cartwright, Tim Choy, Marie de Cenival, Michael Dorsey, Corey Dubin, Lisa Finn, Erik Garcia, Nancy Giuliani, Avery Gordon, Crystal Griffith, Tiffany Willoughby Herard, Phoebe Hirsch, Harriet Hirschorn, Ogaga Ifowodo, Amy Jensen, Laura Johnson, Nina Jusuf, Arlene Keizer, Stacey Langwick, Metsi Makhetha, Chris Newfield, Teeny Parkinson, H. T. L. Quan, Nonie Reyes, Elizabeth and Cedric Robinson, Martha Sheldon, Suran Thrift, Meredeth Turshen, and Virginia Velez.

I am exceptionally grateful to Ken Wissoker, my editor at Duke University Press, who patiently waited for me to figure out what the book was about and who also graciously provided me with exceptional support, even when meeting deadlines seemed impossible to me. I am very lucky to be working with him. With deep gratitude I acknowledge Anitra Grisales, Jeanne Ferris, and S. K. Thrift for expert copyediting and indexing.

My immediate family—and the many wonderful members of my extended family—provided the usual joy and sustenance that one needs for these long hauls. Most especially, I have so much gratitude and appreciation to express to Stephen David Simon, whose sweet spirit has nourished me at every turn. He listened to me read extensive parts of the manuscript out loud, and he then skillfully helped me shape the text. He truly has a natural ability to be an unconditionally superb and loving human being. The book is for him.

## Chemical Multitudes

### Fake Drugs and Pharmaceutical Regulation in Nigeria

Holly Martins looked directly at Harry Lime and asked, "Have you ever visited the children's hospital? Have you ever seen any of your victims?"

"Victims?" replied Harry, pointing to the small children moving below them, appearing as small dots in the far distance. "Would you really feel any pity if one of those dots stopped moving forever? If I said you can have £20,000 for every dot that stops, would you really, old man, tell me to keep my money? Without hesitation?"

—*The Third Man*, directed by Carol Reed, 1949

### *The Problem of Chemical Multitudes*

Between April and August 1990 nearly a hundred infants and children mysteriously died of kidney failure in Plateau State, located in the central part of Nigeria. The Plateau State Ministry of Health, located in the city of Jos, issued a report that listed symptoms indicative of a severe hemorrhagic virus (Alubo 1994).[1] Toward the end of that period, a second wave of deaths occurred in Ibadan, Oyo State, located in southwest Nigeria. There, twenty-six children suffered many of the same symptoms, and twenty-four of them consequently died. Clinicians at the University of Ibadan apparently did not suspect a virus but rather a problem with the drugs they had administered

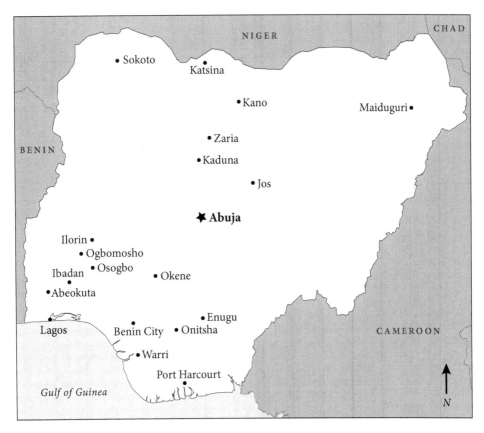

MAP I.1. **Nigeria.** © Daniel Dalet, d-maps.com.

to their young patients.[2] They found that when they withdrew paracetamol syrup (acetaminophen), an over-the-counter pain reliever from the treatment regimen, the symptoms immediately ceased (Alubo 1994).

A federal government study later confirmed these findings, as well as the source of the problem:

> all the paracetamol syrups were prepared in a Plateau State Government pharmacy, from where distribution was made to at least seven government hospitals where the medicine was administered to children.
>
> In the second reported case, the syrups was [sic] prepared in Oluyoro Catholic Hospital, Ibadan where it was administered to the children.
>
> ... the laboratory analysis of the sample of the second reported case has shown that one of the raw materials labeled and sold as *propylene glycol* was in fact *ethylene glycol*, which is known to be very poisonous and gives rise to kidney failure. (quoted in Alubo 1994, 100; his emphasis)

Remarkably, the report also tracked the source of ethylene glycol to a pharmaceutical company in Ibadan, which purchased the raw material from a supplier in Onitsha, in the southeastern part of the country. The chemical's label claimed to originate from the Netherlands. But S. Ogoh Alubo (1994), a medical sociologist, found in his own research that the Dutch company in question had ceased to exist two years prior to the incidents. In fact, the company was not a manufacturer, as the label indicated, but an international wholesale distributor. Ethylene glycol is about twenty times less expensive than propylene glycol, which suggests that it was probably intentionally mislabeled in order to gain a significant profit. The trail went cold after these discoveries; it was never determined who manufactured the chemical, who labeled it, and who distributed it.

As was the case in the classic British film noir *The Third Man*, which portrayed an underground trade in adulterated penicillin after World War II, the fake (intentionally adulterated) drugs that populate the Nigerian pharmaceutical landscape are often viewed only as a problem of sheer greed that distorts an otherwise legitimate trade.[3] In the Nigerian case, greed can be represented as signs of corruption and chronic underdevelopment. Yet events like those described above have occurred elsewhere in the past. The U.S. Food and Drug Administration came into being in 1937 under very similar circumstances: an anti-infective patent medicine made by Massengill had been formulated using diethylene glycol, a poisonous substance very similar to the one used in the paracetamol syrup in Nigeria. In the U.S. case, over a hundred people died throughout the South and the East Coast, generating a national outcry for better consumer protection laws (Carpenter 2010, 73–117). Although these incidents seem like horrors of a distant past to Americans, fake drugs entering the United States have recently caught the attention of the Food and Drug Administration. The agency recognizes the vulnerability of the U.S. pharmaceutical supply and has begun to reorient its approaches to try to regulate pharmaceutical industry offshoring and the transcontinental diffusion of the pharmaceutical supply chain. These activities make regulation highly difficult and therefore drastically complicate U.S. drug safety (U.S. Food and Drug Administration 2011 and 2013).

The same year that the Plateau and Oyo State deaths occurred, a new Nigerian drug regulatory agency, the National Agency for Food and Drug Administration and Control (NAFDAC), was getting newly established and so there were only nascent regulatory policies in place. Since that time, Nigerians have become fully aware of the problems with dangerous pharmaceuticals making their way into the national drug market. They have repeatedly demanded a better-quality drug supply. In turn, since the early 2000s NAFDAC has aggressively clamped down on every aspect of transnational supply, from production to retailing. Nevertheless, the quality of drugs cannot always be guaranteed. This is not due to problems of development, capacity, or know-how, as NAFDAC has received numerous international awards for the work it has done in the realm of fake drugs. Rather, the difficulty in regulating the pharmaceutical supply is a historical outcome of massive economic and structural changes that took place not only in African (and certainly European and North American) states, but also within the pharmaceutical industry.

The death of so many children due to harmful fake drugs occurred at the same moment when Nigeria's economy was spiraling downward as a result of tremendous state and market transformations. Just four years earlier, the country had implemented a structural adjustment program (SAP) that included a significant state and market austerity policy. Following the 1970s recession in the West and the collapse of commodity markets in Africa, implementation of SAP was insisted on by the International Monetary Fund and overseen by the World Bank in exchange for new loans to Nigeria, whose national economy became troubled after the collapse of an oil boom. Economic and state adjustments had profound negative consequences on African economies, including massive job loss, high inflation, and widespread poverty. At the same time, North American and European pharmaceutical companies were manufacturing and distributing drugs for the Nigerian market, then a highly significant one in terms of foreign sales. They abandoned this market when structural adjustment's worst effects kicked in. After the market for brand-name drugs crashed, a new market was built. Now the Nigerian market is a wholesale supplier for West and Central African private drug markets. The total national market value constitutes over $2 billion worth of generic drugs of varying and often low qualities, almost all of which move through unofficial channels.[4]

*Speculative Markets* is about West African pharmaceutical circulation that is integrated into transcontinental trade. It particularly situates the Nigerian drug market and its lively practices squarely in the context of speculative capital, manufacturing off-shoring, and drug marketing. In this regard, Nigeria's pharmaceutical market is also connected to U.S. economic changes since the 1970s–1980s—changes that favored the economic growth and long-term survival of the pharmaceutical and biotechnology industries. The book links market transformations that have occurred at different times and on separate continents to specific movements of capital and the practices of new market makers.[5] This is not only about how a once significant and formerly profitable African pharmaceutical industry collapsed in the face of economic reforms, nor how the American turn to speculative capital during the 1980s shifted transnational business strategies, creating intensified competition in the pharmaceutical industry. Concomitantly, the book shows how all of these occurrences are linked together and localized in the face-to-face exchanges at a major nodal point in Lagos, Nigeria.

One of the key issues arising out of these events is that the practices of a purely so-called legitimate trade and a black-boxed illicit one have become increasingly intermingled. Licit and illicit products are difficult to disentangle, as they may have the same manufacturing origins and travel along the same distribution routes. In both pharmaceutical production and distribution processes, various arbitrage and speculative practices are used to anticipate and bet on positive outcomes that can profitably move pharmaceuticals from producer to consumer. These speculative practices are integral to the licit production and distribution of pharmaceuticals. But they also encourage and fuel the proliferation of low-quality drugs in West

Africa. These blurred activities are a product of severe and chronic market volatility that resonates differently in the brand-name drug industry, Nigerian markets, and the transcontinental supply chain.

By the early 1990s the structure of the pharmaceutical market appeared out of control, as far as Nigerian government officials were concerned. Research studies and reports indicated that just a few years after the implementation of structural adjustment, fake drugs comprised 30–70 percent of the entire national drug market in Nigeria (Atueyi 2004, 38; Uwaezuoke 1991, 20). For this period, reports also indicated that fake drugs were sold in tens of thousands of illegal places in Lagos State (Itueyi 2004, 41). While current reports indicate that Nigeria's fake drug problem has declined since the 1990s, the United Nations recently declared that West Africa has the worst fake drug problem in the world (UNODC 2009). Presently, fake drugs comprise anywhere between 30 to 50 percent of the entire regional market (Yeboah 2013, 6; Taylor et al. 2001, 1934). [6] These numbers and declarations are epistemologically blurred because while fake drugs are perceived as prolific, their numbers cannot actually be counted or ascertained.

Such empirical elusiveness or "phantom epistemology" (Peterson 2009) is something that is both familiar and unknowable as discourse and cultural practice. Within Nigeria, there is a commonsense nature to stories, anecdotes, and rumor about fake drugs, which is very widespread and diffused across society. If one becomes ill after taking a drug, such an experience is almost always linked to "fake" drugs and few questions are asked about an allergic or adverse reaction to that drug. Or if a drug is perceived to not work, a lay diagnosis often blames fake drugs while few questions are asked about drug resistance—a serious widespread problem but one that is not nearly as well known as fake drugs.

While drugs have long been recognized as distinct technological objects in society that are embedded with plenty of social meaning,[7] these Nigerian examples point to significant ontological confusions over the actual substance and clinical meaning of drugs. This makes it easy to fall into a collective effort to complain about an acknowledged national problem such as fake drugs, while other issues like a significant dearth of diagnostic technologies (Okeke 2011) and widespread drug resistance (Lamikanra et al. 2011) remain obscured in such scenarios. Equally, I am interested in these unknowable aspects of drug chemistry in relation to those things that are known or discernible. The very quick circulation of anecdote and rumor about fake drugs and the quantification of drug chemistry in quality control tests each have a lot to say about pharmaceutical landscapes. Scaling the supposed knowns and unknowns in this manner hopefully destabilizes understandings of the empirical while offering new analytical openings into the issues at hand (Peterson 2009, 37–42).

In what follows, I discuss what happens to drugs once they enter Nigeria and, specifically, how fake drugs are dealt with at the level of regulation. NAFDAC encounters complex Nigerian politics because regulation is not purely about legal mandates pertaining to public safety but rather about moral authority and heavy-handed leadership. Although NAFDAC has been lauded for its efforts, I take it for granted that regulation is a near impossibility due to very specific market and political dynamics appearing at various points in the transcontinental supply chain. This introduction describes the social, political, and economic entanglements that characterize the final point of a drug's arrival in Nigerian pharmaceutical markets. The chapters that follow examine just how volatile markets and speculative practices created new transcontinental drug circuits that are now integral to the drug industry and people's lives in Nigeria.

## Fake and Substandard Drugs

On one of my first trips into Idumota market, one of the largest pharmaceutical markets in West Africa, I was with two long-time Lagos pharmacists, Toks and Abiodun.[8] They took me to visit Ikenna, a wholesale pharmaceutical trader, in his market stall. After much discussion of the day's news, the four of us began to talk about fake drugs in Nigeria. I asked Ikenna which products are usually faked.

"Movable products. Fast [selling] products," he said. He then pointed to a few shelves situated behind the wooden stool I was sitting on and said: "All these products are in the same [chemical] range. They are all the same product." Reaching past me, he pulled a boxed antibiotic—a combination of ampicillin and cloxacillin—off the shelf and handed it to me, saying, "For instance, now this is Ampiclox made by Beecham, that we are selling for 5,600 naira." He pulled another drug off the shelf and said: "And this is Ampiclox generic that we are selling for 400 naira.

The brand-name Beecham product is actually manufactured by Glaxo-SmithKline,[9] a brand-name multinational company based in the United Kingdom that is the highest-earning pharmaceutical company listed in the Nigerian stock exchange (Wambebe and Ochekpe 2011). The brand-name product Ikenna handed to me cost roughly $40, and the generic version cost about $3.

As I was translating naira to dollars in my head, Ikenna rhetorically asked: "Is it not the same chemical compound they used in producing the generic and the brand [-name product]?" He then said something that surprised me: "If somebody who wants to buy retail, he brings out his sachet [wallet] . . . and I can't sell this generic. It is the [brand-] name that is selling."

Abiodun immediately jumped into the conversation and said: "Let me tell you something. What he is saying is 100 percent right. Let me compare multivitamin syrup. It has been in the market years even before I was born [in the 1960s]. I remember when I was growing up I was using Multivite. That time there was a lot of advert [advertisements]." He sang the advertising jingle, "Multi, Multi, Multivite!" and then continued: "Compare Multivite to all other multivitamins in the market now. I can assure you that there are some multivitamins that are much more better than Multivite, but because Multivite has made a name—it is only selling its name."

In fact, people with very little money—especially those living with HIV or vulnerable to it, such as sex workers—had often told me while I was conducting research on HIV/AIDS in Nigeria that due to the presence of fake drugs, they prefer to buy brand-name products in spite of the higher cost. They imagine that companies such as Glaxo and Mulitivite's manufacturer have higher-quality products than other companies simply because they were present in the drug market long before fakes became a widespread problem.

Holding up my left hand, I said to Ikenna: "This is the generic." Holding up my right hand, I said: "This is the brand. Will they say the generic is fake because it is cheaper?"

"Some people will say it is fake because they don't know about drugs. But if the brand is fast-moving and sells at 5,600, [fake drug manufacturers] will sell it for lower."

At that point, Toks said to Ikenna: "Let me explain this fake very well." He took the Beecham brand-name Ampiclox out of my hand and asked: "If they take this one now, will they reduce the price if it is fake?"

"They will reduce the price." Pointing to the Beecham product, Ikenna said: "This one [is currently being faked and sold in markets]. It is selling for 1,000 [naira, about $8]."

"So people will rush and say it is the same Ampiclox?" Toks asked.

"They cannot differentiate [between fakes and] the original."

Those facilitating the entry of fake drugs into the country identify which "nonfake" drugs are selling quickly and well—what is commonly referred to as "fast-moving products"—in Nigeria and then place orders for those drugs with overseas manufacturers. Ikenna pointed out that the Beecham Ampiclox had been faked and was circulating in the market for about $8. Brand-name multinational companies like Glaxo bank on their reputation and on habitual prescribing and hospital stocking practices to sell their drugs rather than establishing competitive prices, which remain high compared to generic products on the market. Glaxo has more products for sale in Nigeria than any other brand-name multinational. Ampiclox is an older antibiotic to which most bacterial infections are largely resistant. Yet it is well recognized by the public and is a "fast mover." As Ikenna points out, this makes Beecham Ampiclox a prime candidate to be faked and sold in the market, especially given the fact that low price can be linked to a number of scenarios besides faking.

Although they initially arrived in small amounts, fake drugs began entering Nigeria as early as 1968, when Crown Agents, the main British company charged with national drug distribution since the colonial era, divested. Taking over distribution was the Pharmacists Board of Nigeria, a government agency (Atueyi 2004). Because it was saddled with other tasks, including regulation, it could not meet all the country's distribution needs. It turned distribution over to state governments, which issued patent medicine vendor licenses that were increasingly held by traders. There had been an extreme shortage of pharmacists since independence (Atueyi 2004) and so these licenses were meant to fill this gap. In Idumota market, traders hold patent medicine vendor licenses and import directly from pharmaceutical manufacturers. The increasing diffusion of wholesaling from a centralized body to multitudes of private trading companies was a result of both holdovers from the colonial infrastructure and state reforms in the 1980s. As a result, multiple paths to importation opened up new avenues to smuggle fake drugs into the country.

When fake drugs reach West Africa, they join legitimate generic drugs mostly imported from Asia as well as a smaller percentage of drugs manufactured by Nigerian companies. Fake drugs are quickly dispersed into the market and sold by pharmacists and wholesale pharmaceutical traders (sometimes mistakenly), roadside hawkers, travelling salesmen on buses, and patent medicine sellers in rural areas. In Nigeria many of these drugs are distributed through what are called "open" markets by regulators, which are nonregulated sites located in public yet unofficial market spaces that rapidly emerged and expanded in the immediate aftermath of state and market reforms. Once drugs pass through open markets, they are extremely difficult to trace, much less regulate.[10]

While fake drugs are highly patrolled, substandard drugs are not well regulated. Substandard drugs are not intentionally faked drugs, but ones that have too little or too much active ingredients as a result of shortfalls in the Nigerian or other manufacturing processes.[11] Both fake drugs and substandard ones pose threats to human health, and they cannot always be discerned from each other once they end up in Lagos wholesale markets and retail shops. For example, a story about malaria drugs in Lagos was reported in the national daily newspaper *The Punch,* which subsequently went viral on the Internet. The newspaper article was about a research publication by pharmaceutical chemist, Teddy Ehianeta and his colleagues (Ehianeta et al. 2012) at the University of Lagos. The researchers found that out of the thirteen antimalaria drugs they purchased from Lagos pharmacies, only 15 percent (two drugs) had the required amount of artesunate and amodiaquine, the active pharmaceutical ingredients (API) for standard malaria treatments (Ehianeta et al. 2012, 642).[12] Otherwise known as artemisinin-combination therapies, these chemicals compose the World Health Organization's recommended first-line therapy for malaria in Africa. The researchers, the media, and Internet discussions posited these results as a problem of fake drugs, with no attention given to other possibilities.

Ehianeta and his colleagues compared the weight of the API—amodiaquine and artesunate—listed on the label with the actual weight. To be considered a standard and efficacious product in Nigeria, the API should fall within 90–110 percent of the standard range. A substandard product may contain API that falls short of, or exceeds, this range. Five of these eleven contained inadequate amounts of one active ingredient and too much of another (for example, sample C had 127 percent of the proper amount of amodiaquine and 60 percent of that of artesunate). Four of them had an adequate amount of one ingredient and a low amount of the other (for example, sample F had 98 percent of amodiaquine and 71 percent of artesunate). One sample was on the low end for both (sample A had 76 percent of amodiaquine and 36 percent of artesunate). And one had too much of both (sample G had 134 percent of amodiaquine and 115 percent of artesunate) (Ehianeta et al. 2012, 639). How can these wide variations at both the low and high end of the API range be explained? It may be safe to say that sample A, the only one that had low amounts of both API, is fake. All other malaria drugs tested could be fake, but they could also be a result of shortcomings in the manufacturing process.

An academic pharmacist, Temi, explained to me that too much API is a usual problem for Nigerian manufacturers. Many manufacturing companies are over thirty years old. With very little available capital from financial institutions, a few have been refurbished but many have not, creating problems with manufacturing infrastructure. For example, if a company imports a secondhand scale and uses it for a long period, the weighing accuracy diminishes over time, and there are few auditing mechanisms for such equipment. Temi asserted that manufacturers actually anticipate this problem and do not want to be accused of including unacceptably low API because that would indicate faking. This means that local companies often add too much of the active ingredients to their drug products, which is considered legal although it is substandard. Unfortunately, the problem of fake drugs often overshadows these problems of "good manufacturing practices," which is industry language for very specific standard operating procedures that must be accurately followed in drug production and quality control audits throughout the manufacturing process. In the context of these multiple scenarios, Ehianeta and his colleagues lumped these chemical variations into one category: "fake drugs."

In turning to fake drugs as the primary site of regulation, NAFDAC did something throughout Nigeria that very few regulators around the globe have attempted: it shut down unofficial drug markets. In doing so, it ran a successful and rather stunning national public awareness campaign, but at the same time it put the national, and in effect, West African, drug distribution network at risk of collapsing.

*Drug Market Raids as Drug Regulation*

Professor Dora Akunyili was appointed director general of NAFDAC in 2001. Highly motivated by her own sister's death as a result of taking a fake drug, Akunyili started a very visible national campaign to confiscate and burn fake drugs, accompanied by great media attention and public displays of the drugs' destruction. She also rid the agency of perceived corruption by sacking some of the highest officials at the time, an act that was relatively rare and highly supported by the public. Her work received humanitarian awards and commendations from around the world, including *Time Magazine*'s 2006 "Eighteen Heroes of Our Time." She became a celebrity almost as soon as she took over the agency. During her tenure she was clearly one of the best-known civil servants to emerge in the period immediately after the end of several decades of military rule. The public celebrated her as the embodiment of a new democratic era.

NAFDAC launched massive awareness campaigns that educated the public on the fact that fake drugs—unlike other fake products such as knockoffs of Fendi bags and Samsung mobile phones—enter the human body and have toxic qualities. Drugs and the premises through which they travel must be regulated from the start of manufacturing to the purchase by the end user. A regulatory apparatus that oversees pharmaceuticals even into the postmarketing phase is required. NAFDAC also educated the public on how to tell whether a drug product was registered in Nigeria, by the agency's hologram seal on the packaging: if there is no hologram, the drug should be considered fake. Stricter drug regulation rules and inspection requirements were also implemented. NAFDAC even set up inspection offices in countries whose drug firms export their products to Nigeria, including China and India.[13]

Although these new requirements eliminated unregistered products as a widespread problem, these measures did not eliminate fake drugs. It just became more costly and cumbersome to manufacture and distribute such products as they continue to make their way into Nigeria. Several regulators indicated to me that after Akunyili initiated the crackdown on fake drugs, distributors attempted to register standard and authentic versions of fake products. They accomplished this by submitting samples of high-quality drugs as part of the registration process. But after a drug was registered, distributors reverted to importing the fake version instead. Even though extensive documentation is in place to compare registered with potentially faked products, the postregistration process is difficult to monitor. It is also difficult to tell if a faked yet registered product came from the manufacturer or from the importing distributor, who may have tampered with the product.

Packaging, a seemingly inconsequential issue, is actually one of the most important aspects of drug registration and distribution, and of detecting fake drugs. The lower the API costs, the more money can be budgeted for packaging, which is the largest overhead cost (Bate 2012). These investments are important because they go toward faked logos, fonts, holograms, colors, and so forth that require sophisticated computer graphics and ink matching. If well done, the fakes can easily fool even suspicious regulators. Excellent packaging means better entrance into the more high-end markets and legitimate wholesale systems that include fake papers, fake quality and inspection certificates, and fake custom stamps (Bate 2012).

Before new registration guidelines were implemented by Akunyili, many manufacturers used graphics on the packaging as a way of listing a drug's uses, which appealed particularly to those who cannot read and who are self-medicating. A NAFDAC official told me:

> Look at Napozine [a steroid], for example. Somebody is now putting one man who is carrying [laughs] maybe fifty bags of cement on his head, and he is saying, "Yes! I can do it!" We don't allow this at all. [The packaging] must be free of any pictorial that is indicative of the implication. With it, you can read meaning that somebody is representing. Take Cimetidine [used for ulcers and gastrointestinal hemorrhages]—[someone] just puts a picture of the stomach. That means everybody can go and take it for stomach [laughs]. The picture already tells you what it is used for, and [consumers or patients] may not even consult anybody before going to go and take it. So we disallow pictures, but compliance is always a problem. When registering they would comply, but after registering, now it is a problem. They go back [to using the pictures] and this is a serious challenge— this issue of monitoring what has already been registered.

The port inspection branch of NAFDAC may check for graphics, find fault, and impose a fine. Sometimes the agency even blacklists a foreign company. But once the drugs make it past inspection and into the Nigerian market, they are quickly distributed throughout the country and across West Africa and lost to regulators.

In addition to the administrative and regulatory tactics described above, NAFDAC took a step further by shutting down large unofficial drug markets in Nigeria. This was somewhat unusual, as most countries that try to curb fake drug distribution do not necessarily go after the importers but instead attempt to strengthen the regulatory environment. The largest raids took place in Aba (eastern Nigeria) in 2002, Kano (northern Nigeria) in 2004, and Onitsha (eastern Nigeria) in 2007, which had some of the largest drug markets in Nigeria; others have taken place since then and many of the shutdowns last for a few weeks to a few months. During the first raid in Aba, one official who had worked for NAFDAC at the time told me that the effort required the entire police force of two neighboring states because the traders, whether or not they were selling fake drugs, fought back with great force to protect their livelihoods. The police had to be treated to hotel rooms and well fed in order to discourage them from helping themselves to the raided drugs. Nigerian civil servants often are not paid in a timely manner, and NAFDAC felt that the confiscated drugs would be a great temptation to the police. Inside the market, all the stalls were shut down, and literally tons of drugs were confiscated and burned.

I asked a NAFDAC official how the agency orchestrates a market shutdown. Referring to the raid in Onitsha, in which over a hundred trucks were used to haul away drugs found in the market, the official told me: "It's very strategic, with the assistance of the law enforcement. It's very strategic, and it's usually done uninformed because [the traders] can just pack and go [if they get word that a raid is coming]. So, when you assemble every police officer, they don't even know what they are going to do until you get to that [market]. . . . So that has really made the activity to be very effective. You would even find people doing the things in the act [laughs] [packing their stock as the raid is happening] so it has been wonderful."

"The police don't even know?" I asked.

"Nobody is informed," he said. "The police ask, 'How do we go about this?' And we say, 'We are moving to [a certain] place.' 'For what?' 'When you get to [that] place, report to Mr. X. So when you report to Mr. X, you will get your assignment the next day. [For now], move into this hotel. This is your room. Just sleep.'"

We both laughed. Indeed, the strategy addressed the stereotype of the police, and precautions were taken to ensure that they had no prior knowledge of the raid and so could not take advantage of the situation.

The official looked at me and said: "So nobody is telling you what [the police] are going to do. So the following morning [the police are told]: 'Okay, good morning, everybody, enter this bus [that will take you to the market to be raided].'" Finishing the story, he said: "By the time the traders return [to the market] the next morning, the whole of the place is already fenced with police, already inside."

I asked him how to tell the difference between fake drugs and real ones. He said: "So many ways, [I] am telling you."

"But if you fence off the entire market, how do you know which ones are the real people?"

"Are you telling me that I should ask the faker, 'Is this fake?' He will not tell you."

I laughed out loud at the thought and rephrased my question: "So you go into every shop? You still have to inspect everything."

"You don't know by face until you get there and check every shelf, every item.... Presentation, labeling, everything [should be] the same." Here he was implying that a fake drug would be detected if the packaging, labeling, color of tablets, and so forth was different from the original generic or brand-name drug.

"How do you do the logistics? Do you put them somewhere before taking them to be burned?"

"There are standby trucks."

"But do you assemble them, maybe on the ground before taking them to be burned, or ... ?"

"The trailers are down there. One is a full mobile police trailer that escorts them to the dumping site. Straight [away]. No diversion."

"I thought you normally keep them somewhere." Certainly, the photographs I had seen in the media of stored fake drugs indicated this.

"No diversion," he insisted.

"So what happens at the end of the day once you've finished and everything is destroyed? You leave the ones that look okay behind on the shelf?"

"You have no business with the ones that are okay and you leave it!"

"Well, what a method!"

"And it worked! They could not believe it, how it worked, until tomorrow, they do not understand how it worked."

As a result of these raids, Akunyili and many NAFDAC workers were attacked in markets; there were several car bombs and in December 2003, there was an assassination attempt on Akunyili's life. Shortly thereafter, NAFDAC's offices in Lagos, Kano, and Benin were burned down by arsonists (Olugbenga 2013). The only time I met Professor Akunyili was at a NAFDAC conference in 2005 where I served as a consultant. She entered the room late in the day and took her seat to speak, while her three guards sat off to the side with their automatic weapons.

The same raid in Onitsha that the NAFDAC official described was very significant. It is the largest unofficial drug market in Nigeria, with (according to some in the Idumota market) over five thousand pharmaceutical traders. It is an extraordinary, expansive market that spills out onto the expressway. Even the traders in the congested Idumota market that is home to about 1000 traders in Lagos talk about Onitsha as if it is an exotic, undesirable place to do business. According to them, there is no place to park and there are large, six-story buildings with no ventilation that are so close to each other that "from the window, you can stretch your hand and shake" with someone in the building next door, as Ikenna described it for me. The raid in Onitsha happened in March 2007, and the market was subsequently shut down for four months. It reopened as a result of negotiations between the state governor and NAFDAC. The governor agreed to long-term conditions, including forcing several officers of the market union to step down. Another key condition was the banning of several people from owning and operating shops, especially more than twenty individuals who were identified as leaders of the fake drug trade (Anyanwu 2007).

Prior to the shutdown, Onitsha had its own drug task force. But traders in Idumota claimed it was not very good at deterring the sale of fakes. As far as Akunyili was concerned, Onitsha was a "den of criminals," "a disaster" (quoted in Sowunmi and Dada 2007). Certainly most fake drugs get channeled through unofficial drug markets, and certainly some drug traders in Nigeria are responsible for that process. However, when one large market shuts down, it has a great effect on Nigeria's drug supply. This was especially true in the four-month closing of the Onitsha market. Due to the market's size and its ability to supply countries throughout West and as far as Central Africa, its closing sent shockwaves through the wholesaling distribution chain.

Idumota is considered the main drug market, while Onitsha is the central market. A *main market* means that Idumota traders buy directly from the manufacturers and then sell to large wholesale clients like state hospitals and clinics, retail pharmacies, and corporations with health care facilities in the Lagos area as well as other parts of West Africa. Idumota supplies other pharmaceutical markets such as Onitsha, which as a *central market* supplies eastern Nigeria as well as the bulk of neighboring countries, especially those in closer proximity to Onitsha than Idumota, such as Cameroon, Gabon, and Chad. There are just a handful of Onitsha traders who buy directly from the manufacturers; but the vast majority of them must purchase drugs from Idumota traders. Sometimes there are drug shortages in Lagos because as soon as the drugs arrive in Idumota, they are sent off to Onitsha. Small-time Lagos traders who rely on better-off Idumota distributors with direct ties to manufacturers sometimes have to travel to Onitsha to get the products they need.

When the market in Onitsha was shut down, fewer traders came to buy in Idumota, and the ones who did come bought in smaller amounts. Because their shops were closed down in Onitsha, I was told, many of them were going on the road to hawk their products. One of the wealthiest Idumota traders told me that he had eleven million naira (about $90,000) trapped in Onitsha. In other words, some goods were distributed on credit, and because items were not selling, he was not getting any return on his money. On top of that, he was losing two million naira (about $15,000) per day in sales. The cash flow of small-time traders was even more impeded.

Abiodun was part of a study team that analyzed the impact of market shutdowns, whether they resulted from NAFDAC actions or other reasons (usually fires or riots). He told me that when Idumota shut down for several days in 2001 due to a riot, the team estimated that 850 million naira ($6.8 million) per day were lost in traded sales.[14] All sales, including those on credit, halted. And as Abiodun pointed out, "if you lose Onitsha market and you lose Lagos market, then the business is finished." Unofficial drug markets are home to both fake drugs and West Africa's wholesale distribution system. Thus, while shutting down markets does lower the rate of fake drug distribution, it also puts the regional distribution of drugs in serious jeopardy.

### Sanitizing Wholesaling: Moral Authority and "Nigerian Factors"

Pharmacists and traders alike praised NAFDAC's dramatic awareness campaigns about fake drugs. People began to ask questions about the drugs they were consuming and they became savvy in identifying fake drugs from packaging alone. These actions were facilitated by a great deal of highly favorable media coverage, which helped to expand public awareness. Despite these efforts, Toks stressed a point that many people I interviewed concurred with:

> In my opinion Akunyili's achievement was genuine but overblown. I think she didn't carry the reform to an appropriate level. For instance, she did not prosecute anyone throughout her tenure—not one person—and really that is the deterrence. When you prosecute, the [fake drug] guy next door realizes that that guy is in jail because of that, so let's be careful [meaning that other fakers will become more cautious]. And that's what she did with NAFDAC and that is

an issue. . . . In 2004, one man lost 10 billion naira [about $8 million] in one day. He lives two hours away from here [Lagos]. Ten billion! He had packaged the fake drugs in Nigeria and was sending them to Côte d'Ivoire. He was arrested, his shop was locked up for some time, but really he was not prosecuted. That why he's living "next door" . . . [laughs].

Prosecution is viewed by pharmacists as a successful deterrent to the importation of fake drugs. But the fact that prosecution is not widely pursued is commonly referred to as one of many "Nigerian factors," and not necessarily the executive actions taken by Akunyili. *Nigerian factors* in this case meant that shutting down markets and prosecuting the big men who are traders in fake drugs involves conflicts with layers of politics and connections that can have nothing to do with the actual illegality at hand. Some pharmacists who shared their analysis with me claimed that because Akunyili did not shut down markets on her home turf in Lagos, she was not successful with prosecutions elsewhere. It is not simply that one must have "political will" to enforce regulatory law. Rather, when state authorities take action in the name of public safety, they inevitably face complex political issues—especially when those issues are tied to commerce. Commercial constituencies that depend on unofficial activities, such as trader and other labor associations, can be linked to more powerful people by home region or professional organizations who can act on their behalf when their livelihoods are threatened.

For example, an industry pharmacist told me the following story, meant to demonstrate the entanglement of complex politics with law enforcement in Nigeria: At one point along the expressway from Lagos to Ibadan (a stretch of about 150 kilometers), there are long-haul transport trucks parked along the shoulder of the road for many miles, forming informal depots. Truck drivers are always visible here—resting, working on engines, and socializing. A market has formed in this area, which catches the business of the truckers as well as expressway traffic that often must slow down to pass the parked trucks. The governor of Ogun State, through which this expressway passes, went to the federal inspector general of police to request the removal of the long queue of trucks on the road, which presented safety concerns because many of the trucks transport fuel. The inspector general was from the same home region as most of the truckers and this connection prompted him to go directly to the president of Nigeria. The inspector general complained to the president that he had helped the Ogun State governor get elected, and now he was making impossible requests. So the president blocked the governor's attempts to remove the trucks, which still remain on the road.

These stories of failed action were often compared to the efforts of Governor Babatunde Fashola of Lagos State, who cleared out many interstitial urban areas for which no residential or commercial permits existed. People on the Lagos street talk about how the first illegal premise that Fashola destroyed was his own mother's permit-less shop. Or maybe it was his father's house that sat too close to the road. The story is never precisely the same, but it has an extraordinary appeal: if you dare to act first against your own family or others to whom you have social, financial, or political obligations, as Fashola was at one time praised for doing, you are viewed as serious and someone who is not to be messed with. This kind of heavy-handedness is often seen as the best, if not at times the only, way to ensure justice and public safety.

These two very different stories are important because they are typical of the kinds of narratives that people commonly tell about the entanglement of "Nigerian factors," law enforcement, and how "things don't work" in Nigeria. Taking action in the name of regulation may lead those to whom you are indebted to move against you. Or it may create more enemies, because clearing an expressway or breaking up a shop without a permit or shutting down a market can often result in outright violence as well as displacing people who have nowhere to go (except back to their villages) because alternatives are usually not created for them. So those responsible for regulation and public safety must either contend with or rely on networks of political and social obligations. These networks cannot be avoided because they include social debts that are far more powerful than the law on the books; and these debts can be traded, hedged, or destroyed (as Governor Fashola did) in lieu of regulatory practices. With these politics in mind, NAFDAC recognized that drug regulation required moral authority to gain any traction. The dangers of fake drugs and the discourse of evil fakers are what give drug regulation its moral authority and so they remain prolific tropes of the problem at hand. But regulation is never a fait accompli because the complex politics of social networks always turns up in the mix.

These are sometimes notorious, sometimes banal Nigerian stories and challenges. No matter their particularities, they are connected, and even completely intertwined, with long-term historical precedents as well as transcontinental politics that animate Nigerian complexities at multiple scales. Fake drugs, regulation, and "Nigerian factors" are just a few small parts of a much broader story that animate the lively world of drug circulation in and outside of Nigeria.

## The Making of Speculative Markets

The elements and actions of the state, law, manufacturers, traders, pharmacists, and so forth facilitate and contend with elaborate drug circuits. Generally, drug circuits constitute an assemblage of indirect and lateral paths that comprise transcontinental drug manufacturing and distribution. Geopolitics, trading relationships, regulation, and consumer purchasing power help determine the extensive routes through which drugs are made and distributed.

Drug circuits in Nigeria represent a betrayal of not just the promise of a 1970s vibrant economy but also a vision of a nascent postcolonial future. In a very short period of time (1960s–1980s), a number of events converged to reconfigure Africa's place in the global economy.[15] At the beginning of this period, independence as both an idea and a reality gained importance because it allowed people to imagine the possibilities of how life could be lived.[16] Freedom's imaginary was located in massive state investments in building schools, roads, and health care facilities, and in expanding manufacturing, such as that of pharmaceuticals. This newly built infrastructure was accompanied by the idea that education, literacy, health care, and job opportunities would be available to the masses (see especially Awolowo 1966). But these independence-inspired visions were quickly thwarted. Civil war in the late 1960s threatened to undo the new postcolonial Nigerian state, and then the 1970s oil boom reoriented Nigeria's pan-African visions of prosperity (Apter 2005). With new state oil wealth, extraordinary limitlessness was projected into the future, but it came up against another event that emerged at nearly the same time: the neoliberal revolution.[17]

Visions of independence and neoliberal reforms were at tremendous odds with each other. The temporal nature of this intersection was completely disoriented by the exuberance of the visions of possibility and their destruction near simultaneous. This book captures these historical conjunctures that produced long-term economic turbulence. Pharmaceutical markets in Nigeria are exemplary of such turbulence and continue to embody the aftereffects of a seemingly endless decline.[18]

Beginning in chapter 1 I examine several historical convergences that took place within Nigeria that made it possible for the control over national drug distribution to switch from Nigerian pharmacists and North American and European multinational drug companies to Igbo traders (from the eastern part of Nigeria) and generic drug manufacturers located mostly in China and India. These historical convergences are as disparate in time as they are in events, spanning post–late 1960s civil war migration to the rise of an oil boom and its subsequent bust in the late 1970s. They had the effect of bringing pharmaceutical traders and pharmacists together into the same professional, yet rather tense political realms that became solidified at the height of Nigeria's economic crisis in the 1980s.

After structural adjustment was implemented in 1986, the citizenry and markets got remade into newly discernible risks via military governance and corporate practices, what I describe as *risky populations* in chapter 2. In terms of governance, the 1970s Nigerian state went from investing in public goods to violently repressing social movements that opposed economic austerity in the 1980s. The newly rendered widespread poverty generated by structural adjustment also meant that the vast majority of Nigerians could no longer afford brand-name drug products. As a result, the brand-name companies abandoned the Nigerian pharmaceutical market. I draw on the story of two brand-name manufacturers, Upjohn and Pfizer. Here I describe how market abandonment was simultaneously tied to the pharmaceutical industry's pursuit of speculative capital—the industry's primary survival strategy in a highly competitive business environment. Nigerian market abandonment and the industry's speculative practices are both responses to crises in the late 1970s global economy, and ones that pertain to very different economic and political circumstances within the United States and Nigeria. They converged to dramatically transform the Nigerian pharmaceutical market into the stressed and volatile condition it is today.

After the brand-name market crashed in the 1990s, Nigerians involved in the international narcotics trade reportedly built a new generic market; this generic market also attracted Asian pharmaceutical firms, which I describe in chapter 3. The remaking of the pharmaceutical market not only altered trading circuits, it also gave rise to new professional relationships and market formations within Nigeria. Pharmaceuticals were largely ejected from formal trading circuits and relocated to legally defined "illicit" unofficial markets that grew tremendously in the interstices of urban space, that is, within neighborhood public space, on the side of the road, in traffic jams. The ontology of these markets is constantly questioned in sites of exchange and even the courts: Are they legal? Illegal? Can they be called markets? Because of their liminal nature, markets as a legal category are difficult to discern and, as a result, become difficult to regulate. I illustrate how these problems of discernment emerged in one particular court case that not only contested regulatory jurisdiction but also animated subsequent claims over who is entitled to control this enormous and highly profitable unofficial market.

Inside the unofficial markets, labor, changing credit structures, debt negotiations, high-risk entrepreneurialism, and quite importantly pricing strategies and price wars all encountered new scaling and forms of valuation occurring within unpredictable and profound market volatility. In chapter 4 I describe how these dynamics are fused with actors' hustling the day in the pursuit of cash. These actions rely upon anticipating and speculating on chronic market volatility as well as life's chances, what I refer to as *derivative life*. I situate these dynamics within non-equilibrium and entrepreneurial theories of the market—specifically Yoruba and Igbo as well as Chicago and Austrian neoliberal market theory—which have converged in ways that negotiate the chronic uncertainty of market life.

The Nigerian pharmaceutical market provides 60 percent of the health products consumed by all West African states by volume (Wambebe and Ochekbe 2011, 64). The bulk of drugs found on this market include antibiotics, analgesics, antimalarials, and nutritional supplements. The shape of market structure does not match needed treatment for high burdens of both chronic (such as hypertension) and neglected tropical diseases (such as schistosomiasis). I describe in chapter 5 how this market structure is directly connected to downward pricing dynamics, transcontinental outsourcing of drug production by the brand-name industry, and the consumption capacity of low-income West African consumers. These intertwined scenarios also drive the distribution chains. Transporting low cost drugs from mostly Asian firms to Nigerian markets is facilitated not only by price arbitrage but also by arbitraging drug chemistry itself. This raises constant concerns and social anxiety over national drug safety, what I refer to as a *social life of bioequivalence*.

In chapter 6, I describe how pharmaceutical marketers in this environment invent drug markets and help to develop the contours of the markets' structure. Multinational brand-name companies compete alongside generic companies by selling simple drug formulations and over the counter medication like aspirin and multivitamins rather than marketing more complex and patented formulations for hypertension, HIV, and cancer. I show how these specific marketing strategies only become possible within the context of debt regimes and trade related intellectual property law. As such, marketing strategies in Nigeria are key to securing protected drug markets in Europe and North America for brand-name companies, which shapes the current formations of global drug monopolies. Potential industrial competition posed by a drug industry such as Nigeria's raises questions about future promises and desires to secure drug supplies and poor people's access to them.

In conducting this research during the summers of 2005, 2007, 2009, and 2010, I got to know Nigerian regulators, pharmaceutical traders, pharmacists, marketers, and management staff members at Nigerian and multinational pharmaceutical companies. I conducted extensive interviews, shadowed many of their activities, and observed transactions in retail pharmacies as well as Idumota market, located on Lagos Island. I also did extensive archival work in medical libraries, government agencies, and industry associations, which helped me understand the complex convergences of history and circumstance that made the market what it is today. The very generous people with whom I spent a great deal of time witnessed, experienced, and survived the civil war, the oil bust, structural adjustment, military rule, and now chronic market turbulence and protracted economic decline—the things that string their disparate lives together. When I began this project, I did not know how much these different events that span several decades would come to bear so significantly on the pharmaceutical worlds these people now occupy. Following their lead, I have endeavored to situate Nigeria as a geographically centralized place from which we can see just how the rest of the pharmaceutical and their related worlds have come into being.

# 01

## Idumota
### Pharmacists, Traders, and the New Free Market

The traditional markets are the only places where Africans of all ethnic origins and classes, from the country and the city meet and assert their humanity and historicity through consumption.

—Manthia Diawara, "Toward a Regional Imaginary in Africa"

### Idumota: A Historical Convergence

There is a neighborhood on Lagos Island that in many ways holds the history of Nigeria as much as it forecasts the country's future. Idumota is adjacent to the Lagos port that facilitated the slave trade (Mann 2007), and later, under British indirect rule, it surrendered to exports that fueled the colonial enterprise (Mabogunje 1964). Once a strictly residential neighborhood, Idumota is now home to one of the largest markets in West Africa and accommodates the substantial inflow of imported goods, which some people say are linked to the demise of the country. This market became a thriving site of exchange, enabled by several significant and conjoined moments in

FIGURE 1.1. View of Idumota market from the Third Mainland Bridge, which connects Lagos Island to the mainland suburbs. Photo by the author.

Nigeria's history. The palm-oil trade, colonial governance, and postindependent political and social life resulted in an economic integration that connects Nigerians to both local and distant economies.

At one end of Idumota is the main market for pharmaceutical distribution in West Africa (figure 1.1). As an unofficial (that is, untaxed and unregulated) market, it is not peripheral to global networks of drug distribution but integral to them. The bulk of pharmaceuticals imported from abroad are routed often first through Idumota and then on to other markets throughout Nigeria and the rest of West Africa. The energy of private Idumota wholesalers facilitates this activity, where up to millions of dollars' worth of wholesale stock is bought and sold every day. Surrounding this pharmaceutical wholesaling is a thriving "popular economy"—a multiplicity of actors as well as official and unofficial commercial activities found in unofficial markets—whose existence is completely dependent on the lucrative trade.[1] There is a constant, pumping rhythm in Idumota that greatly outpaces the usual hyperstimulation found in large cities, such as Lagos, whose population currently exceeds 20 million residents.

Former Brazilian slaves known as Agudas crossed the Atlantic twice in a single lifetime. After being freed from slavery, they settled on this small island with their children and helped develop it just before British occupation took a firm hold.[2] The Brazilian architectural sensibilities and artful façades remain robust and muscular; the buildings are packed close together and are as densely occupied as the streets (figure 1.2).[3] The extensive commercial activity takes place on the first floor of nearly all the buildings, while the upper floors are largely residential. Hanging laundry, flags, and signboards advertising businesses and items for sale adorn the buildings (figure 1.3).

The entrance to the wholesalers' pharmaceutical distribution section is located at the intersection of Adeniji Adele and Iga Idunganran Streets, at the northeast end of the island and facing the mainland, which is less than one kilometer away. The major distributors, whose clients are located across West Africa, have shops on the main road, while smaller operators work on narrower paths that move deeper into the neighborhood (figures 1.4 and 1.5). The gaps between buildings are narrow and often allow only one person to pass at a time. It takes quick and agile footwork, as well as a great deal of head ducking and maneuvering, to negotiate the extremely dense foot traffic, okadas, and other vehicular traffic that fills the streets.

From floor to ceiling, large stacks of boxes containing drugs line the inside and outside of pharmaceutical shop stalls (figure 1.6). Some licensed patent medicine dealers, or traders, as they are called, have been here for years, and some are second- or third-generation traders who command the wholesale system. There are always others, almost all Igbos, who have just arrived from the eastern part of the country to start work as apprentices for an older relative who owns a pharmaceutical shop. Other labor, performed by indigenous Lagosians—mostly Yorubas—is less formalized in this market. Here the space of exchange outside the drug shops significantly contributes to this local economy, a social system comprised of petty trade and informal payments that provide a livelihood for those not engaged in more formal commercial activity involving pharmaceuticals.

The first time I went to Idumota it was not to the pharmaceutical section but to the cloth market, which appeared to be a massive labyrinth. I was with a friend, her sister, and five other people who were shopping for Ashoka cloth for a traditional wedding. We passed through the sections that sold spare parts, DVDs, housewares, and shoes. Nothing could have prepared me for what turned out to be one of the most unique and stimulating experiences I have ever had. Through the mass of people moving in and out of shops, with groups of bodies effortlessly crossing each other's paths, we walked single file as if on a mission. We rapidly stepped into the

FIGURES 1.2–1.3. *Top:* Buildings on Iga Idunganran Street in Idumota market. Residents of the neighborhood live on the upper floors, and drug shops are on the bottom floor. Photo by the author. *Above:* A large side street off Iga Idunganran Street in Idumota market. Shops are on the bottom floor on each side of the street. The boxes up and down the street contain bulk quantities of pharmaceuticals or dietary supplements. Photo by the author.

FIGURES 1.4–1.5.
*Top:* Near the entrance to Idumota market in the morning. Photo by the author. *Left:* Locked up pharmaceutical shops in an alley in Idumota market, before the market has opened in the morning. Photo by the author.

FIGURE 1.6. A small drug shop on an Idumota street corner. Photo by the author.

muddied footprints of the person ahead, keeping one eye on the road and the other on approaching foot traffic, occasionally losing sight of the path and of each other amid shoppers and sellers also forging through the market with the same intensity. I returned many times on my own to Idumota, always getting lost, always needing assistance to find the way out, despite admonitions from friends to not lose my way.

What makes a city appear fast paced is the density of its layers, the way that social and commercial activities are stacked on top of each other, the way they overwhelm our capacity for discernment. How the layers work is difficult to apprehend at first, especially to someone who is new to the place and whose senses are inexperienced. In a large city such as Lagos, what appears to be a dense and nonsensical mass of activity over time reveals itself to be made up of discrete socialities with their own logics of singularity and interconnection. In this environment, traders may expect few customers among thousands of visitors to the neighborhood, and one must expect to encounter myriad stressors that are related to business and not simply the environment. This is a life that the trader lives and the sometimes intense experience that a visitor or customer expects. With each return trip and with more time spent in shops, the intensity of the place was no longer overwhelming. In a corporeal sense, I realized that what we think of as normal is adjustable.

My research partner, Olatubosun Obileye, introduced me to the pharmaceutical section of Idumota in 2005. 'Tubosun and I had met at a month-long biotechnology workshop for West African scientists and lawyers in Ibadan while I was doing my dissertation research on Nigerian AIDS politics in 2000–2001. We got to know each other during his tenure at Médecins Sans Frontières, where he worked for the organization's Access Campaign as a pharmacist with expertise in the new World Trade Organization policies, specifically intellectual property law.[4] Since then we have been conducting research and writing policy documents together. I introduced him to the world of AIDS activism in Lagos, and he introduced me to the world of drugs. When I returned to Lagos in 2005 after having been away for three years, he took me to Idumota. That is where I first really understood what pharmacists meant by a chaotic—meaning ad hoc or random—drug distribution system. But with return trips and visits over the years, I have come to understand that business life in Idumota is anything but arbitrary.[5]

When 'Tubosun and I park at the entrance of the market, we greet Tunde, who is in charge of four parking spaces. He collects 200 naira (about $1.40) from us and anyone else parking there, making about 5,000–10,000 naira per day. If you drive into the market itself, usually because you have come to buy huge stocks of drugs, and, God help you, attempt to maneuver through the traffic and the narrow street, you will pay a higher fee. As I wait for 'Tubosun to park, I greet and chat with the group of women who are always there, selling drinks or credit for mobile phone cards; their activities serve larger acts of exchange and consumption in Idumota. Before I move further into the market, at least one of the women always switches out of Yoruba and asks me in English, "What do you have for us?" indicating that I should consider giving her some pocket change.

Many unemployed young men—indigenes of Lagos Island who are marginalized in this economy—lean against the cars parked up and down the street. They chat and wait for small jobs that the drug shops occasionally offer. In the struggle to survive in the world of this market, they exemplify how "the propulsion of bodies outward in the arduous completion of basic tasks and in the pursuit of some unreasonable dream constitutes an economy of transactions, of continuously realigned affiliations and exchanges" (Simone 2011, 111).

The bit of evidence linking these shops to life in the surrounding neighborhood is boxes of drugs that are either being hustled off boats (usually by men) or into vehicles (usually by women) or that have been discarded. Often the boxes are reused for other purposes up and down the street. These recycled containers retain former identities that point to overseas origins. A woman uses a box labeled "Novartis" and bearing Chinese characters to display plastic containers on sale. Other boxes are used as plates to cool puff pastries (deep-fried and sweetened dough) being sold to people passing by. Still others are used in the aftermath of a rainstorm to soak up the wet ground, providing a dry walkway between shops.

Linking together the larger relations of obligation and exchange that make up the structure of the market is the presence of the extraordinary residence of the *oba* (traditional ruler) of Lagos, Chief Akiolu. The building dates back to the early seventeenth century, when the Portuguese traded here. It has gone through a number of modernization projects and serves today as a tourist attraction. The size and grandeur of the palace mocks the decaying buildings around it. The palaces of other traditional rulers along or around Iga Idunganran Street (the Oluwa, Ashogbon, and, a few blocks west, Onisemo Palaces) are somewhat dilapidated, and for the most part their former occupants no longer reside here. But collectively these members of the Yoruba elite own most of the property in the neighborhood. As landlords, they too are engaged in processes of extraction and accumulation, although they operate on a scale a great deal larger than that of their impoverished neighbors, scrambling to stay afloat in this tenuous economy.

In front of the Oluwa Palace is a food joint where people gather for lunch in the afternoon. Beyond that and up the street is a row of buildings, all of which are occupied by pharmaceutical shops—usually four small ones, but sometimes two or three bigger ones, on the ground floor. Some of these old buildings, the ones that are rented by the indigenes, have seen much better days. The ones occupied by wealthier businessmen can be quite posh. The third-floor office of a wealthy trader I visited was in a fully renovated suite with nice office furniture, the luxury of air-conditioning, and brand new leather chairs.

A block further up Iga Idunganran Street is an Anglican church that conducts many of its services in Yoruba. During the day amplified music and the singing of a choir can be heard down the road. Just across the street from the church is a parking lot filled with vans, or buses as they are called, loading up pharmaceutical supplies, all of which are transported to neighboring West African countries. Drivers and their comrades hang out, using stacked drug boxes as chairs and beds as they wait to journey onward. There is no air-conditioning, no fans, and no awnings to ward off the hot sun, so as the drivers wait, socialize, or nap, the efficacy of the contents of their pharmaceutical loads declines at differing rates. Interspersed throughout the different sites of activity is a branch of every major bank in Nigeria. The banks recognize the extraordinary amount of cash that trades hands here in the course of a day. Their sole objective is to extract as much money as they can from drug product sales in this unofficial market and transfer it to the banking sector. Amid this market activity that provides one of the few promises for a decent livelihood, Idumota is a place where some people make a fortune while others just make their way.

How did this old neighborhood become transformed into one of the largest West African points of drug distribution, facilitating the exchange of pharmaceuticals and other commodities from all over the world? In the 1970s Idumota was strictly residential and had none of the market character it has today. But since the 1980s the businesses in this neighborhood have slowly grown from three "lock-up" or retail shops to over 1,000 wholesale pharmaceutical traders, with upward of $250 million worth of drug stock (maybe significantly more) passing through this market each year.[6]

This chapter tells the story of this transformation. It draws on oral histories I collected from pharmacists and traders, who highlighted factors as disparate as migration after the Nigerian civil war; the oil boom driven by the Organization of Petroleum Exporting Countries (OPEC), the dominant organization of oil-producing countries in the 1970s, of which Nigeria is a founding member; and its subsequent bust. These events in the 1970s helped bring Idumota market into being, as did structural adjustment in the 1980s. They created the conditions that made it possible for the entire Nigerian pharmaceutical market—the actors, the drugs, and the distribution networks—to transform itself.

I draw on Achille Mbembe's creative use of "time" as a helpful conceptual and methodological tool. Mbembe argues that Western philosophical traditions and colonial binaries are inappropriate for apprehending or rendering an analysis of the postcolony and postcolonial subjectivity. Instead, he deploys the terms *age* and *durée*, with *age* being "not a simple category of time but a number of relationships and a configuration of events. . . . As an *age*, the postcolony encloses multiple *durées* made up of discontinuities, reversals, inertias, and swings that overlay one another, interpenetrate one another, and envelope one another: an entanglement" (2001, 14). In Mbembe's view, although slavery and colonialism, for example, come to an end, there are always remnants of these *durées* hauled into and expressed in the present moment.

In this case, the postwar migration (which gave rise to drug market traders) and the oil boom (which significantly remade the professional pharmacist and attracted multinational companies into Nigeria) began at the same moment, but on different trajectories. Their paths crossed and came into conflict beginning in the 1980s, as pharmaceutical markets, manufacturing, and distribution were becoming transformed worldwide.[7] Ultimately, these events converged to alter the formal drug distribution system into one that dispersed drugs widely into rapidly expanding unofficial markets like Idumota. I describe these different moments by first examining Igbo market workers and their arrival in Lagos as drug traders. Most of the Igbo traders who have controlled drug distribution in Nigeria through Idumota since the 1980s came from one small town in the eastern part of the country in the immediate aftermath of the civil war.[8] There is little recorded data on this particular historical aspect of 1970s postwar migration, so I tell it here by piecing together oral histories with information about labor and business practices that traders in Idumota related to me.

I then turn to the beginning of Nigeria's oil boom, which was directly responsible for the increase in the status and prestige of pharmacists that took place in concert with a massive expansion of the multinational pharmaceutical industry in West Africa. As a result of newly garnered wealth that led to industrial expansion, the boom forged important relationships between Nigerian pharmacists and the multinational brand-name industry, which together controlled national drug distribution during the 1970s. Older pharmacists narrated to me their experiences of massive financial decline (and structural adjustment, discussed in the next chapter) in the early 1980s, when new forms of risk and uncertainty were simultaneously brought to bear on markets and drugs.

## Igbo Pharmaceutical Entrepreneurialism after the Civil War

A bloody and violent civil war broke out in Nigeria in 1967 and lasted until 1970. The fighting took place in the eastern part of the country, which had seceded from the Nigerian state and declared itself to be the new country of Biafra. A complicated series of events, including a 1966 military coup, a countercoup, and violent massacres, set the civil war in motion.[9] This war garnered a great deal of international media attention, which focused on what would become the first modern paradigmatic example of a humanitarian crisis that, in controversial and complex ways, demanded external intervention (Wiseberg 1973; Redfield 2013). The local government area of Orlu—located in what is now Imo State, in the predominantly Igbo eastern part of the country—served as a main site of international relief efforts, where organizations such as the Red Cross, Oxfam, and especially Protestant and Catholic churches tended to a civilian population facing starvation and immense loss of life (Wiseberg 1973). These devastating events would ironically lead to new livelihoods for Igbos in the pharmaceutical world.

Ikenna is a trader whose volume of drugs is one of the largest in Idumota and whose clients extend across Anglophone and Francophone West Africa. He explained: "So there and then my father was part of the trained staff that were giving medical attention to people who probably had gunshot wounds, people that were, you know, [fleeing from the] war situation. So there and then they came to know what drugs are—paracetamol, analgine, chloroquine. So when eventually the war ended, they've come to know these things, and they've come to enjoy doing it." Ikenna's pharmaceutical shop is on the main road in Idumota, where the largest shops are located. To enter his shop, you must step up on a cement slab that eases its way into the first floor of the building. Inside, drugs are neatly stacked from floor to ceiling. Fans blow air across the room, and a single bulb makes a futile attempt to illuminate a three-by-three-meter room. In the dim light at the back of the first room is a door that leads to another room housing just as many drugs as the first. Customers and workers are milling around in this second room, some examining drugs on the shelves, some sitting on benches against the wall. Behind that room is a one-by-one-meter room where Ikenna sits—always looking a bit weary—with his calculator and accounting books, facilitating the nonstop movement of visitors and apprentices. The first time we met, he was so busy that I found it impossible to finish a sentence with him. As in all the shops in the market, a generator was running noisily. At that moment, Idumota "had no light"—a phrase that Nigerians use to refer to the many power outages experienced during a typical day.

Ikenna's family's pharmaceutical business in Idumota grew out of the evolving movement of commerce fueled by postwar migration. His father, who is from Orlu, served the Biafran cause. He was trained by the Catholic Church to administer pharmaceuticals and emergency medical care to people fleeing eastern Nigeria. Amid a great deal of destruction and an estimated 1.8 million refugees, many people from Orlu took the skills they had acquired in the war and migrated to Lagos and other Nigerian cities. There they obtained patent medicine licenses, enabling them to sell over-the-counter (not prescription) medication. People like Ikenna's father set up shop and began distributing drugs, a practice that has expanded into postwar, multigenerational family businesses:

> Way back after the war, they [people in Ikenna's father's generation] continued treating people, knowing about drugs, selling drugs. Because they did not go past that primary education, their scope was limited. So when some came to Lagos . . . they wanted [their] child to be a pharmacist today. That's what is happening now. Most of us, we find in a family that we either have two, three medical doctors, one pharmacist—everybody is in the medical line. Just like I said in my own family, now I have two aspiring pharmacists. If you go to probably my father's friend, he has a son or daughter that is a pharmacist. So it is growing, it's evolving, and we're moving from there. And if you look at it, it becomes a norm in my part of the country; from Orlu, 50 to 60 percent of us are into pharmaceuticals. That is what is happening now, and if you go to that market, that the Idumota market, let's say 40 to 50 percent of the people that are there are from this local government area.[10]

The market for many products, including pharmaceuticals, often grows in the midst of economic restructuring. For example, the Igbo diaspora was largely built via entrepreneurial activities. It was in the making long before the British arrived and was linked to manufacturing and other non-agricultural-based industries facilitated by long-term Atlantic commerce (Berry 1985; Northrup 1978).

There is an extensive and fascinating history of market making and entrepreneurship in early Nigeria (Dike [1956] 1981; Isichei 1973; Kilby 1969; Forrest 1995; Olutayo 1999), where power in and control over markets shifted with the growing objectives of the colonial state. In the early twentieth century, indigenous Africans were largely kept out of monopoly capitalism, and the rapidly increasing profits from exporting cash crops led to the emergence of investment and other opportunities for colonial officers (Kilby 1969; Williams 1985). New forms of competition arose simply because local agents were needed to make room for burgeoning capitalist expansion. Consequently, barriers to new sellers were greatly reduced, and Nigerians moved into some sectors of trade and profited from increasing imports, although they were still dependent on British capital, banking, and shipping.

Olanrewaju Olutayo (1999) and others argue that these beginnings were key to the survival and developing entrepreneurial activity of Igbos because they faced increasing land shortages and pressures to migrate.[11] As markets began to grow in Nigeria, Igbos migrated in large numbers to urban areas all over the country, creating an increasingly well-established, multigenerational diaspora. The eastern towns and cities of Enugu, Onitsha, Umuahia, Port Harcourt, and Aba all emerged with European contact (Olatayo 1999) that facilitated entrepreneurial activity. As a result, Igbo entrepreneurship got strongly shaped by ties between rural and urban kin, circulatory migration, and investment flows (Chukwuezi 2001).

By the end of the civil war, all the major cities in Igboland had been nearly destroyed, and patterns of business ownership had changed in other major Nigerian cities (E. Nnadozie 2002). Biafra was dissolved, and the Nigerian state remained intact. It is estimated that between half a million and three million lives were lost. The Nigerian postwar reconciliation policy took a "neither victor, nor vanquished" approach, but Igbos faced systematic obstacles in purchasing property and occupying government positions (Chukwuezi 2001; E. Nnadozie 2002).[12] Kate Meagher argues that although the civil war devastated Igbo business activities across Nigeria and precipitated a mass return of migrants to their home area, it also laid the foundation for the consolidation and rapid development of Igbo informal enterprise.[13] Drawing on networks and linkages that had been in place prior to the war, Igbos began to take up residence throughout the eastern part of Nigeria, as well as other parts of the country, to conduct business once again in the immediate aftermath of war (Meagher 2009). Many businesses had to start over, because Igbo traders had sustained heavy financial losses, and they drew on the Igbo diaspora outside of the country for fresh injections of capital (Forrest 1994). The diaspora was also the base of new trading networks that formed throughout West Africa, developing commercial links with Hausa traders from the north (Hashim and Meagher 1999). Despite heavy wartime losses, a vibrant commerce expanded both during and after the war in the 1970s.

In addition to the Igbos' historical turn to trading, one of the main factors holding their diasporic entrepreneurial networks together is the apprenticeship system in Igbo business practices. West African apprenticeship has been described as key to artistic development and business acumen. Writing about tailors in Liberia, Jean Lave (2011) argues that apprenticeship is deeply intertwined in evolving social relationships (see also Egbue 2006). Certainly, apprenticeship in Nigeria has long existed via kin relations, and the practice has adapted to major twentieth-century events. Apprenticeships have been common in industries such as weaving, shoe making, and the manufacture of auto parts; and they have boomed under conditions of great material loss and political marginalization, which have actually led to the creation of new business activity (Bräutigam 1997; Forrest 1994 and 1995; Meagher 2007 and 2009). The case of pharmaceuticals is somewhat different. In contrast to industries that have long operated in a space of political marginalization, the pharmaceutical industry was incorporated into a state-run centralized system of distribution that gave way to the rise of a few private operators in the aftermath of colonialism and the advent of the oil boom. After structural adjustment, this all changed. Pharmaceuticals were ejected from the formal system and into Igbo entrepreneurial networks, and Igbo apprenticeship became one of the few forms of labor attached to multinational corporations.

In this scenario of apprenticeship labor and trading in the popular economy, members of the Igbo diaspora send their returns on investment back home to build village infrastructure, including schools and medical clinics (Chukwuezi 2001). Investing back home is also investing in future apprentices for diverse industries across the country. Sending money home has been encouraged and practiced since the civil war, as the fear of marginalization and the history of massacres have encouraged Igbos to maintain businesses and residences in their home area. Thus, the aftermath of the war generated a renewed emphasis on kin-business dynamics. Apprentices in Idumota are based on a kinship structure dependent on migration patterns between home—Igboland—and other parts of the country. The career pattern usually begins after secondary school (Tobin-West and Adeniji 2012). Young apprentices go to work for a relative, often leaving the eastern part of Nigeria for Lagos or other cities where older family members trade in pharmaceuticals and other products. Family relations play a key role in matching the apprentice with his master and thus are the main basis for labor recruitment. In addition to vocational training, an apprenticeship also provides socialization in existing and potential entrepreneurial networks.

Most of the small shops that now occupy Idumota have emerged because the apprenticeship system helped expand market volume. People newly released from their own apprenticeships bring in a new generation of apprentices. For example, Chidi and Nweke are third-generation shop owners. They do business past Ikenna's shop, off the main road, on an eroded dirt pathway. Their stall is less than one meter wide and about three meters deep. They make full use of the compact space by tightly stacking drug products throughout the stall. Chidi and Nweke were apprentices together for seven years. Since then, they have worked in this shop, which their master opened for them ten years ago. They had been living in the east, near the city of Onitsha, when a relative of one of them came home looking for new recruits. They felt lucky to be recommended to the relative, who became their master. He brought them to Lagos, where they worked in his shop and lived with him throughout their apprenticeship.

Like other apprentices, they did not learn about the principles of pharmacy but about how to do business in the drug trade. During Chidi and Nweke's apprenticeship, their master imported drugs from Brazil, the United States, and Turkey. Their training included learning about the products that their master traded, his local and overseas suppliers, mandatory drug registration, customer relations, bookkeeping, and how, as Chidi put it, to "make sure his money is safe." Now Chidi and Nweke take on as many as three apprentices at a time. As new apprentices get "settled"—meaning released and ideally (although not always) given a small payment to help them start out on their own—they may stay in Idumota or venture out to other parts of the city. If successful, they will bring on their own apprentices, and the cycle continues, tending to expand the market exponentially.

In Idumota only the big operators on the main road are generalists who stock and sell an array of medicines. The small-timers almost always specialize in a particular drug class or drug type, like tablets, liquid medications, or injections. Although they get to know their own products intimately, they may not know anything about other drugs. But their neighbor might know. Any customer looking for a particular product will be led to someone else in the trader's network, which could have developed during his apprenticeship period. For example, Odili specializes in liquids (antimalarials, antibiotics, and flucanozole, for fungal infections) and imports from only one company. He finished secondary school at the age of nineteen, trained as an apprentice for seven years, has worked for distributor companies, and has been on his own for over a decade. His extremely small shop—about one by two meters—is sparsely stocked with various liquids. It is located not far from Chidi and Nweke's shop, yet it is further off the main road. Around his shop there is a mix of people living in the neighborhood, other shop owners, customers, and traders selling drinks and food. Even though this part of the drug market is more crowded than others, it has more of a neighborhood feel, with people nearby doing laundry, conducting morning church services (which I sometimes found Chidi and Nweke doing), and preparing the day's meals. The wholesale clients of Ikenna, Chidi, Nweke, and Odili include hospitals, health centers, health clinics, parastatal organizations, pharmacy retail shops, police clinics, and the military. Although these shops sometimes make retail sales, it is more common for them to provide less expensive bulk products to medical institutions, and such sales potentially constitute very large accounts for these traders.

But in an earlier period, a very different wholesale distribution system existed that did not require extensive private markets. Instead, pharmacists who worked as marketers for the multinational drug industry once had, but ultimately lost, control of the wholesale system.

*Pharmacists, Drug Companies, and the 1970s Oil Boom*

Mr. Adebayo began working as a medical representative—marketer or detail man in industry lingo—for Upjohn, one of the world's largest multinational companies, in the early 1980s. Back then, many drug markets like Idumota did not exist. As with many other medical representatives working for global companies at the time, Mr. Adebayo was assigned a particular territory, where he worked with wholesale distributors, corporations, and state apparatuses. He liaised with a distributor not far from Idumota who was the only major player in the area during that period. Over time, he was promoted and became a marketing strategist for Upjohn in West Africa. He not only helped develop marketing strategies for Upjohn's existing products but was also responsible for developing product lines that would suit the health needs of the Nigerian population.

His former employee, Toks, is a generation younger. Toks was attending university while market reforms were underway in the 1980s. Like many others, he has plenty of stories to share about the dramatic changes that took place during this period. Subsidies for what are now considered luxury goods in any university, like three meals a day, were instantly revoked—an indication of what was still to come after students graduated. Toks earned his degree and fulfilled his civil service obligations—mandatory for all university graduates—working as a dispensing pharmacist for a state hospital. Eventually he found his way to the private sector, where he worked as a marketer for both the global companies and large local distributorships. After fifteen years of employment in the pharmaceutical marketing world (including a stint with Mr. Adebayo), he decided to create his own business selling drugs and other products. Toks and Mr. Adebayo's experience show how pharmacists across the board were professionally shaped, a process that was largely driven by a massive oil boom in Nigeria, which began in 1970, in the immediate aftermath of the Nigerian civil war and lasted until the end of the decade.[14] In less than ten years, the oil boom made Nigeria wealthier than had seemed possible at the end of colonial rule.[15]

The oil boom completely remade the structure of the national economy.[16] One of the most dramatic changes was the increased imported consumer goods, some of which quickly overwhelmed the existing infrastructure.[17] Ultimately, oil became the predominant component of the national economy, while industries that had been part of the previously diversified economy declined drastically. Bill Freund points out that "the oil export boom led to a significant shift in emphasis from planning for industry to primary product export, if not actually to deindustrialisation" (1978, 96). The new oil revenue did not do much to expand Nigeria's aspirations for development, but it did enrich the postcolonial state. The existing merchant class that had been growing since the beginning of the palm-oil trade dove head first with foreign companies into the oil bonanza.

During this period, multinational brand-name drug companies were expanding their operations beyond North America and Europe. Indeed, sales outside of the companies' home regions amounted to more than one-half of their global revenue (Silverman and Lee 1992, 27). Oil played a significant role in attracting brand-name companies to Nigeria, which greatly expanded pharmaceutical manufacturing in the country. Companies such as May and Baker, Pfizer, and Glaxo set up Nigerian distribution outlets as early as the 1940s and 1950s, and others, such as Ciba, Bayer, Wellcome, Hoechst, Boots, Roche, Imperial Chemical Industries, and Parke Davis, arrived in the 1960s. By the 1970s they had scaled their business activities up, via either packaged distribution or manufacturing, as they saw the postindependence oil-rich markets as lucrative. Indeed, they manufactured drug products that were distributed and sold within Nigeria and throughout West Africa rather than for export to Europe or the United States. This approach took advantage of the relative wealth of the Nigerian middle class, made up of ordinary people who could afford luxury goods and whose sensibilities were oriented toward the high symbolic value associated with brand-name drugs. With few exceptions, virtually no generic drugs were marketed at this time. By 1973, industry earnings were $48 million (Carlson 1982, 78). In 1980, they were about $200 million and nearly 10,000 Nigerians were employed by the drug industry (Adenika 1982, 7; see also Andelusi-Adeluyi 1982).

The arrival of the multinationals led to an increase in the professionalization of pharmacists, especially those who worked as marketers for brand-name pharmaceutical companies. Industry pharmacists were enticed by much bigger salaries than their community and hospital pharmacist counterparts received, and the companies provided them with perks such as housing allowances and chauffeur-driven cars (Adenika 1998, 84). They received extensive marketing training and were flown around the world to attend conferences and seminars. Eventually, many pharmacists ventured out on their own, maintaining their relationships with their former company employers as retailers and distributors of company products. Pharmacists-turned-retailers identified specific clients they could work with over time, establishing shops to cater to those clients' needs. They might also have a secure contract with an oil company or a federal hospital. Once you were in that situation, as Mr. Adebayo put it to me, "you are done!" By this he meant that pharmacists could procure good incomes by establishing clients who consistently placed large orders. In such situations, drug companies provided generous credit relationships and bulk discounts (Mgbokwere 1984) and pharmacists routinely recouped a price markup on imported drugs, which was as high as 33% at that time (Okereke 1988, 12). The link between industrial labor and Western capital and the lifestyles echoing oil-boom extravagance meant that all pharmacists in the private and public sector had high prestige and were well regarded in society.

Although the transnational Indian company Ranbaxy has been manufacturing and distributing drugs in Nigeria since the oil boom, global Asian companies were not yet major suppliers. Despite the fact that Indian and Chinese companies now dominate the Nigerian and West African market, pharmacists do not view them with the same kind of respect that North American and European companies receive. In the 1970s, Indian companies did not provide the kind of lavish salaries and training support their North American and European counterparts did, which greatly influenced pharmacists' choices in seeking employment with the manufacturers. The oil boom facilitated lasting relationships between first-generation postcolonial (and later) pharmacists and global companies that would shape future definitions of quality in drugs and the drug distribution systems that move products from manufacturer to consumer.

The extravagant turn in the pharmacy profession was a far cry from its more humble origins. Roman Catholic missions introduced pharmaceuticals to precolonial Nigeria in the 1860s, and a British citizen, Richard Bailey, trained the first generation of drug dispensers in the early twentieth century (Adenika 1998). These early pharmacists were jacks-of-all-trades: dispensers of medicines, sanitary officers, and anesthetists in operating theaters. Indeed, pharmacy itself was not professionalized or standardized until 1964, four years after independence.[18] Pharmacy expanded throughout Nigeria's colonial period, with the building of pharmacy schools, the founding of professional organizations, and new legislation regulating drug sales and dispensers. At that time, pharmacists were concentrated in Lagos and a few other urban areas, where they worked mostly in government hospitals. The wholesale drug trade and large private colonial retail businesses grew during the early colonial period, and private wholesale and retail businesses only became established in the later colonial period and during the early years of independence (Adenika 1998; Carlson 1982).

The numerous pharmacists I interviewed think of the colonial period as a golden era for their profession, when the Central Medical Store in the Oshodi neighborhood of Lagos served as a centralized point of distribution for the entire colony. According to the late academic pharmacist Fred Adenika (1998), the British trading company Crown Agents provided all the supplies, and the Central Medical Store controlled their distribution to provincial hospitals. The supply of medical stores expanded with the establishment of colonial regional governments. Adenika (1998) and others have claimed that drug stocks were known to last for at least a year and that there were no known drug shortages. Whether or not the distribution chain was this efficient, the system catered mostly to colonial officials and Nigerians employed by the colony; nevertheless, pharmacists idealize it now.

These stories of nostalgia refer to a time of increasing drug industry and state wealth that led to new business practices. While the multinationals were in full manufacturing mode, Nigeria implemented an indigenization policy in 1972.[19] The term *indigenization* differs from economic nationalization. Nationalization is usually understood as full state retention of private industry. But indigenization represents a partial transfer of transnational assets, after which the parent companies and their newly mandated subsidiaries have continuing working relationships. The indigenization policy originated in nationalist movements for independence that sought full control of an autonomous national economy (Ogbuagu 1983). It mandated that by 1977, 60 percent of transnational corporate assets had to be sold to Nigerian indigenes, who, in practice, were members of the business elite (Apter 2005). As a result, a number of subsidiary pharmaceutical companies emerged, which produced most of the medicines on the market at the time (Adenika 1998).[20] The state set up manufacturing facilities in Nigeria, and indigenous companies began to manufacture simple dosage forms.

These relationships often facilitated the same kind of transfer pricing found in previous colonial eras. This means that the pricing structure was such that import prices remained high. Nigerian subsidiaries could not (or were not supposed to) make a profit but only pay the bills for its imports. The profits themselves are repatriated to the parent company. Both Nigerian and overseas businesses were "overpricing imports and underpricing exports in order to shift money out of the continent and into foreign bank accounts" (Baker 2012, 59). Nevertheless, the state and businesses viewed the policy as favorable for the country's investors and its economy.

The systematic expansion of the pharmaceutical industry was filled with structural contradictions that were laid bare once the oil boom began its decline. At the time of industrial indigenization, Nigeria did not specify how companies should upgrade their technology, nor did it establish any policy about how to generate new know-how or use the newly available massive assets to meet the nation's drug needs. For example, Adenika refers to the feeder industries that did not, and in some instances still do not, exist for the most part (1998). These industries provide the basic materials needed for manufacturing, such as capsules, alcohol, machinery, and glass bottles, as well as materials for suspending, binding, preserving, and packaging drugs.[21] One visit I took to a drug-manufacturing premises included a trip to the shop, where glass bottles and other equipment are manufactured on site. Everything had to be built from the ground up, as did basic communication, electricity, and water infrastructure.

Moreover, the state under late colonialism promoted import-substitution industrialization that was largely owned and managed by foreign companies. Adebayo Olukoshi (1992 and 1996) and Bjorn Beckman (1982) show that these policies meant that all parts and inputs required to facilitate manufacturing were imported from abroad, a structural holdover from colonialism. All the raw materials—materials that are either unprocessed or minimally processed such as chemicals—required for pharmaceutical manufacturing are still imported. Although import substitution was never meant to be an end in and of itself, just a stage in full-scale manufacturing of industrial goods (Mkandawire and Soludo 1998), its implementation did not change the structure of drug manufacturing much, and it encouraged light or secondary manufacturing that a comprador class was largely responsible for organizing. So when the oil boom ended, manufacturing industries, such as steel, iron, textiles, and pharmaceuticals, were still either nascent or completely stagnant and began to decline (Freund 1978; Olukoshi 1992).

### Import Licenses and New Forms of Accumulation

The oil boom and its subsequent bust, which occurred at the end of the 1970s, greatly affected the circulation of pharmaceuticals in Nigeria. These events cannot be understood without examining several points of activity in the global economy at the time, when U.S. policy was quite important. While Nigeria and other OPEC members were earning windfall profits, the United States was experiencing severe economic contraction and recession. By the late 1960s U.S. manufacturing industries had begun to face intense overseas competition, especially from Japan and Germany, and profits were waning. The United States was also confronting increasing indebtedness and a balance-of-payments problem, a result of excessive expenditures on the Vietnam War (Arrighi 2003).

In 1971 President Richard Nixon took the United States off the gold standard in order to stabilize the U.S. economy. This action helped to end the Bretton Woods system of international financial exchange. At that time, the U.S. dollar was pegged to gold, while all other currencies were pegged to the U.S. dollar. Foreign banks held more in dollars than the U.S. held in gold reserves and the U.S. feared a run on its gold. Other industrialized nations had already or soon followed the United States and floated their own currencies. Anticipating the stabilization of international currencies, the U.S. increased its reserves by printing more money. These events led to the devaluation of the U.S. dollar. Because oil was priced in dollars, oil-producing states found themselves receiving less real income. In an attempt to protect itself from this decline, OPEC increased the price of crude oil fourfold and pegged oil to gold instead of the dollar. These actions dramatically increased the wealth of OPEC members but sparked further economic problems for the United States.

The United States implemented several policies to deal with its financial crisis by the end of the 1970s. Namely, the U.S. government stopped pumping the economic system with liquidity. Instead, it aggressively competed for capital by increasing interest rates; lowering taxes for corporations, speculators, and the wealthy; and lifting restrictions on capitalist enterprise. Crucially, these measures provoked an appreciation of the dollar, which attracted capital back into the United States. In effect, the direction of capital flows—that is, the economic gains of Nigeria (and other oil-producing states in the global South) and the economic contraction of the United States—were reversed. Giovanni Arrighi asserts:

> This was a reversal of historic proportions that reflected an extraordinary, absolute and relative capacity of the U.S. political economy to attract capital from all over the world. It is likely that this was the single most important determinant of the contemporaneous reversal in the economic fortunes of North America and of the bifurcation in the economic fortunes of Third World regions. For the redirection of capital flows to the United States reflated both effective demand and investment in North America, while deflating it in the rest of the world. At the same time, this redirection enabled the United States to run large deficits in its balance of trade that created an expanding demand for imports of those goods that North American businesses no longer found profitable to produce. (2002, 22)[22]

Nigeria was severely affected by the global recession, both because much of the country's reserves were U.S. dollars, which were declining in value, and because the United States was searching for new supplies of oil during its energy crisis. Additionally, between 1974 and 1978 Nigeria's oil exports, which made up a significant portion of the nation's revenue, declined by over two-thirds (Freund 1978, 98–99). By 1977 the country's oil industry had been forced to enter into agreements with foreign companies, especially Shell Oil, to finance oil exploration under unfavorable terms that looked like subsidies for the North American and European oil companies at a time when oil prices were falling (Freund 1978, 98).[23] The key point here is that the OPEC strategies and U.S. monetary policies employed to cope with recession throughout the 1970s reduced both Nigeria's autonomy and its power in OPEC to set the terms of oil prices and production; and it made the country more beholden to North American and European oil companies.

In Nigeria all these events amounted to what was commonly known as "foreign exchange scarcity"—a term used by almost every pharmacist who discussed this period with me. It refers to the drying up of money for imports due to a lack of oil output, but also to the flight of industrial capital from Nigeria. Indeed, there was a huge strain on all business in Nigeria, including brand-name drug companies, and pharmaceuticals that once had been abundant quickly became scarce. The Nigerian government responded by implementing what was known as the import license policy in late 1983. The intention was to allocate foreign exchange to manufacturing companies, trading companies, and distributors to import what became classified as "essential commodities," which included pharmaceuticals.

According to industry journalist Abieye Kalu (1985), the Pharmaceutical Trade Group of the Lagos Chamber of Commerce and Industry suggested that several criteria be set up for award consideration. These included awarding companies with drug manufacturing and importation experience, focusing on very vital classes of drugs (such as vaccines, anti-hypertensives, anti-cancers), and creating incentives to keep workers employed in the industry (Kalu 1985). For these drug industry members, the ultimate aim was to use the import license as a temporary measure whereby more emphasis on local drug production could be established while phasing out imports ("Issue Import Licenses Now" 1985).

However, things did not go that smoothly. In the beginning of this period of austerity, holding an import license opened new opportunities to engage in what is often referred to as "corrupt" money-making practices (Fadahunsi 1993).[24] Licenses were awarded to a select few firms and individuals, many who had never imported drugs in the past ("Shortfall in Drug Import Caused by Fake Companies" 1985). In 1984—the first round of distribution—only N55 million out of N100 million was used to import drugs; the remaining balance was diverted to "fake" companies that funneled the money to other means according to *Pharmanews,* the leading industry monthly news magazine, which cited the minister of health's findings on diversion (Ujumadu 1986, 6). Many health care services collapsed as a result.[25] With each round of foreign exchange administration, pharmacists and smaller scale drug companies were increasingly edged out of the importation and distribution of drugs ("Shortfall in Drug Import Caused by Fake Companies" 1985).

Indeed, between 1983 and 1984 the pharmaceutical labor force was cut nearly in half as a result of the policy, falling from 13,000 workers in 1983 to 7,000 in 1984 (Atueyi 1985, 3). These incredible figures were matched by an acute shortage of drugs all over the country. In his capacity as a marketer for a multinational company that manufactured drugs in Nigeria, Mr. Adebayo described to me the process of obtaining an import license and the way it helped to deindustrialize manufacturing while expanding trading:

> There was bidding and there was money for the manufacturers. The problem was that manufacturing takes a lot of money and time to yield a dividend. And [the drug companies] needed to be careful. [The Nigerian government] gets the highest bidder and the highest bidder gets the foreign exchange. If I am a manufacturer and I know that with all the problems—electricity problems, water problems, infrastructure problems—I can't manufacture at this foreign exchange rate and make [a] gain. So my bidding will be low and I might not get [the import license], while the traders bid high and they get it. That is actually what killed manufacturing. . . . The cost of production is just too much compared to what [the traders] bring in. It encouraged trading. Bring it in, sell it off immediately, dump it into the market; people buy, you collect your money back. You don't have any infrastructure, you don't have any staff, you don't have any equipment, you don't have anything to pay.

As the cost of large-scale manufacturing increased dramatically,[26] trading in imports became far less expensive and quickly proliferated. Because the import licenses were allocated to the highest bidders, those who needed the least amount of foreign exchange were the ones most favored to receive it. Most companies that did not receive a license went out of business. And so corruption became both a matter of buoyancy and a matter of monopoly. For those who did get licenses, they purchased low-cost drugs that would make a profit, such as antibiotics, rather than other, essential but less profitable drugs, such as anti-diabetes medications (Obinwanne 1986, 26). Toks encountered this situation when he graduated from university. He viewed it as "a practice in Nigerian diplomacy," meaning that awarding an import license to Pfizer or other drug companies that had long been responsible for creating the national drug market was viewed by some as a form of bilateral trade, with histories of obligation attached to it.

Toks told me that in addition to perceived favoritism and institutionalized corruption, a new and more personalized financialization was on the rise:

> At the time [the government] gave the import license to companies that would either resell the license to somebody else or do whatever they wanted to do.... You know that this thing was a racket. [The government] will protect the multinationals. [The import license recipients] were not interested in trading, they just wanted to *round trip* the money [my emphasis]. Bring it out and sell at a higher price and that is it. ... Since they are going to get government rates and sell at black-market prices to anybody who can pay, they [fake] the documentation to reflect that they sold it at the right price.

Round-tripping, a form of currency arbitrage, proliferated in the Nigerian economy in the early 1980s.[27] In the pharmaceutical industry, trading companies awarded an import license did not necessarily do direct trading (as was mandated by the terms of the license); rather, they moved products through different tiers of officially established and black-market exchange rates that varied substantially at that time.[28] These activities were made possible by the government's invention of a two-tier exchange market: the lower exchange rate was reserved for paying off government debts, and the higher exchange rate was for everything else, to which black-market activities were directed. The diversion of money from the productive sector to more lucrative trading had a number of consequences. The most immediate was that it led to drug stockpiling and incredibly severe drug shortages, because government-administered foreign exchange was not used to buy the goods it was intended to secure. Many pharmacists at the time referred to these impacts of the import license as "market distortion." Indeed, they began to become quite adept with the languages of markets and importation during this period.

Just as the indigenization policy was beginning to create dramatic growth in the number of locally produced drugs,[29] the import license reversed that success. In 1976, for example, 31 percent of all drugs were locally manufactured, but by 1990 that number had plummeted to 10 percent ("PSN wades in import license crisis" 1984, 1; see also Kalu 1984a).[30] The lack of petrochemical plants needed to produce raw materials in an oil-producing country—a result of colonial import-substitution policies—did not help the situation (Kalu 1984b). As importation of especially fast-moving products scaled up, a wide variety of drugs that Nigerians were not accustomed to seeing entered the country, including generic drugs as well as substandard and intentionally adulterated products.

### Restructuring the Pharmaceutical Industry

The foreign exchange problem, the use of import licenses, infrastructure problems, and the fact that importation was rapidly outpacing manufacturing all converged in a short time period, roughly between 1980 and 1985. This was a turning point and the beginning of market restructuring. Pharmacists, who had had the major hold on pharmaceutical distribution, began losing ground. Mr. Adebayo, Toks, and others told similar stories of how the relationship between pharmacists and drug companies broke down. In addition to losing out on import licenses, a common theme had to do with the large volume of money and drugs that passed through retail stores during the oil boom. Pharmacists working under supervisors could be responsible for handling a minimum of $10,000 worth of goods, all on credit. Much of this could not be paid off once the economic crunch bore down hard on industry players. I was told that some pharmacists, pressured with mounting debts, turned to round-tripping advanced credit. They diverted the money meant for drugs into other quick-return business opportunities, expecting to make the money back and easily pay off short-term debts, which often did not happen.

With the deterioration of the economy, the multinationals ended credit advances and required cash up front for goods. Wholesale and retail pharmacists had developed their businesses on the basis of receiving credit from the companies and could not cope with the changing circumstances. As a result, there was a huge gap in the process of importing drugs into the country. Igbo traders recognized this gap and were eager to fill it. But initially the multinationals were not willing to sell to them: the traders had patent medicine licenses enabling them to sell over-the-counter drugs, but they did not have pharmacists' licenses, a requirement at the time. The scarcity both of drugs and of foreign exchange put human resources and distribution systems under extraordinary pressure.

As a response to the substantial scarcity of drugs, the government dismantled key pharmacy regulatory laws. Deregulation was a result of panic, not just an unpleasant answer to a worsening drug supply situation. One obscure, yet key, example was that prior to deregulation, pharmacists were not legally allowed to open their own retail shops until after five years of on-the-job experience with an established retailer or company. The government's lifting of that requirement initiated the transformation of the wholesale drug distribution system. Mr. Adebayo laments:

> And so there were a lot of challenges, and because of issues that were bordering on getting jobs for pharmacists—because the situation was so tight then economically for most pharmacists—they lifted that ban based on a minimum of five years [of] experience before [you can get your own] retail shop. They lifted it after you may have finished your internship and done your youth service.[31] And because of that situation, Igbo boys were ready. They now found a large pool of pharmacists who can register them. They also told pharmacists that they don't have to be coming all the time [to the place of work], that you can just register for us, we'll give you [such and such an] amount, and you can still go and work somewhere else. So what they wanted was for the pharmacist to license their premises so that they can buy directly from the manufacturer, with the pharmacist playing a ghost role.

The pharmacists who lost control of the drug distribution system in which they had been partners of the brand-name companies were not displaced completely. Rather, they were reincorporated into a new system and business paradigm. But this occurred at a cost to their sense of professional integrity. Their high social status began to wither as they lost control of the wholesale system and as fake and substandard drugs entered the country with the establishment of the import license—something greatly discussed in industry and academic literature (see for example Egbuonu 2000; Nuhu 2002; Ohaeri 2002; Okereke 1988). The traders who took over the wholesale market needed pharmacists to register their premises. In exchange, the traders agreed to pay up to a year's salary, in cash up front, which gave pharmacists new access to capital. This enabled the incoming wholesalers to conduct their own businesses, with pharmacists connected only in an "on the books" way.

These up-and-coming traders were not all completely flush with cash, but their system of apprenticeship labor—with its built-in systems of exchange involving credit and debt—allowed them to adapt to the situation more easily than pharmacists, who were struggling with debt and losing their relationships with the brand-name companies. Ultimately, the brand-name manufacturers retreated from the credit structure they themselves had created; traders then transformed it by inventing and implementing their own systems of exchange, related to the apprenticeship arrangement. The brand-name companies also adapted by eviscerating their own drug markets and then aggressively selling over-the-counter drugs in competition with generic companies from all over the world. All drug companies had to form new relationships with traders in order to make the destruction and renewal of markets a fruitful enterprise.

All these events provided the initial spark that brought Idumota market and others like it into being. The national economy continued to spiral downward; and in a short period of time, new state militarism ushered in political and economic reforms that changed the people's lives and the pharmaceutical scene for good.

# 02

## Risky Populations
### Drug Industry Divestment and Militarized Austerity

Our pathfinders were held down with copper thongs
in fields swept by the spillage of black gold
when we bought debts as candles to light our way
to the worship of the many-handed goddess
to whom the boys from Chicago made love
testing the manhood of their tribes
in the affrays of our century

—Odia Ofeimun, "A Kind of Lovemaking"

### Austerity as Speculative Anticipation

The situation of pharmacists, traders, and drug distribution soon became untenable as capital and drugs became increasingly scarce. By the early 1980s the Nigerian economic crisis was in full swing, following the crash of the global commodity and oil markets. The financialization of a highly troubled U.S. economy brought capital back to the United States, but the oil glut and unpaid debts in Nigeria set in motion economic turbulence that has yet to abate. In this scenario of reversal, U.S. foreign policy, especially from 1973 on, must be explained in terms of oil and financialization. The massive surplus gained from the oil profits of the Organization of Petroleum

Exporting Countries (OPEC), stored abroad in Western banks, created a new layer of privately controlled liquidity. That money was used for financial speculation and the creation of new credit outside publicly controlled channels (Arrighi 2003; Harvey 2007). It was converted into highly favorable loans to other African countries, with little concern about their ability to repay. During the oil boom, Nigeria borrowed heavily to finance the infrastructure that the citizenry demanded (to provide education, health care, transportation, and so forth). But when the boom ended, Nigeria suddenly had not only a revenue problem but also a severe debt problem.

The government attempted to secure new loans to cover shortfalls in expected revenue. But the loans that had flowed easily out of Western financial institutions in the 1970s halted in the 1980s, and Africa's creditors insisted on a number of austerity measures in exchange for new loans.[1] Overseen by the International Monetary Fund (IMF) and the World Bank, these measures were known as structural adjustment programs (SAPs).[2] Nigeria's SAP was designed to alter and restructure the consumption and production patterns of the country's economy by eliminating price distortions, reducing the importation of goods and dependence on exporting crude oil, and increasing private-sector growth. Policies of subsidy removal, health and education privatization, high taxes and severe restrictions on imports, banking deregulation, and currency devaluation dramatically inflated prices for consumer goods and resulted in massive job loss, plummeting most Nigerians into poverty.[3]

Yusuf Bangura points out that "African governments lost effective control over economic policy making to the international financial institutions, having enjoyed relative autonomy in this area for only about two decades of independence from colonial rule" (1994, 786). Moreover, the implementation of the SAP in Nigeria was widely unpopular and met with social movement activism and a national prodemocracy movement (Edozie 2002), mostly because devaluation led to significantly decreased earnings and the quadrupling of food prices within months. Primary health care services collapsed because the IMF had expected to recover all costs from patients who could not afford even basic food commodities (Salako 1997).

Multinational drug companies, which had commanded almost all of the Nigerian market, could no longer operate in Nigeria because the country's currency, the naira, was rapidly losing its value, leading to a general decline in sales (Peterson 2012a). Within ten years of the implementation of the

SAP, all brand-name companies divested themselves of their Nigerian businesses, which generated a massive shortage of drugs. By 1990 the domestic production of pharmaceuticals had almost entirely ceased throughout Africa (Samba 2004). Most pharmaceutical and medical supply companies were pushed into bankruptcy, and medical workers fled the public sector for private-sector jobs both elsewhere in Africa and beyond (Turshen 1999). The civilian government could not manage to force reforms through. Rather, reforms were made possible by military dictatorships that unleashed unprecedented levels of violence on the population.

When I started conducting research for this book in 2005, it was not clear to me why a multimillion-dollar brand-name pharmaceutical industry would risk one of its largest sites of foreign and international sales (for some products) to the forces of structural adjustment. The drug industry could hardly absorb such a financial loss, especially since the early 1980s its profits were declining and a great many drug patents were expiring (Kanji et al. 1992). Nigerian pharmacists and drug marketers posited that the industry's acceptance of the SAP had something to do with Cold War politics: some suggested it was politically important for the companies to move operations out of Africa and set up shop in, say, South Korea, as a strategic positioning against North Korea or China; others thought that because the Soviet Union was breaking up new marketing opportunities were becoming available to the brand-name industry. One former marketer for a European-based global company suggested that SAP was not about Cold War politics. Rather it was about taking a strategic decision to emphasize access to oil in Nigeria, realizing that drug manufacturing could be relocated. These were not the reasons for implementing SAP, but in the aftermath of liberalization, Nigerian oil certainly got remade, and new markets opening up at the end of the Cold War became important sites to the pharmaceutical industry.

The 1980s and 1990s were a time of flexible accumulation in global market restructuring (Harvey 1991).[4] But flexibility was not simply about capital's ability to move effortlessly across deregulated national borders in search of ever-cheaper labor. It was also about strategic trade calculations that appeared to give something up, like a massive drug market, in favor of something else, like the prospect of building new markets outside of Nigeria that (perhaps inadvertently) helped substantially expand and consolidate extraction, particularly in the oil industry.[5] Importantly, the moment that a once highly successful market was crashing rapidly due to 1970s and 1980s

U.S. monetary policies, as well as to structural adjustment, new forms of capital speculation appeared on the horizon, promising fantastic, profitable growth in the stagnating pharmaceutical industry. Speculative capital and speculative drug-industry practices included mergers, acquisitions, and buyouts that were buttressed by deregulation, new laws pertaining to intellectual property, and start-up companies that had no products to sell but whose stock was traded based on promises of future growth (M. Fortun 2008; Sunder Rajan 2006). At the moment the drug industry got tied to the speculative marketplace, companies also cut their losses, which included abandoning Nigeria's entire national drug market, an important strategy that the companies used to stay economically afloat.

Drawing on these events, I use the term *risky populations* to describe citizens and markets that were exposed to newly discernible risks via military governance and corporate practices. In terms of governance, the 1970s Nigerian state switched from investing in infrastructure[6] and human capital to violently managing a population resistant to economic reforms. In other words, after Nigerian independence, development efforts had attempted to reduce human risk by establishing new public goods; but with structural adjustment the population itself became a risk to the state's plans to implement austerity.[7] Moreover, the logics of state militarization were about paving the way for new orders of capital, and various forms of extraction and accumulation emerged in many sectors, including pharmaceuticals.[8] To illustrate, I relate encounters with state militarism in Idumota drug market and the specters that remain well after the end of dictatorship.

I link risk and military governance to histories of West African marketing and divestment that were told to me by Nigerian pharmacists who had been working as marketers—or medical representatives, as they are called—for several global companies at the time of structural adjustment. Although medical representatives in the 1970s attempted to meet Nigerians' health needs by providing drugs for illnesses with both high and low morbidity, devaluation and impoverishment meant that Nigerian consumers could no longer afford pharmaceutical products. This low purchasing power made it too much of a risk for drug companies to continue to participate in the Nigerian market. The companies had focused on expanding their product profiles to meet human health needs, but with the onset of SAP they saw chiefly a consumer population whose new impoverishment meant that the country's pharmaceutical market was no longer sustainable. To illustrate, I focus on the U.S.-based companies Upjohn and Pfizer, both of which fled Nigeria within a decade of SAP implementation. Pfizer consolidated its speculative and productive practices to become the largest drug company in the world. In contrast, although Upjohn became the ninth-largest drug company in the world, it was devoured by other companies, including Pfizer.

Speculative capital and investor promises of renewed and even extraordinary growth, as well as the plummeting value of Nigerian currency and spiraling household poverty, rendered African brand-name markets both irredeemable and unnecessary to brand-name manufacturers. Subsequently, the way was paved for Nigerian pharmaceutical market abandonment to become inseparable from drug-industry speculation.

*Risky Populations and the Spectacle of Dictatorship*

One day I was sitting in Odili's very small market stall, often leaning one way or another as people moving through the market passed or stepped over me. Odili did not have many products on his shelves, unlike some of his wealthier counterparts on the main road in Idumota. However, the small-time players in this alleyway buried deeper in the market can still earn a decent income. That day I was conducting the only taped interview I did with Odili. Toks, the pharmacist who had several retail outlets, was there as well. Both Odili and Toks are in their forties and had entered the pharmaceutical business in the 1980s, at the onset of structural adjustment. Toks, as already noted, had gone to university and was trained as a pharmacist. Odili had been an apprentice for Ikenna, who works on the main road in Idumota. Odili and Toks had done business together on and off in the past, and both participated in the conversation. What started off as a discussion about market structure took an unexpected turn when they began reminiscing about a number of terrifying days that they had experienced during the dictatorship of General Sani Abacha in the late 1990s, one of Nigeria's most horrific eras of governance.

Odili turned to Toks and asked: "You don forget the day wey they carry me and you go? [You haven't forgotten the day when they came and took us away?]"

"Ah! *That* day!" Toks exclaimed, as they both laughed at the uncomfortable memory. Toks turned to me and asked: "Do you know that they arrested us? Nigerian Drug Law Enforcement Agency" (NDLEA).

"For what?" I asked.

"They just wanted money! It was horrible," he replied.

"Did you go to jail?"

"No, they took us to their camp, their redemption camp for hardened criminals."

"No!"

"Oh, [I am] serious, both of us," he replied, moving his finger between himself and Odili, who was standing over us as Toks and I sat together on a small wooden bench. "Ah ha! They wanted money. They handcuffed us. They handcuffed me," he declared.

Odili punctuated Toks's account with "1998!"—the year it happened. This simple yet somewhat detached utterance hung in the air as if the encounter was still within his grasp. "1998. 1998."

Toks continued: "And the guy told me, 'Look, we are just going to make you suffer here. I know you will [pay up] at the end of the day. If you don't want to suffer just give us money.'" He was referring to the threats of torture used in this instance to extort cash. "It was just terrible. Do you know I still saw the guy [years later]?"

Odili said: "I [saw and spoke to] him [on the street] now."[9] Indeed, they had both encountered the man after the country had returned to civilian rule in 2000.

Toks looked at me and said: "The guy was begging [years later]. He said, 'Ah, sorry.'" Toks recalled the later encounter as if he were living it all over again: "In fact I would have dealt with him that day.... Number one is windscreen, I would have destroyed it. I would have deflated the tire so that he cannot move. Then I would just go and call the police."

Returning to the original point, Odili said to me: "[Violence was] the religion. 1998. Terrible. Terrible situation."

Toks picked up from where he had left off: "He now started begging me, he started begging me: during Abacha there is nothing he could do, he said." Suddenly Toks began to imitate the words and gestures of the agents who arrested them: "Nobody would know you are here!"

Odili interjected: "And that is it, oh! Do you know how much we spent? Four hundred thousand [naira]."

Toks said: "These guys, I know they wanted . . ."

"*Four hundred thousand!*" exclaimed Odili, finishing Toks's sentence.

"I mean they collected [a large amount of extortion money] *then!*" declared Toks. Turning to Odili, he asked, "That was how many years ago?"

"1998."

"When [the] naira was still very valuable."

"1998."

Toks explained to me: "I spent, they took—you know, I wanted to come and buy [pharmaceutical stock]. I was supplying [hospitals and retail outlets]."

Getting ahead of the story, Odili asked Toks: "Was it sixty thousand [naira]?"

Knowing precisely what Odili was referring to, Toks said: "They took all the sixty thousand from me, and that was all the money I had in my life."

By this point I was lost. I asked Toks if the day they were arrested he had been coming to shop for pharmaceuticals or if he had made a previous arrangement to purchase something.[10] He said that he had come to purchase drugs from Odili's company. But the NDLEA agents, Toks explained, had said, "We are dealing with hard drugs and in Nigeria if they say you are dealing with hard drugs, [it] is a serious offence." Indeed, just a few years earlier, the military government began executing narcotics dealers, so the threat of being framed set the tone for the rest of the encounter. When we got to this part in the story, we sat in silence for a moment, with just the hum of the generators and the sounds of familiar market activities in the background. We were soon interrupted with the ring of Odili's phone. As he took the call, I turned to Toks and said, "My God, I didn't know."

"There are so many things in my life," he laughed. "Oh, it was a sad experience, the first time in my life I cried. Even when my father died I didn't cry. I cried that day because it is a serious offence; they can kill you."

Off the phone now, Odili picked up the conversation again effortlessly. Looking at me, he said: "Many people died there [at the redemption camp]. . . . Now you know before [the agents] came to our own [business] they took [others who died] to that place. That was why everybody was panicking and that was why we pay that money."

"So you can die there and nobody would ask of [about] you. Nobody. It was notorious then. Cocaine was death penalty then. They kill them. Anyway, it was a terrible time," added Toks.

"That's military for you," said Odili.

"It was a terrible time," responded Toks.

"That's the military for you," said Odili. They continued to echo each other until Toks pulled himself back to the moment when his life savings were taken from him: "All the money I have in my life! You know I used to do supply. So what I do, I come to the market, buy drugs and sell to hospitals.

[The agents] took everything I had. So it's either that, or you stay [in detention]. You would go to court but before you get to court nobody would know you have suffered—they would tell you that."

"That is what they said now," Odili said, affirming Toks's account.

"You would suffer; you would even almost die. They would release you, but you would suffer and it's true what they are saying, it's actually true you would suffer," Toks said, recalling the physical violence and torture that many people had experienced in the camp.

I asked: "How would they collect the money? Did you have to call someone to bring it?"

Toks answered: "No, I had the money. No, they knew what they were doing, now. They know that [Odili's employer at the time] is a big pharmaceutical business. So the NDLEA knew [Odili's company] had money. But me, before they knew I wanted to come [to see Odili], they'd been watching me, [they knew] that I had some money on me. You know they search you, they search everybody, get everybody . . ."

Odili looked at me and asked: "Do you know what they did? [The agents entered the building and] they said all the people inside should not go out."

Toks imitated the agents again, this time yelling: "Nobody should go out!"

Also imitating the agents, Odili shouted: "All of you remain inside." Then he turned to Toks and said: "You were wondering—I was telling you to go."

"But they were carrying guns and I don't want them to go and shoot me. You know I almost escaped, really, but they could have—I don't want them to go and shoot me."

"Because I know if you are not involved I would have . . ."

Raising his voice, Toks said: "We were on handcuff all through out! They paraded us [through the market]; people were watching and saying, 'Oh, oh!'"

"It was . . . yeah."

"They tore my shirt, slapped me so many times."

Caught up in their emotion, I said: "Oh, God, no!"

"It was terrible. I wish not to see that kind of thing again," said Odili.

"I said I cried; in my life, [I] have never cried like that."

"It was terrible," Odili said. "It was terrible. I have—have never seen in my life. I never wish to remember that thing."

Turning to Odili, I asked: "how long were you there?"

"Eh, four days, four days."

"And how long were you there?" I asked Toks. But Odili interrupted, to return to an unfinished part of the conversation: "It wasn't even him [Toks] they wanted, it was the company they wanted."

"It was by chance that they saw me," confirmed Toks.

Referring to Toks, Odili said to me: "But now that he was there, [the agents] noticed he has money."

"If not, I would have gone. They were the target."

"You were the target?" I asked Odili.

Toks answered for him: "Yes, because they wanted the company to pay big money; he was working for the company."

We paused for a moment, absorbing it all. I broke the silence by asking Toks how long he stayed in the camp.

"Just an hour or so."

"How long did you stay?" I asked Odili again.

"For about four days. Four days."

"[He was there for that long] because they have to go and find the money. Four hundred thousand," Toks explained.

"Is it not money they want?" Odili asked, rhetorically.

"Naira was very heavy [valuable]," Toks said, reminding us of the more favorable rate of exchange with the dollar at that time.

"1998."

"Very valuable."

"Am telling you. 1998."

"Naira was very valuable."

I interrupted this sequence of echoes: "1998. That was maybe ten naira to one dollar, at least, no?"[11]

"Naira was very strong, a lot of money," said Toks.

Only then did I begin to grasp the actual amount involved, based on the exchange rate at the time. "That's over $100,000," I said. I got the exchange rate wrong; in fact, it was more like $50,000. But then I returned to the emotion of the moment: "My God. Ah, sorry oh. Pele [sorry]!"

Odili began to imitate the agents again: "If you mention the thing [extortion], if you mention . . ."

Toks explained to me: "They will even tell you, if you tell the thing [extortion] to anybody—[he too began to imitate the agents] 'Do you know we have your identity [identification card]? . . . If you mention it, you are dead.'"

After a pause, I asked Toks: "But you now saw this man afterwards."

"Yes, I saw him, he started apologizing."

Odili added: "At the end [of the day], he will say that he was sent, he was doing his job."

"Yeah, he said he was sent. It was his oga ["boss" in Yoruba] that sent him. He was not the one. I just left him to God."

The conversation is repetitive, and the two men moved in and out of the past when speaking of their detention, as if they were still experiencing it. There are many specters, many histories here. The drug enforcement agency that threw them into detention was a branch of the military government. The NDLEA agents were trained by the staff of the U.S. Drug Enforcement Administration and adopted a policy similar to the war on drugs initiated by President Ronald Reagan (Klantschnig 2013). It was an approach that criminalized drug use and targeted production rather than addressing problems with consumption. By the 1990s the United States sanctioned the Nigerian government, which coincided with scaled-up repression carried out by the NDLEA, of which Odili and Toks were just two of numerous targets (see Klantschnig 2013). Indeed, new forms of accumulation became possible in Nigeria through elite capture of privatized resources as well as extracting payments from the citizenry. Lower-level officials were kept out of large-scale deals that were made among military and civilian elites. But they found their own ways of extracting money, targeting nonelite players such as Odili and Toks.

The Abacha dictatorship they referred to had followed several Nigerian dictatorships sparked by a tanking economy in the 1980s. Although Nigeria had previous coups d'état, the period coinciding with the SAP was especially turbulent. In the span of just ten years, military officials carried out four coups d'état: in 1983, 1985, 1990 (a failed one), and 1993.[12] Immediately after the 1985 coup General Ibrahim Babangida cited corruption and the government's failure to deal with the worsening economic crisis in his justification for the coup, even though various forms of economic austerity had been implemented under prior regimes.[13] Once Babangida took office, he set up what was billed as a public debate on the question of SAP. The idea was to appear to go through a democratic decision-making process, but the public response was overwhelmingly against the IMF's proposals. Despite the attempt to appease the public, Babangida created a home-grown SAP that included unpopular austerity measures, some of which were worse than those the IMF had originally proposed (see Jega 2000; Olukoshi 1993). The previous coups were welcomed by some sectors of society because the new rulers promised to restore order. However, Babangida's regime began a new wave of violence and corruption in Nigeria that was strongly correlated with unfolding austerity and privatization programs. In 1993 General Sani Abacha took over and implemented violence on an unprecedented scale, which was met with a massive prodemocracy movement that resisted austerity and dictatorship throughout the 1990s.[14] Indeed, when translated to militaristic governance, the repressive methods of Nigeria's war on drugs additionally reflected the state's attempt to control popular protests calling for the end of military rule (Klein 1999).

As austerity and dictatorship formed a necessary intimacy, the state was faced with immediate and high levels of unemployment resulting from structural adjustment. The unemployment in this case did not quite amount to "floating populations" described by Karl Marx ([1867] 1992; cf. Berry 1985) that were detached from their previous anchors of livelihood. In Marx's description of primitive accumulation, people living on common lands in England were forcibly removed via the Enclosure Acts of the seventeenth and eighteenth centuries, which drove people into waged factory work and turned them into a new kind of laborer. In other words, privatizing formerly communal land created a labor force for nearby industrialization (Marx [1867] 1992). Under structural adjustment, however, people who became unemployed—some who had already been waged workers for either the state or industry—did not become available for new forms of industrialization or any other forms of formal work. Instead, labor was transformed into surplus. Austerity measures did not attempt to put labor back to work but focused on putting capital to work: massive capital flight, new forms of debt, and industry consolidation were made possible as markets and labor were also being restructured on a global scale.

The task of governing under such circumstances certainly has the features of necropolitics, which Achille Mbembe describes as subjugating life to the power of death. The foundation of Mbembe's necropolitics is "the generalized instrumentalization of human existence and the material destruction of human bodies and populations" (2003, 14) as a central project of state sovereignty, with actual state systems being able to function only in a state of emergency.[15] Mbembe draws on, yet distinguishes necropolitics from, a European biopolitics described by Michel Foucault in which populations of liberal subjects are seen as being "at risk," and thus for the purposes of industrialization much work must be invested in the biological survival and healthiness of the population (Foucault 1990).[16] In necropolitics, however, the population becomes subjected to the prospect of death. Although the threat of terror looms large in military governance, in necropolitical analysis the question of surplus labor and the actual prospects of working receive less attention. But as Mbembe points out, resource extraction has been increasingly emphasized, which is directly linked to what he calls "management of the multitudes" (2003, 34).

The Nigerian military government had to face a population that was already imagining itself as participating in a social contract, and that was expecting to have—indeed, was already receiving—public goods like education and pensions (Freund 1978). The short-lived postcolonial "at risk" population gave way to *risky populations* who aggressively protested reforms and whose sense of security was rapidly eroding, posing risks to the military state. Yusuf Bangura and Bjorn Beckman's (1993) analysis of African workers and structural adjustment is important here. The authors carefully demonstrate how workers consistently showed up as "obstacles" to the state, whether as labor that was deemed too costly or as the citizenry's outright resistance to austerity. My use of the term *risky populations* was not adopted by the state, nor does it refer only to premeditated actions taken by the military government, even though censorship, including shutting down newspapers; political assassinations; and quotidian extractions like the one that Odili and Toks experienced were part of a calculus of sorts. Rather, I use the term to capture a diffuse sensibility practiced up and down the military state, one that reacted to various threats and competition within the state, whose political and economic survival was at stake. It was a sensibility that was violently displaced entirely onto the social body, which led to a tension between the state retaining its international line of credit and the prospect that the middle class and, certainly, the majority of Nigerians would fall into poverty.

Indeed, the social body was being reworked via micro practices and enactments of militarized power as internal power struggles and social inequalities mediated new fiscal relationships. These included following creditors' prescriptions; allowing markets to be abandoned; competition within the military state over the seizing of public assets during the privatization process; and identifying new derivative forms of money making, whether they be the round-tripping discussed in chapter 1, the outright disappearance of funds, or new extractions. Although political patrons and their respective clients were propped up, as Daniel Smith (2008) described, these social and economic formations became inseparable from the way in which militarized state sovereignty and the citizenry were reordered.

A population becomes "risky" when it attempts to reconnect to old regimes of living or gain recognition in new ones (Collier and Lakoff 2005), but must come to terms with new ethics, subjectivities, and economic orders. Theories of risk in liberal societies must be distinguished here. In fifteenth- and sixteenth-century Europe, risk was perceived to be outside of human control and located instead in natural disasters (Ewald 1993; Luhmann 2005). This notion of risk shifted during the eighteenth and nineteenth centuries, when it was linked to technological development (Beck 1992) and could be calculated for the purpose of regulating society (Foucault 1990; Hacking 1990). By the twentieth century, human conduct could be modified to mediate risk (Lupton 1999). European and American notions of risk assume that some kind of stability or ground exists, for which safety or security is juxtaposed with deviated notions of risk. Insurance works largely in this vein because it presupposes that there is some kind of "normal" in people's lives for which things like accidents or the unexpected can be calculated as outside of an imagined standard.

But none of these transformations or expectations of risk translate well in Nigeria. They are tied to the development of the European nation-state, so my usage of risk actually differs from this genealogy. Rather, looking at histories of colonialism is more apropos. The kind of agency that liberal risk paradigms afford does not exist for people subjected to colonial governance. As Frantz Fanon (2005) observed, the very body of the colonized person is not marked by a notion of liberal (much less human) will, agency, or subjectivity. When it becomes permissible to violently alter the lives of entire populations, whether under colonial governance or in military regimes, the privilege of liberal risk does not necessarily belong to populations as some kind of lived ontology. Rather, it belongs to those who govern, those who discern the risk that the multitudes pose to state interests and to those in power.

In managing the multitudes that become risky populations and in privileging the interests of international creditors, structural adjustment had the effect of finishing off the Nigerian multinational brand-name drug market. If necropolitics connotes being subjugated to death, then pharmaceuticals are an apt way to think about life-and-death politics. Indeed, with the new speculative door opening, drug companies saw Nigeria's ever-declining standard of living as a threat to what had once been a thriving pharmaceutical market. The corporate headquarters of North American and European drug companies had to estimate risk in a distinctly different way than the military government of Nigeria. Companies had to calculate risk in terms of speculative market practices, a Nigerian consumer population newly seen to be risky, and a market whose value was tanking. Nigerians' newly impoverished status was essentially weighed against new competitive strategies.

### Drug Industry Divestment in Nigeria

Industry pharmacists recruited by global companies as medical representatives in the 1970s faced enormous problems in the 1980s. Local manufacturers could no longer invest or reinvest in raw materials. Thanks to import substitution policies, all petrochemical-based raw materials needed for drug manufacture are imported to Nigeria, despite the fact that the country is an oil producer. With devaluation, the cost of importing raw materials skyrocketed, defying the IMF's original claim that the SAP would be sustainable. Important was the 1972 indigenization policy, which appropriated transnational assets to build local industry that ended with the implementation of the SAP. A former worker for Roche, the Swiss drug company, explained to me:

> The Structural Adjustment Program—of course you know it was World Bank–fashioned—discouraged [the indigenization policy], and if you have free enterprises or free markets it means that this "hostile" regime [the indigenization policy] has been withdrawn, and there's the possibility that people will come and try their luck in investing in the market. Nigeria has a very big market, 120 million [people], so if you want to do business in Africa you will think about that. The whole of all West African countries combined together is still a fraction of our population. So you could just go to one country rather than thirteen [different West African states].

The SAP discourse of free markets designated for African economies meant that either state-run industries or those industries that were built out of transnational capital repatriation would open up to new actors vying to grab the remnants of breaking systems. It produced precisely the opposite effect, especially with mandatory currency devaluation. A local executive for Glaxo Nigeria told me how both import substitution and the rapid decline of the naira had affected his company.

We were importing raw materials from the parent company. We bought raw materials, produced, distributed on market, would sell, and collect the money back. We have expatriates who were here in this country. We had to pay the salaries of expatriates, pay everybody and repatriate, if I may use the word, the income back home where the company is. . . . [Y]ou import your raw materials, packaging, and everything at 100 naira to a dollar and then before you finish selling the same batch of goods between one month and two months, the exchange rate has gone to about 130. That is about 30 percent, so automatically the physical money you are going to repatriate overseas makes no sense then. They were operating at a loss. So they said, "Gentlemen, what are you doing in this country? Pack and come back." Most expatriate staff were asked to come back because it was not sustainable, because you can see why we have to pay so much and get nothing. So that is also one of the areas that were IMF-affected, and [it] made sure that companies who were here quickly [sold] off and kept skeletal services here because it was easier at that time to import than manufacture.

The now high cost of imported raw materials and currency devaluation, combined with rising prices, meant that consumers had much less money to spend. The ever-widening exchange rate meant that drug companies could not sell their stock and continued to let workers go, while all drug companies were steadily losing profits. A marketer who had been working for Ciba Geigy, the Swiss pharmaceutical company, at the time explained:

I know most companies left the country during the IMF SAP policy, which devalued the naira. And at the point of devaluation you cannot meet up with turnover. Before devaluation of the naira, Ciba Geigy Nigeria was number three worldwide [in terms of sales] because the naira was strong, at times challenging the dollar. With heavy deregulation, Ciba sold off their plants. You need to sell a lot more to meet turnover in dollars. But was the economy able to support this? It was not. So companies started forming decisions on how to do business in the country. I could remember my company sponsored a meeting here in the Sheraton [Hotel] on how to do business in Africa, and they started looking through each therapeutic area and what the population could afford. And of course price still remains an issue when you have a population where 70 percent live below the poverty line. And this was a result of IMF SAP policy.

Another medical representative, who worked for Pfizer, remembered:

I was just joining Pfizer then [1985–87], and it was a very serious issue for the multinationals. We had lots of stock that we could not sell with the raw materials that we brought in and trying to adjust themselves with pricing. The prices were really on the high side, and this equally encouraged the [smuggling of lower-priced and faked products]. They could not cope with the overhead and the price increase because definitely there was resistance from the drugs that were being sold because of the price. I mean we were buying at one naira, and it turned into four naira per dollar. It was sure a big jump for you to be able to cope. And equally [I] remember that time it was an issue that led to Pfizer eventually taking a decision in 1996–97 to sell off the company; management buy over took place. They had to sell to Neimeth [the Nigerian subsidiary] and just create a scientific office; and in case it gets better, we could come back fully. Because we were looking at what we were [earning] in the '80s [compared] to what we were doing in the '90s because of this devaluation of the naira. You were [earning] five million dollars some ten years back. You suddenly discover that you are doing two million or one million dollars. It was a serious, big issue. The policy was a serious problem for companies.

Devaluation created fairly dramatic transformations, in which successful drug-market niches suddenly encountered substantial financial losses. This had an impact on the relationships between parent and subsidiary companies. Although Nigeria indigenized companies' assets in the early 1970s, expatriate and Nigerian workers' relationships remained fairly close because indigenization simply created Nigerian-owned subsidiary companies, sometimes employing expatriate staff members. Moreover, these companies relied on raw materials from the parent company rather than manufacturing their own.

Nigerian workers for the pharmaceutical industry consistently speak fondly of their time during the oil boom heyday, when "Nigeria was Nigeria," as some are apt to say. The prestige of their Nigerian education and their employment status was recognized beyond their profession as pharmacists, and their corporate employers were highly regarded in society. They did not view themselves as small players in the pharmaceutical world, and they had long maintained amiable connections to their parent companies. Despite the congenial relationships between parent and subsidiary firms, pharmaceutical companies had to calculate new circuits of accumulation, recognize a new increase in standards of living outside of Africa, and at the same time rapidly identify sites of dispossession that global recessions and structural adjustment had generated. Drug companies adapted quickly, and pharmaceuticals were entirely rerouted and aligned to these new logics of labor and capital. As a marketer who had worked for Roche during the 1990s put it: "Basically it's a matter of economics or calculation. You have two options you weigh. There are companies like Shell, oil companies doing good business, and you look at what they bring in compared with the pharmaceutical industry. You lose here and you gain more there. It's not about pharmaceutical policy or the interest of Nigerians." "You lose here and you gain more there"—this is what it boiled down to for those drug companies with large worldwide market shares located in the Nigerian market.

Some former medical representatives told me that managers in the parent companies were concerned about losing the entirety of the Nigerian market and advocated for staying put. But at the end of the day, these long-term partnerships, and the social and economic investments that had developed those relationships over time, were structurally severed—a decision taken by managers at companies' headquarters. And so, a new type of calculation immediately took hold. It was not about trying to save a market, a steady line of profit. It was about being smart about flexibility in an environment that was changing the game of global competitiveness. The companies understood what needed to shut down and what needed to move, what ties needed to be cut; they responded to the new inducements to move from one country to the next. Every foreign drug company that had been manufacturing in Nigeria packed up and moved abroad (many to Asia), shut down, or expanded their operations at existing sites and manufacturing plants in Europe and the United States. The companies that divested or ended their operations in Nigeria included Imperial Chemical Industries, Bayer, Upjohn, Parke-Davis, Boots, Wellcome, and Hoechst. Pfizer divested after a forty-year presence in Nigeria. The Nigerian market was rapidly disappearing.

Reading through industry news and academic journal articles from this period, one cannot help seeing the panic on the horizon. Within the first two years after the implementation of SAP, approximately 1,500 pharmacists left Nigeria for the United Kingdom or the United States to seek employment, amounting to nearly 20 percent of the workforce (Samba 2004).

Drugs and other aspects of health care had once been subsidized, but the SAP required the introduction of user fees, increasing consumer costs; drug prices rose astronomically. Furthermore, in a short amount of time, fake drugs began to outcompete genuine products. In fact, *Pharmanews*, the industry magazine, reported that in 1987, 70 percent of the entire Nigerian drug supply to the local market was composed of fake drugs ("Only 30% Drugs in Nigeria are Genuine" 1987). Dire health problems were one result. For example, Ebrahim Samba (2004) presents evidence that the number of malaria deaths quadrupled shortly after the SAP was implemented simply because drugs had become scarce and unaffordable. In order to cope with this emerging situation, companies adjusted their marketing strategies to try to compete with the fakes that were rapidly accounting for the bulk of sales. This included implementing more efficient and aggressive selling techniques; introducing targeted marketing; placing more representatives in the field; selling drugs for fewer health indications; developing improved products; developing new products for foreign markets; modifying existing products for new markets; and the use of aggressive advertising that put competitors on the defensive (Adenika 2000).

As the squeeze on foreign exchange continued, desperate attempts to market and sell products became intertwined with prescribing practices. For example, drug companies whose products were moving much more slowly than usual began to require customers to purchase certain pharmaceuticals before purchasing others (Okereke 1987). Some companies were selling drugs for less than their recommended price because they made a faster profit that way (Okereke 1987). Ben Olaoye (1991) documents how coping strategies included inventing new doses and selling lower doses at higher prices. Aside from price differentials, pharmacists were concerned about how changes in prescribing would affect drug absorption (via digestion), as well as other health concerns. These prescribing practices were linked to the problem of high prices, maintaining adequate stocks of drugs, and drug availability. Although these practices were a direct result of deregulation and market restructuring, they eventually became standard in drug-company marketing.

These scenarios created some alarm for pharmacist-policy makers because toward the end of the oil boom funding had been slated to expand drug distribution and the national health infrastructure. Especially problematic was a dearth of pharmacists, which was beginning to put tight constraints on the health care system as well as nascent plans to build new university-level pharmacy schools. But these plans put a great deal of pressure on the system because drugs, infrastructure, and professional human resources were all contracting at once (Adenika 1998).[17] As drug chemistry and dosage became tied to changing marketing strategies, companies had to ascertain the risk of going under, the risk of a massive scarcity of medicines, and the new sorts of risks that patients encountered. But seen on the global scale, risk took on a different meaning in the new speculative world of pharmaceuticals.

### The Speculative Turn: Upjohn and Pfizer

In the 1980s, at the same time that SAPs were being implemented across Africa, brand-name pharmaceutical earnings were slipping across the globe. Generic versions of drugs were already flooding world markets in the 1970s, which posed significant competition to brand-name companies, whose foreign sales amounted to more than one-half of total company revenue (Silverman and Lee 1992, 27). The emergence of competitive generics was accompanied by new international policies regarding rational drug use. Notable among them was the World Health Organization's Essential Drug List, which posed new competitive threats to brand-name drug companies because of its advocacy of generic substitution (Greene 2011). Moreover, future industry revenue was in jeopardy because companies, on the whole, had few promising drug research pipelines and numerous company products were facing patent expirations—research and patenting being critical sources of income (Kanji et al. 1992).

By the 1980s, the Reagan administration responded by budgeting more money for life sciences research (most of which went to the National Institutes of Health), "which henceforth would become the most heavily funded area of basic science research in the United States apart from defense" (M. Cooper 2008, 27). In 1980, the U.S. Congress also passed the Bayh-Dole Act, which enabled smoother technology transfers between research-based academia and biotechnology companies (M. Cooper 2008; Greene 2011). That same year, the U.S. Supreme Court ruled in *Diamond v. Chakrabarty* that patent rights could be applied to genetically modified organisms, playing "a seminal role in the commercialization of biotechnology" (Jasanoff 1995, 206).

Critically, all of these events enabled the drug industry to remake itself by becoming intricately tied to the speculative marketplace, and the industry pursued speculative capital via the NASDAQ Stock Market as a way out of stagnation (M. Cooper 2008; M. Fortun 2008). The standard of pharmaceutical value became entirely set by the investment community. Specifically, it values drug companies not simply by the amount of profit earned but also, and more importantly, by rates of growth, with expectations pegged as high as 13 percent per year (Sunder Rajan 2012, 323). As Kaushik Sunder Rajan (2012) points out, companies do not produce enough new drugs to achieve these growth rates, which amounts to an inherent structural contradiction. To meet the growth expectations of the investment community would require that a company bring to market multiple drugs each year—a highly difficult, if not impossible, goal to achieve because it takes up to fifteen years to develop a drug and bring it to market.[18] This is why companies come to rely on blockbuster drugs that make over $1 billion per year as well as producing "me-too" drugs—drugs that are chemically similar to existing marketed products—that are easy to develop, although not always easy to sell in a highly competitive environment (Sunder Rajan 2012).

During the 1990s stock market investment was the only source of revenue for many start-up companies, many of which were attached to the brand-name pharmaceutical industry via licensing agreements (Sunder Rajan 2006).[19] As Melinda Cooper notes, the NASDAQ listed high-risk firms that had yet to make a profit, and they were allowed to include a range of intangible speculative assets in their portfolios. These included patents on not yet commercialized products, which amounted to claims of future profits (2008). As Wall Street orchestrated companies' market valuations, there emerged a highly competitive scramble in the realm of drug discovery (M. Fortun 2004; Sunder Rajan 2006). In short, the industry was completely reshaped through financial speculation, new property regimes, new molecular technologies, and new entrants into the field that manage the industrialization of life itself—a field in which, Cooper argues, the rise of biotechnology became inseparable from the rise of neoliberalism (2008, 19).

It was at this time that Wall Street's "takeover movement" began (Ho 2009, 123–68). As Karen Ho explains, Wall Street accomplished this takeover by "putting corporations 'in play,' . . . where all the largest corporations were up for grabs to the highest stock-price bidder, thus forcing them to be immediately responsive to the exigencies of the stock market" (2009, 129). Ho describes how market booms and busts are associated with a particular corporate culture that, in turn, is tied to the construction of shareholder value—a business term that connotes that the ultimate measure of a company's success is measured by how much it enriches its shareholders. For example, mergers and acquisitions are commonly pushed to obtain immediate gains when company earnings cannot meet investors' expectations of high growth. But over the long term, these deals can bring the value of shares down and possibly help undermine the productivity of the corporate clients that investment banks advise (Ho 2009, 126). Wall Street dictates led the drug industry into a frenzy of consolidations during the 1990s, which made international news. But less attention was paid to an equally important strategy to survive competition and unrealistic investor expectations: asset dumping in foreign markets. Two prominent companies that had a significant presence in Nigeria—Upjohn and Pfizer—carried out company consolidation and asset dumping in exemplary ways.

In the 1980s Upjohn, a U.S.-based company, had two major offices: the company's headquarters in Kalamazoo, Michigan, and a European office in Brussels, Belgium. The Brussels office coordinated Upjohn's activities in Europe, Africa, and the Middle East, and once Nigeria's economy began its severe contraction, Upjohn's Brussels office moved what was left of its assets in Nigeria to Europe. Mr. Adebayo, one of Upjohn's directors, was still working at the company at that time. He explained to me that although Upjohn was making millions elsewhere (and even making roughly $500,000 in Nigeria each year), the Nigerian market was beginning to slump severely. At the same time that Nigeria was restricting imports, as mandated by the SAP, brand-name drug companies had opportunities to invest in Russia, as the Soviet Union was breaking apart. Part of Upjohn's problem was that the company had just built a manufacturing facility in Ibadan, about 150 kilometers north of Lagos, so it was not easy to pick up and leave overnight. Operations were scaled down to minimal levels but kept going in the hope that a comeback would be eventually possible.

All the multinationals decided to divest themselves of holdings in Africa, which Mr. Adebayo refers to as the "voluntary collapse" of a significantly large foreign market. A "voluntary collapse" of a drug market is very different from the "market failure" described by welfare economists (see, for example, Pigou [1920] 2012) and their neoliberal critics in the Chicago school (see, for example, Coase 1960). Markets "fail" when allocated goods in a free market are not efficient—specifically, when no person can be better off without making some others worse off (a state commonly known in economics as Pareto efficiency). Markets are also understood to fail when they are noncompetitive because they are monopolized by one or a few businesses or when production results in externalities—that is, unintended third-party costs and benefits.[20] In the latter part of the twentieth century economists debated the extent to which—and in what context—a national government can or should intervene through regulation to offset market failure.

But these debates do not account for the kind of activity and events I am describing here. Market failure as defined in economic theory is concerned with an ideal equilibrium reached between those directly engaged in exchange, for which externalities (Coase 1960) must be mitigated.[21] Actors' subjectivity and their positions of power are absent here, and monopolies and externalities are thus decontextualized. Events in Nigeria do not reflect failure in the traditional economic sense—practices of exchange and the problems of social costs. Rather they reflect outright market abandonment, which is not accounted for in this economic paradigm.

The impacts of voluntary collapse or market abandonment were substantial. For example, Mr. Adebayo marketed Togamycin, a brand-name version of spectinomycin. It was used in Africa in the late 1970s and early 1980s as a second-line antibiotic for the treatment of gonorrhea and other infections (Obaseiki-Ebor et al. 1985). It had become standard treatment in the United States after strains of such infections developed resistance to penicillin (Savage 1973). In Nigeria two million units of the drug were sold per year; according to Adebayo, that amounted to 15 percent of its global sales, making Nigeria the number-one market in the world at the time. A demand for Togamycin did not emerge in other places, which meant that 15 percent of its worldwide sales could not be absorbed elsewhere. Marketing and planning on a global level were disrupted because they had to revolve around transnational stock planning, supplies of raw materials, and manufacturing output. Upjohn decided to simply stop marketing Togamycin in Nigeria. Moreover, the company had also just launched Unicap M, which within one year had become the top-selling oral multivitamin in Nigeria. It was designed to be the first drug product wholly produced locally, from manufacture through packing to marketing. But one year after establishing this marketing plan, the import license system was imposed, followed by structural adjustment, and Unicap M was never manufactured in Nigeria.

Outside of the tanking Nigerian market, Upjohn's global earnings were on the rise, but it faced a number of challenges. For example, its best-selling drug, Motrin, was widely prescribed for arthritis and menstrual cramps in the mid-1980s. Motrin accounted for 40 percent of Upjohn's total earnings, but by the mid-1980s it was facing intense competition in the U.S. market, its largest site of sale: Motrin lost 25 percent of its market share to a product from Boots, a British-based company. However, Upjohn's sales were increasing during this period in large part due to another best-selling drug, Xanax, which was used to treat anxiety disorders. In 1985 Xanax's worldwide sales doubled, from $82.2 million to $152.4 million. By 1979, it had earned over $400 million in revenue, which continued in the 1990s when the drug was also approved for use with panic disorders. But Xanax was accused of being highly addictive, and its sales soon became sluggish (Funding Universe n.d.).

During this same period, Upjohn began marketing Rogaine, a product used to reverse hair loss, which had low sales in the mid-1980s. The company decided to bypass its usual marketing to doctors and launched direct-to-consumer advertising, spending $50 million solely on Rogaine advertising in 1987, which boosted sales. But the company faced other serious problems. For example, another drug, Halcion, a sleep-inducing agent that earned seventeen million prescriptions per year, got bad press for causing memory lapses and addiction and provoked over a hundred lawsuits. At the end of the 1980s, patents were about to expire for many of Upjohn's critical revenue-earning products, including Xanax, Micronase (for diabetes), and Cleocin (for cholesterol reduction). By 1992 Upjohn had the lowest sales in the research and development industry (Funding Universe n.d.).

The company responded in several ways, including speeding up its research efforts; working to develop high-selling over-the-counter drugs; and, like other companies, increasing its pharmaceutical prices. But importantly, in the midst of these events, drug companies were merging, consolidating, and getting bigger. Upjohn merged with Pharmacia, a Swedish company, and the new entity became the ninth-largest company in the world, with $7 billion in sales. Its U.S. sales were in a slump, but it expanded research operations in Europe and Japan, moving into health products for animals, and it sold off many of its subsidiaries. However, the merger did not bring in the expected revenue or huge projected growth (Funding Universe n.d.). So in 2000 Pharmacia and Upjohn Company merged with Monsanto and Searle. Three years later, Pfizer bought Pharmacia.

Pfizer, a global giant, began operations in Nigeria in 1954 and by 1974 had established a full-fledged plant in Lagos (Okoli n.d.).[22] Highly profitable, the company provided many perks to its African employees, including annual travel awards for up to 250 Nigerian workers and marketers to go to conferences and seminars around the world ("Pfizer Products PLC" 1992). A former Pfizer worker told me about his subsidized housing and chauffeur-driven car—and the incredible training and travel available to him and his colleagues (Mr. Adebayo reported receiving similar benefits from Upjohn). During the early 1980s Pfizer's growth, like that of other companies in the industry, was stagnant. Pfizer's coping strategy was to increase its research and development budgets by 100 percent. In addition to acquiring Warner-Lambert,[23] which made Pfizer the wealthiest pharmaceutical company in the world, it also initiated a licensing program with foreign companies, paying them royalties in exchange for marketing rights on their newly developed drugs (Reference for Business n.d.).

At the same time, Pfizer's Nigerian sales began to slow, mostly due to currency devaluation and the high cost of raw materials in the country. During the oil boom, Pfizer, like other multinational companies, had charged high prices for its products because many Nigerian customers had the capacity to pay them. But after earning power was depleted and currency devaluation set in, the company was no longer earning upward of $5 million per year in Nigeria. Like other European and U.S. pharmaceutical companies doing business in the country, Pfizer was unwilling to lower prices even for a society that was plummeting into ever-expanding poverty. By 1997 Pfizer had halted all manufacturing in Nigeria and divested itself of its holdings in the country. Unlike Upjohn, Neimeth—Pfizer's Nigerian subsidiary—orchestrated a buyout. Mazi Sam Ohuabunwa, Pfizer's CEO for West Africa, raised 270 million naira to pay for Pfizer's assets in Nigeria ("Pfizer Divests, Neimeth Is Born"1997, 1). Many subsidiaries bought out their parent companies.

These dramatic changes in the industry exacerbated some existing problems that Mr. Adebayo and other high-level managers identified in the structure of the Nigerian drug market. As a product manager, Mr. Adebayo attempted to fill the gap between available drug products and health care needs that had received less attention. Certainly some products were marketed as ways to prevent or treat diseases with high morbidity, like malaria, and those products sold well. However, drugs for worm infections such as schistosomiasis and leishmaniasis were also far less available. This was due to the fact that pharmaceutical companies did not prioritize such drugs then—nor do they even now. But there were also less prevalent diseases such as hypertension and cancer for which there were few available products. Although companies were selling literally millions of bottles of antidiarrheal medication, the only hypertensive drug on the market, Minoxidil, was "coming in trickles" to Nigeria, according to Mr. Adebayo. As Nigerian pharmacists knew back then, morbidity related to malaria and diarrhea was very high, and the tendency is to overlook a broader disease landscape, one that also includes cancer, hypertension, and diabetes, to name just a few diseases.[24]

In addition to their desire to draw attention to neglected diseases, Nigerian pharmacists saw themselves as educating medical professionals in their country about new medications as they reached the market. Mr. Adebayo described this as "concept selling" and said that with the release of new drug products in the 1960s and 1970s, new learning curves were established across medical fields and continents. At that time, Upjohn sponsored lectures for physicians on new medical findings coupled with pharmaceutical treatments throughout the United States. Mr. Adebayo's work for Upjohn did much of the same thing in Nigeria:

> When you talk to the doctor about anaerobic infections, he said, "yes, tetanus," [and] that's all he knew. And we said, "No, we are not talking about tetanus, we are talking *Staphylococcus*, *Peptostreptococcus*, etc." You begin to teach doctors that there is aerobic *Staph* [*Staphylococcus*] and there is anaerobic *Staph*; and the anaerobic organisms are in deep-seated wounds because they don't operate on the surface. They are the causes of gangrene, they are the causes of slow-healing wounds. . . . We got [the doctors] gradually, we convinced [them]. . . . We did the education on anaerobic infections and we [marketed] Clindamycin [an antibiotic especially effective against anaerobic bacteria]. Today everybody uses Flagyl [an antibiotic and antiparasitic] because it was only when we had done the education that [the British multinational company] May and Baker now came in with Flagyl. Because Flagyl is very effective against anaerobes—very effective—you could see that it was really moving on, and we were getting results. We knew if that had not happened, today Upjohn [would have] been wonderfully big here. Also, because we were preparing the ground, we had anticancers. But today, Roche (and some generics) makes a lot of money from anticancers. Roche was not even a player in the anticancer market [back] then. Upjohn was the only company going 'round teaching the doctors all these things, but [Upjohn] didn't last long enough to benefit from it.

Selling pharmaceuticals at this point in the 1970s was a combination of education and seeing how Upjohn could expand its market share by addressing national disease burdens. As Mr. Adebayo pointed out, it was not simply a matter of marketing drugs that appeared to be useful in a particular market. In fact, that market had to be created; public, professional, and corporate knowledge had to be produced along with new market strategies. The mismatch between disease burdens and the products available in the market began the moment that foreign companies began exporting drugs to West Africa. And although Mr. Adebayo and others tried to remedy the problem, divestment halted their efforts, and a long-term pattern of mismatch was established.

Indeed, prior to drug company divestment, Pfizer's development strategies in Nigeria included work on infectious, cardiovascular, and inflammatory diseases, as well as diabetes ("Pfizer Products PLC" 1992). But former company directors at Neimeth indicated to me that product priority plans had to change. Importantly, Neimeth aimed to identify new potential markets as the economy was being radically transformed. Not only did Neimeth move away from manufacturing products it had once marketed in Nigeria, but it also began to import less-expensive drugs and distribute them. For example, drugs such as Loxin (a combination of ampicillin and cloxacillin used as an antibacterial) and Unaben (albendazole, an anthelmintic used to combat tapeworms and other worms) were manufactured by Korean United Pharmaceuticals in Korea but distributed by Neimeth. So by the time the economy had become fully contracted, it was difficult to introduce new drugs; all companies found it less expensive to import drugs than to manufacture them in Nigeria.[25]

Despite these dire events in Nigeria, Pfizer managed to release thirty-seven products, eight of which were blockbusters.[26] Less than a year after Pfizer left Nigeria, it also sold off several subsidiaries around the world for a total of $4.35 billion.[27] In the same year, it launched Viagra, earning nearly another billion dollars. During this same period, Pfizer increased its research and development budget sixfold, reaching nearly $2.8 billion by 1999, a sum equivalent to more than 17 percent of the company's sales. In 2000 Pfizer had earned an unprecedented $29 billion.[28]

Upjohn disappeared through mergers, and Pfizer became the largest drug company in the world. But both, along with all other foreign drug companies that had been operating in Nigeria, abandoned the Nigerian market. Ultimately, market abandonment must be understood not only as a response to the pressure of the speculative marketplace for which companies dump failing assets in order to survive intense competition. But market abandonment was also profoundly postcolonial because it dismantled the possibility of future Nigerian drug industry competition. Just four years after the SAP's implementation, Nigeria—a country that had once been a great consumer of brand-name drug products—accepted a loan from the World Bank for $20 million to purchase essential drugs to make up for the pharmaceutical shortfall in hospitals as well the high cost of drugs ("Mrs. Okoli Pleads for Indigenous Producers" 1990, 1; Okoli and Ebere 2001).[29] By 2000, after the bulk of consolidations and asset dumping took place, the five top companies' wealth amounted to twice that of the gross domestic product for all of sub-Saharan Africa (Borger 2001).

CORPORATIONS' AND MILITARY governance's management of risky populations had effects that lasted well into the future. With the market for brand-name drugs drying up after the implementation of the SAP, Nigerians had to build a new drug market and new livelihoods. The pharmaceutical market was reconfigured to meet the needs of a newly impoverished consumer base. It was also reconstructed to meet the needs of companies, which had to ascertain what could sell in Nigeria in light of the reduction in customers' purchasing power.

In no time, generic drugs from around the world would be imported into Nigeria through new unofficial markets, like Idumota, places that many Nigerians—especially Igbo traders—gravitated to in search of work. In the process, the Nigerian wholesale distribution system underwent a momentous transformation in ways that would impact future drug distribution and availability not only in Nigeria but throughout West Africa. As the public suppliers disappeared, wholesaling got re-established within unofficial markets. Over the years, these markets have rapidly expanded, creating disputes over drug regulation as well as over who is entitled to control the drug distribution system.

## Regulation as a Problem of Discernment

### *Open Markets in the Making*

[The state] must not dream that one day it will be the empire of the last day.
—Michel Foucault, *The Birth of Biopolitics*

*Markets in Newly Made Urban Space*

The financial crisis, militarism, devaluation, and market abandonment all produced devastating effects that resonated throughout the Nigerian economy, throwing people's lives into disarray. During the late 1980s and early 1990s, as foreign capital was rapidly being emptied out of Nigeria, the brand-name drug market was eviscerated. As a result, the public and the state were faced with an immense drug scarcity problem that prompted new private actors to step in. Drug traders not only helped facilitate bringing pharmaceuticals into the country but also helped create new markets and a national drug distribution system.

In the 1970s multinational manufacturers of brand-name drugs that were based in the United States and Europe controlled the distribution chain. At that time in Nigeria, they supplied their products only to registered pharmaceutical wholesalers (who were always pharmacists) throughout the country, and they in turn supplied registered community pharmacies and hospitals. This three-point distribution system evolved out of an imperial relationship that emphasized multinational corporate control of the national economy, a relationship that propped up an elite class of professionals.

By the late 1980s wholesaling was relocated from formal distribution channels to unofficial markets. Crucially, the process of privatization and devaluation under structural adjustment wiped out most (but not all) pharmacist wholesalers in the previous distribution chain. It was not simply that Igbo traders replaced these wholesalers. The physical space of wholesaling also had to be reinvented to accommodate new actors seeking new livelihoods. Unofficial markets grew in the interstices of urban space, providing new physical sites for retailing and wholesaling. Interstitial space used for market building included unexpected places falling into legally overlooked public or state-owned space: around bus stops, in the middle of traffic jams, under and around bridges, inside public transport, between private and public space in neighborhoods, and at the side of roads and expressways.[1] The new unofficial markets that were built in these different spaces were not just simply sites of exchange: in essence, they were forced to stitch the crashing public and private sectors together with new private activities. In the process, the market was reconfigured in ways that make it difficult to separate official and unofficial activity.

Unofficial markets in Nigeria grew exponentially with the onset of liberalization, and they now anchor Africa's largest popular economy. The pharmaceutical market was no exception to the incredible market growth that occurred, and Idumota became the main drug market—meaning that traders there imported drugs directly from the manufacturers. With the exception of some wholesale pharmacists who work outside of unofficial markets, few other traders in other Nigerian markets have this relationship with manufacturers. Subsequently, Idumota is often the first stop in Nigeria in the wholesale chain. Pharmaceuticals then move to other significant unofficial markets in the country that distribute drugs regionally, including Ariria in Aba (in the southeast), Sabongari in Kano (north), and Niger River Head Bridge in Onitsha (southeast).[2] Onitsha is considered the central market, getting most of its drugs from Idumota and then distributing them more widely to West Africa; it is perhaps the largest drug market in the region. The making and expanding of markets in the interstices of urban space literally grounded market conditions. These markets are powerful points in the national and regional distribution of goods.

Once pharmaceuticals began to circulate in unofficial Nigerian markets, new concerns arose because fake drugs were flooding into the country and constituted the majority of drug sales by the mid-1990s. This raised serious concerns about drug safety, especially because drug regulatory authority in Nigeria was getting newly established at the time of drug industry divestment; so controlling these substances was nearly impossible.[3] As a result, tensions grew between pharmacists and traders. Pharmacists blamed the influx of fake drugs on traders and unofficial markets, while traders accused pharmacists of being envious of traders' successful takeover of drug wholesaling. These disputes continue to play out quite extensively in the media and in academic and industry literature. But they also played out within a new regulatory regime. That is, even when SAP demanded deregulation of sorts, the state soon faced questions of drug safety and attempted to regulate a largely unrestricted environment by adopting several new regulatory laws[4] as well as creating two drug regulatory agencies—the National Agency for Food and Drug Administration and Control (NAFDAC) in 1990 and the Pharmacists Council of Nigeria (PCN) in 1992.

But new regulation encountered an expected problem. As shifting urban infrastructures accommodated new inflows of labor and new orientations toward global trade, the conceptual boundaries of institutions such as markets, state agencies, and banks were redrawn. At stake in transforming urban space was the very ontology of markets. Julie Livingston points out that "historians and philosophers of science and medicine use the term ontology to explain how scientific objects . . . became recognizable as distinct entities. It takes an array of technological, intellectual, social, political, and economic circumstances to perceive these entities and make them widely accepted as facts" (2012, 52). Markets became difficult to discern as actual entities or actual legal categories. This meant that they became difficult to regulate.

Africanist scholars have described how institutions and commercial exchange have occupied two realms—specifically, the formal and informal sectors. These scholars have studied how money and various other media of exchange have largely circulated outside formal institutions in Africa.[5]

The term *formal* usually connotes regulated capital and institutional practices that pass through banking circuits and state regulatory functions. *Informal* connotes capital, goods, and practices that largely bypass state oversight; this could include indigenous credit and banking institutions or unregulated and unofficial markets. It may at times help to use these terms to discern the circulation of goods and capital. But at other times they imply too much about what is being distributed, how things circulate, and the venues through which they move.[6] For instance, both licit and illicit pharmaceuticals travel through unofficial Nigerian markets where drugs are regulated but the premises are not. Some traders who sell pharmaceuticals in these markets are members of registered professional organizations representing legally constituted trading companies, while there are other traders at the same site who do not have such institutional representation. Such official professional organizations perform unofficial daily drug inspections that search out fake drugs in traders' shops alongside official drug market inspections conducted by NAFDAC, the federal drug regulatory agency.

The terms *informality* and *formality* may describe practices occurring within the popular economy but they do not entirely capture this interconnection between the official and unofficial. As Filip de Boeck (2013) points out, formal and informal deserve rethinking because there is a constant, active re-territorializing and reclaiming of urban space that gives rise to practices that do not fit in these categories.

Institutions were also spatially reconfigured, with contradictory meanings emerging via processes of regulation. Institutions are not so much about grounding established (legal) orders but about adapting to always shifting conditions. Several authors have discussed the production of space that is mediated by social dynamics and exchange relations that, in turn, are materially mediated by infrastructures (Choy 2011; Larkin 2008; Lefebvre 1991). Regimes of capital destroy and remake infrastructure according to how new forms of capital take root and reconstruct space (Harvey 2001). Henri Lefebvre argues that destroyed space does not go away; instead, networks and infrastructures are layered on top of old space to match new dynamics (1991; see also Larkin 2008). What these thinkers describe largely matches the way that urban space was reformatted in Nigeria. At stake are the kinds of politics and tensions that emerged as a result.

I begin by discussing the process of making new markets. A critical aspect to rebuilding the Nigerian drug market was the 1980s international narcotics trade and Nigerian money laundering. Through these activities, illicit capital contributed to making new markets and new travel routes for drug products while inventing an unofficial drug distribution system. Moreover, companies from Asia and elsewhere (Brazil and Turkey for example) also recognized the vacuum and slowly took control of the market. As new drugs poured into reformatted urban space, formal institutional activities—particularly banking and federal customs inspection—became intertwined with unofficial drug markets and unregulated activity.

From different viewpoints, scholars such as Brenda Chalfin (2010) and Janet Roitman (2005) both show how regulation and state power were diffused in nonhierarchical ways and discuss how various publics negotiated state power. In contrast, rather than negotiate the intricacies of state power, pharmacists as a public body took hold of state authority via the Pharmacists Council of Nigeria (PCN) in an attempt to reclaim the drug distribution system. To illustrate, I describe a court case (Felix Ugbojiaku & 2 Ors v Attorney General of the Federation & 4 Ors 2001) between Idumota traders and the PCN that arose when the newly established agency saw urban space as a new site of regulation—specifically, the pharmaceutical premises located in unofficial markets. In PCN's attempt to render this interstitial space illegal, an unexpected problem emerged: the definition and ontological status of a market was completely unclear and up for debate. As a result, drug regulation became a problem of discernment, because legal categories could not adjust to new realms of urban space and human agency responding to widespread turbulence and instability. I am not so much interested in diagnosing whether drug regulation is actually successful—although I believe that it rarely is at a systemic level. Rather, I am interested in what new forms of regulation actually mean or what they constitute in the immediate aftermath of massive deregulation. Moreover and importantly, regulatory processes are used to contest who is entitled to control and accumulate potentially great wealth in large, high-volume traded markets.

*Rebuilding the Market in the Aftermath of Reforms*

In June 2007 I flew to Abuja, Nigeria's capital, to attend a conference and follow up on my previous interviews with state officials about pharmaceuticals and markets. After my business was done and the conference had concluded, a friend drove me to a taxi stand so that I could get a ride to the Abuja airport and fly back to Lagos. Felix, the first available taxi driver, put my bag in the back of his somewhat beat up early 1990s Mercedes, and we began our forty-five-minute journey to the airport. Felix's Bible was on the dashboard. It was open and marked in pen; pieces of paper with scribbled notes were tucked into much of the New Testament. In a very excitable and testimonial manner, Felix told me that he used to live in Europe. The conversation went something like this:

"What did you do there?" I asked.

"Ah! I sold [illegal] drugs!" With a lyrical emphasis on the word *drugs*, he pivoted to his right to look at me in the back seat, laughing and smiling.

"Really?" I asked, laughing back at him though I was slightly shocked at his candor.

"Yes, now! How do you think I got this car?"

"And how long ago was that?"

"About ten years now."

"But you decided to come home?"

"Ah, sometimes you can't go back. . . ." I suspected he was referring to some legal trouble he may have had in Europe.

"And so you drive a taxi instead?"

"You see, I am a preacher now. . . ."

The underground narcotics trade was a significant factor in the immediate aftermath of adjustment and devaluation. Crucially, part of the new, massive flow of generic and brand-name pharmaceuticals into Nigeria was initially facilitated by money laundering of transnational narcotics sales. Nigeria's involvement in the narcotics trade was documented as early as the 1960s. With the onset of liberalization in the 1980s, these activities were scaled up when many Nigerian entrepreneurs inserted themselves into the trade at a global level (Ellis 2009; Klantschnig 2013). What began as a site of local cannabis production and small-scale trade expanded quite rapidly into significant global transportation of heroin and cocaine. Nigeria evolved into a key player for illicit narcotics trafficking just as traditional trading routes were opening up to new networks and new players. In particular, the country became a staging point between two important sites of production and distribution: Asia's Golden Triangle,[7] which distributes opium to markets in North America; and Latin America, which sends coca to Europe. That is, Nigeria managed to become a central point of distribution on both ends of these chains (Bayart, Ellis, and Hibou 1999). In Lagos these drugs were repackaged and redistributed to lucrative consumption sites in Europe and the United States.

Narcotics trading and drug-money laundering had several methods and effects, as I learned from people I met while living in Lagos, whom I describe below. They were either directly or marginally involved with, or somehow in the know about, this proliferating business. Although these activities take place in shadow economies (Nordstrom 2004; Ferguson 2006), they make their way into common urban tales, probably because illicit activity proliferated as a survival option. In many of the stories I heard, long-term unemployment was a key driver of participation in such activity.[8]

When I first moved to Lagos, I found a place to live in the back of a house in the neighborhood of Ikeja. In the front of the house were several men who were involved in some kinds of illicit activity—the kind I only understood through winks and nods. They had spent time in countries such as the United States, Germany, and Russia. I quickly discovered that one of the men, who was about my age, spoke German—a language I had learned as a foreign exchange student and he had learned working in unofficial businesses. Because I did not speak his native language, nor was I fluent in Pidgin English at the time, German was a comfortable middle ground for us. Some of these people, like many others, were combining a number of illicit and licit strategies to stay afloat in a rather expensive and unforgiving city. Others, like my taxi driver, Felix, had found God and were simply trying to live a recovered life. *Recovered* here means either that they now reflected on their past in moral terms or simply that they were drawing on the buoyancy of their work as drug couriers and sellers in the 1980s and 1990s, channeling what was left of their earnings into entrepreneurial activities and highly creative ways of surviving.

John, someone I knew who lived in another part of Lagos, told me how couriers got into that line of work, but he never spoke of his own experience. Instead, he simply moved in and out of second and third person:

> You can imagine. After five years of no work, a guy takes you [unemployed person] to the Big Man [drug baron]. And the [unemployed] guy now sees the big house with all the luxury cars and he gets excited. After about one or two bottles of champagne, the Big Man will now give him, say 5,000 or 10,000 naira [in the 1980s, worth about $250–$500], and he'll take it home. He probably didn't have more than 200 naira [in the 1980s, worth about $10] in his pocket and now he's got this. So he wants to come back the next day, and he forgets that there is no free lunch. You see, this Big Man, he makes you smell

wealth, makes you see opulence, and then he makes you begin to dream.[9]

After about a month of "dreaming" and getting enticements like the cash at the first meeting, money emerges for a passport, travel expenses, and a visa to Europe. According to John, before a courier boards that flight to somewhere in Europe, she or he is handed a package and may or may not know that it contains narcotics. If all goes well the first time and the courier returns, she or he could be awarded $10,000 or more—and at that moment is told about the narcotics.[10]

Narcotics traders, whether drug barons or couriers, found clever ways of repatriating earned cash from narcotics deals, as explained to me by both former narcotics dealers and those involved in present-day pharmaceutical distribution. The following accounts present common understandings of money laundering that those working in pharmaceuticals also understand as the history of unofficial market rebuilding. In what Gernot Klantschnig (2013, 44) states is called "money pick-up" by those involved in the industry, narcotics dealers purchased personal computers on a massive scale at cheap bulk rates in Europe or elsewhere and shipped them to Nigeria, dumping them into newly emerging and expanding markets like Idumota. The dealers quickly expanded their purchases, including pharmaceuticals and used luxury cars—all of which are considered products that sell easily.

Because it was too risky to simply pack up the profits made in Europe and travel back to Nigeria with them, or to move them through the banking system, narcotics traders organized an infrastructure for the inflow of licit pharmaceuticals and other goods and the outflow of illicit narcotics. Klantschnig's research into National Drug Law Enforcement Agency files and interviews with imprisoned Nigerian smugglers indicate that narcotics distributive networks originate in existing exporting and importing networks (2013, 43–45). For example, a used-car dealership in Baltimore, Maryland, or a pharmaceutical wholesaler in Amsterdam, the Netherlands, could be involved in the capillary money-laundering infrastructure that is critical to moving both licit and illicit products along similar distribution routes. John told me about such transactions. He explained that even though the companies may not know that they are part of an international arbitrage network that converts drug cash into legitimate products, they must at least break some regulations or rules on taxes—such as when a car dealer ignores the cap on the amount of cash he or she can receive in payments.

Cash from selling narcotics used to buy
pharmaceuticals which are sold in Nigeria

In these transactions, accumulating cash was and remains the primary goal. Traders extended an all-cash Nigerian economy into both licit and illicit realms outside of the country. Because a narcotics trader wants to instantly convert goods, like pharmaceuticals, into cash (the drug expiration date partly motivates this conversion), he must offer those goods at a discount to the pharmaceutical traders in the markets. Without the discount, he has little chance of getting cash. The discount means losing about 10 percent of the sales made in Europe. I was uniformly told that this was an acceptable loss because, as far as narcotics traders are concerned, the markup was already built into the narcotics sale in Europe instead of the pharmaceutical sale in Nigeria.

Narcotics and money laundering were not the only things that helped restock Nigeria with pharmaceuticals. Companies in China and India also scaled up existing business ties with Nigerians. In 2009, I met Mr. Kumar through a mutual friend one late afternoon at an Indian-run hotel and restaurant in a quiet upscale neighborhood in Lagos. Mr. Kumar is a pharmacist from Chennai, India, and a CEO of an Indian pharmaceutical company importing drugs into Nigeria. He started out in Nigeria working as a product manager for an Indian pharmaceutical company in the early 1990s. His company, like other Indian businesses, looked to Nigeria for investment and trading opportunities as the multinational manufacturers of brand-name drugs were pulling out of the country. Over the years Indian companies have supplied Nigeria with many generic drugs. They have also been responsible, along with a few Nigerian firms, for establishing more advanced and expensive therapies, such as those for HIV and cancer. Mr. Kumar told me that his company had just been getting off the ground at that time. He joked that he had been the product manager for a company that had no products. Because he had "no work to do," he had a lot of time to learn the business culture of the Nigerian pharmaceutical industry, practices of Nigerian businessmen, and the state of the country's health care sector:

> So that first year, I had a lot of time. I was able to understand and come to grips with this entire scenerio of what exactly is going on in this country. Mind you, this was the time that the entire regulatory authority was getting set up. The earliest registration of products had started only in the year 1990. So everything was at a very, very embryonic stage and this gave us an understanding as to what was

happening in this country. . . . I've grown in this country and today, of course, I have my own pharmaceutical company which exports from India into Nigeria.

Indian companies now provide over 50 percent of all the drugs on the Nigerian market. India and Nigeria had established ties based on historical links, since both had been British colonies. With Nigerian independence in 1960, the two countries established political links that were quickly dashed in the late 1960s, during Nigeria's civil war. Since then, the links between the two countries have primarily been made through trade (Vasuvendan 2010). Like India, China also has extensive business relations with Nigeria: Chinese companies dominate the medical technology market and supply Nigerian drug manufacturers with almost all the raw materials they need. Indeed, goods from China have been exported on a rather large scale to Nigeria over the last couple of decades (Igué 2003, cited in Baxerres and Le Hesran 2011). For example, in a remarkable tracking of Nigerian-Chinese commercial relations, Deborah Bräutigam (2003) analyzes the formation of Nigerian and Chinese networks through the small manufacturing town of Nnewi in the eastern part of Nigeria. Nnewi developed a famous and prosperous spare-parts industry during the era of liberalization, and Bräutigam shows how Nigerian entrepreneurs "used their connections to Chinese trading networks (mainly in Taiwan) to assist in the transition from importing auto spare parts, to producing them, creating a small industrial boom" (2003, 448). Like pharmaceuticals, spare parts were first imported from Europe. But by the 1960s Asian distributors had entered the market and begun offering to produce copies of spare parts. By the 1970s Nigerian traders had begun traveling to Taiwan to conduct business. These initial trading networks in spare parts gradually extended into other sectors of the import economy, including pharmaceuticals.

*Infrastructure and the Ontological Problems of Institutions*
It was left to the popular economy to build new networks and infrastructure that would facilitate national consumption and livelihoods in Nigeria. In his remarkable corpus of work on cities and urban African space, AbdouMaliq Simone has shown how the infrastructure needed to distribute private goods, or to get access to them, requires "people as infrastructure" (2004)—meaning that the actors in the popular economy substantially

anchor systems and networks. Like good or bad roads, people can be obstacles to or facilitators of transactions. Brian Larkin describes how gray- and black-market economies were tacked on to these new systems. In his work on media piracy and infrastructure in northern Nigeria, Larkin argues that "pirate infrastructure expresses a paradigmatic shift in Nigeria's economy and capital, extending the logic of privatization into everyday life" (2008, 218). Larkin and other scholars (de Boeck and Plissart 2004; de Boeck 2013; Guyer 2002; Mbembe and Roitman 1995; Simone 2001 and 2004) have argued that unregulated goods and the circulatory infrastructures the support their trade have migrated into the mainstream, extending social experience and demonstrating how the "shadow economy has *reconfigured the state itself*" (Larkin 2008, 225; my emphasis).

The political scientist Claude Ake describes this reconfigured state very well:

> The state in Africa has been a maze of antinomies of form and content: the person who holds office may not exercise its powers, the person who exercises the powers of a given office may not be its holder, informal relations often override formal relations, the formal hierarchies of bureaucratic structure and political power are not always the clue to decisionmaking [*sic*] power. Positions that seem to be held by persons are in fact held by kinship groups; at one point the public is privatized and at another the private is "publicized," and two or more political systems and political cultures in conflict may coexist in the same social formation. (1996, 14; see also Mamdani 1996)

Within this "maze of antinomies," state agencies became intertwined with new private endeavors. An example is the Nigerian Customs Service, which inspects all imported products entering Nigeria. Importers may choose to fly drugs into the country simply to ensure sufficient time to market drugs before they expire. In Lagos, these products must pass through customs inspection at Murtala Muhammed International Airport.

I met Victor, a "clearing agent" for customs inspections at the airport. Victor can facilitate the customs processing for all pharmaceuticals (and other products) that someone imports into Nigeria. This includes "sensitive" products, as he calls them, meaning those that are legally banned from entering the country.[11] He also delivers importers' products once they have cleared customs. But Victor is not employed by the Nigerian Customs Service. Rather, he works in a parallel industry composed of what are called clearing and forwarding agencies that have been built around, and literally within, the customs inspection process. He is essentially a middleman between customs officials and importers. Although the clearing and forwarding industry existed before structural adjustment, its incorporation into formal state functions is fairly new. Large, well-established companies in the industry offer services such as freight delivery, cargo insurance, inland container depot operations (for large container goods arriving at seaports), warehousing, transportation, and consultations on export and imports. They boast of providing hassle-free logistics and an extensive network of coordinating offices.

Victor's work site is just outside of the airport customs clearing section in Lagos. Here hundreds of small-time clearing agents have set up shop outdoors in an open field under tent canopies like those used for outdoor parties and weddings. The agents have their legally registered business names, like "Fastclear," displayed over each tent. The scene is lively because a literal market—a robust service economy—has formed around these businesses, abounding with people selling food, drinks, and time credit for mobile phones. For importers, it is nearly impossible to bypass the clearing industry. Clearing agents' fees for services are bundled with the official import duties and taxes, so the importer is charged a single fee. The shipping address includes an "in care of" insignia naming the clearing agent, who works closely with a specific customs official to quickly facilitate goods through customs. These official and unofficial intertwined layers that move drugs into the national distribution system have the effect of moving licit products quickly, enabling fake and banned ones to easily follow.

The layering of the state and the popular economy has created new jobs and new services, but it has also created a number of problems. According to the World Trade Organization, "the multiplicity of import documents and of agencies involved has been recognized as an unnecessary complication for importers. Several agencies operating at the ports also appear to impede trade flows: the authorities estimate that illegal discharging levies increase the cost of imports by up to 45 percent. As a result, large volumes of trade are being diverted to neighboring ports and a significant share of Nigeria's regional trade takes place on an informal basis" (1998).[12] Indeed, both pharmacists and traders have indicated to me that the fees and the red tape can be stifling. I once witnessed Toks agonize for days over an endless text-messaging match with his clearing agent. The dispute was over fees. If one ships by air, the fees can be as high as 50 percent on the purchased price of goods, leaving little incentive to do business; it is this high because the fees are distributed among the clearing agent, his company, and the customs officials—who all know that the pharmaceutical trade is lucrative. Toks argued with his clearing agent that if his business was wiped out, there would be no way for the agent to make more money from him. But at the end of the day, the importer has to figure out how to make money when faced with either breaking even or losing everything.

Like customs officials, banks are also dependent on interactive, unofficial forms of activity in the popular economy (Soyibo 1997). Banks also need a ready source of cash, and the popular economy is one of the best ways to access it. The acute need for cash can be traced back to the 1980s, when the SAP mandated bank deregulation.[13] The number of banks then tripled, but many of them were no more than *bureaux de change* that took advantage of the multiple exchange rates and round-tripping practices (Stein et al. 2002). As Yahaya Hashim and Kate Meagher (1999) point out, the objective of bank liberalization was to eliminate cross-border trade and parallel currency trading. Instead, these activities in the popular economy overwhelmed the formal private sector.

Most of the money that changes hands in Nigeria moves outside of formal circuits in the popular economy. Because banks cannot regulate or restrict money supplies or direct cash into capitalist enterprises, as Jane Guyer has pointed out (2004), the popular economy, not the banks, tends to drive commercial practices (Diawara 1998). Undeniably, it is black-market money exchangers who set the real price of the Nigerian currency, not the Central Bank of Nigeria—whose role is to establish a formal rate of exchange, which is largely ignored in daily exchanges. On my first trip to Nigeria I naively attempted to exchange U.S. dollars for naira inside one of Nigeria's most prosperous banks. The teller refused to help me and told me to "go outside," indicating that I should exchange my money on the black market. It did not take me long to figure out that I needed to find a trustworthy money changer whom I could call on to meet me inside of my own bank branch, where I could do the exchange and then deposit my cash where the tellers would not blink an eye.[14]

Almost all major Nigerian banks have set up branches in Idumota, so they can tap into the wealth that flows through the market. I came to know a bank manager who once managed a branch based in Idumota. He told me that the purpose of positioning banks inside large unofficial markets is to "convert the black market into the mainstream, formal economy."

The banks themselves depend on both the insecurity and the ease of a cash-only economy. That is, they rely on the traders who are at the very top of the income hierarchy in Idumota. These include the manufacturers and wealthier wholesalers who largely control drug distribution; they are primary depositors and have anywhere between 10–50 million naira ($80,000–$400,000) in cash on any given day. Getting access to their deposits is quite critical to banks, which treat wealthy traders to generous letters of credit. Because of their position as distributors in the market, and because of their wealth, the various fees they are charged by banks are no big deal to them. "They can pack it [a fee] on," as my bank manager friend in Idumota put it.

But other traders, those who are barely making it from day to day, may be deterred from using banks for many reasons, especially the multiple fees for things like cost of transaction, movement costs, and insurance costs. The cost of transaction, for example, is widely bemoaned because on average most banks charge roughly 5 naira for every 1,000 naira withdrawn. Moreover, each bank branch employs between ten to twenty staff members who do nothing but count chronically devalued notes, and the bank extracts a fee from customers for this work. For small-time operators who turn over less than several thousand naira per day, much of their profits can be lost to these fees. It is much easier for these traders to use cash than checks because a check can take up to four days to clear, and their transactions must move at a faster tempo. Needless to say, the average trader juggling credit obligations may not have a bank account. And if a small-time trader does have an account, it is not the kind of big money that bank employees, as spelled out in their job descriptions, are supposed to bring in.

As liberalization produced a blurring between formal and informal sectors, practices in formal institutions did not disappear but were extended into the popular economy. As Guyer (2004, 155–79) points out, people experience formality as papers and not as principles or institutions. Documents, licenses, receipts, letters written to either state officials or officials who work in unofficial markets (such as union or market leaders), perform or represent work as well as status in different institutions. In fact, the customs documents and bank notes needed to import drugs carry the official status across both official and unofficial realms that are needed to carry out transactions. Documents and practices that flow across institutions index the ways people attempt to move through multiple layers and intertwined sectors in a system. This is not a matter of being explicitly connected to state or private formal institutions. Rather, it is a matter of what gets practiced in new and reconfigured networks and systems. The stability of the system comes from repertoires of practice, not institutions whose shifting boundaries can produce both legal and ontological confusions.

### The Elusiveness of the Market

Repertoires of practice are completely intertwined with the infrastructure of pharmaceutical premises. Consider the following two sites of pharmaceutical sales.

Mr. Wale, a longtime and well-regarded Lagos pharmacist, has a large retail pharmaceutical shop located in Yaba—a busy and partly commercial neighborhood in mainland Lagos. His store occupies a spacious two-story building, employs a number of administrative workers, and enjoys much success. The offices are carpeted, and the store's air-conditioning welcomes visitors as they enter, escaping from the sweltering Lagos heat. One day Mr. Wale proudly showed me a new cold-storage room for drug stock that he had just built. The government supplies electricity only intermittently and unpredictably. Thus, cold-storage rooms must run on generators when the electricity is off, which is expensive.

In contrast, when I visit Chidi and Nweke, I squeeze myself in their one-by-three-meter stall in Idumota market, with shelves reaching from the floor to the ceiling. The shelves are full of medicines and nutritional supplements arranged by drug and medicinal class, including both brand-name and generic products. It is a hot day. As Chidi and Nweke engage in high-energy discussions with multiple customers at once, I gaze at the fan attached to the generator behind the stall. I cannot help thinking about the day before, when I was hanging out in the office of a friend who is a pharmacology professor. He was chatting with two of his graduate students after delivering a lecture I had attended. It was a fascinating discussion of the latest studies conducted on the rapid deterioration of drugs' efficacy once they are exposed to heat.

Even though Mr. Wale's and Chidi and Nweke's shops serve the wholesale level of distribution, they inhabit different regulatory sensibilities determined by the PCN. Mr. Wale's shop meets all the regulatory requirements of a retail shop, such as having cold storage; his business is not allowed to be located inside a market. Chidi and Nweke use fans and do not have cold storage; they are viewed as selling products in a market.

The regulatory rules are meant to create a streamlined drug distribution system. But instead they give rise to differing opinions among traders and pharmacists about not just problems of the safety of the country's drug supply but also who should be the gatekeepers of distribution. For example, pharmacists correctly point to the fact that fake drugs enter the country through unofficial markets, often identifying traders as the source of the problem. However, most traders recognize that fake drugs are a huge problem and see them as bad for business. Traders assert that pharmacists do not have the capital to operate a pharmaceutical business; pharmacists insist that traders are not qualified to do so. Both want market "sanitization," which refers to ridding the wholesale system of fake drugs. But traders imagine this to mean that those with existing licenses could consolidate in a central and highly regulated market that would ban those who traded in fake drugs. In contrast, pharmacists imagine sanitization to mean that the traders would be largely ejected from the wholesale system because of their lack of pharmaceutical expertise. Because unofficial markets are at the center of these disputes, they were the basis for an early 1990s lawsuit between Idumota traders and the PCN (called Felix Ugbojiaku & 2 Ors v Attorney General of the Federation & 4 Ors).

The PCN was created in 1992 to regulate not drugs themselves but the premises where drugs are sold, in an attempt to control the drug trade that was flourishing in unofficial markets. The PCN is completely staffed by pharmacists. As they lost ground to traders, establishing a state regulatory authority that had the power to shut down premises deemed illegal was one way for pharmacists to regain control of the distribution chain while establishing authority over regulation itself. One of the key things that distinguished Idumota as illegal was the PCN's definition of illegal sites of sale known as *open markets*. Open markets are nearly the same as unofficial markets, only this nomenclature usually applies to pharmaceuticals. Regulators characterize them not only by the physical space of drug premises but also by the physical characteristics of reformatted urban space found in unofficial markets.

Markets in Lagos are legally zoned, physical sites of exchange where stalls are owned or rented and are operated at specific days and times. A local or state government issues licenses for private operators to use stalls and regulates, charges fees, and taxes these markets. In contrast, open markets are characterized by their mobility or their unofficial and often unregulated status. Most open markets are in overlooked parts of public, government-owned land. These public spaces are converted into use for flourishing private endeavors.[15] For example, rather than occupying a state-designated block of land dedicated to an actual public market, Idumota is situated in rented spaces in residential buildings, and buying and selling spill out onto the sidewalks and into neighboring streets, where other activities—from doing laundry to holding church services—also take place. Open markets can be impromptu sites of exchange, embodying a fluidity that matches the hour-by-hour rhythm of the city. They can spontaneously emerge at a time when traffic gets congested. Traders walk—or even run—between the lanes of slowly moving traffic to make quick sales; traders may also appear on long-distance buses where they construct clever performances in order to sell their goods. Open markets can manifest in places where pedestrian traffic is heavy, such as under or on top of bridges or near public transport hubs. They can literally encroach on the road, intentionally slowing the movement of traffic so that a driver or passenger can make an exchange with a trader through a car or bus window.

For years, one of the two main expressways in Lagos, Apapa-Oshodi, was congested with private bus depots and traders who vied for various spots along the highway. But in spite of the congestion, there was a complicated hierarchical system of exchange and extraction that involved private transport, traders, and "area boys"—the equivalent of young gang members—who extracted payments from people selling their goods or from those who were simply trying to move with the flow of traffic. In addition to the bus depots, the most coveted places for trading in this once-thriving market were on the highway itself. Traders set up their merchandise one behind the other, and their layers encroached on the outer lanes of the highway; traffic in the single lane that remained open in each direction always moved at a snail's pace. (In 2009 the Lagos State governor, Babatunde Fashola, completely shut down and cleared away this bustling activity to the great relief of most Lagosians.) It was this kind of market that the law was designed to prevent when it explicitly designated places of sale for pharmaceuticals.

In August 1992 PCN, as the newly anointed regulator of drug sellers' premises, announced in the *Nigeria Guardian* that sellers in Idumota would no longer be issued licenses because they did not meet the PCN's new legal criteria. The agency also sent letters to traders in Idumota containing the same information. Licenses to sell over-the-counter and prescription drugs had long been issued by several different entities, including local government institutions as well as the Inspectorate Division of the Ministry of Health in Lagos. How each of these institutions conducted inspections and issued licenses had varied over time. But due to drug shortages in the early 1980s, pharmacy laws were deregulated then to allow traders to sell prescription drugs alongside herbal formulations and over-the-counter medications. They had to have a pharmacist listed on the business license in order to make their operations legitimate. So by the time the PCN was established, traders followed a legal routine of hiring a pharmacist, paying the fees, and getting inspected.

In response to the revocation of their licenses, the traders sued PCN, insisting that their licenses be reinstated.[16] In court, PCN claimed that the traders operated in an illegal open market. The traders countered that *they did not sell in a market*. As Chidi put it:

> This is not a market. In Nigeria we have traditional rulers and we respect our traditional rulers. The oba [Adeyinka Oyekan, the traditional ruler] of Lagos is staying [living] here. Oba cannot stay in the market. You understand. Anybody that is saying this is a market, which means oba of Lagos is living in market, this is an insult [laughter from those listening in]. . . . They should ask oba of Lagos whether he is [living] in the market [more laughter]. . . . We told them here is not a marketplace. Here is a street. Up there [he points to the residences occupying the floors above him], people are living there. The other street, people living; all these buildings [continues pointing to buildings around him], people are living there. It is not a marketplace. If it is a marketplace, people cannot live here. That is that.

As much as this conversation elicited winks and nods, the point was seriously entertained in the courtroom: establishing whether Idumota was a market became a central aspect of the case. The oba's presence was key here, as it connoted the sense of a residential area and not a dense and highly active market. When I brought this argument up with pharmacists, one jokingly retorted, "Oba, face it, you live in a market!" The traders, however, claimed that their businesses were located in a neighborhood and, moreover, that they did not sell on the road, under bridges, or in any other place considered an open market. Displaying and hawking products is also characteristic of an open market. The traders claimed that they did not engage in the kinds of activities that they imagined to take place on roadsides and buses, as opposed to their shops. Ikenna, the trader who inherited his father's very successful business, had indicated to me that Idumota should not be considered a market but rather part of a wholesaling system. Defining Idumota not as a specific place but as a system captured the way drugs were transferred from formal to unofficial circulation under liberalization, and to a certain extent the court accepted that definition.

PCN floundered under cross-examination and in making its case. Perhaps surprised by the dispute over the definition of a market, the agency attempted to argue that the Lagos State Medicine Dealers Association (LSMDA), the union constituting Idumota traders, did not exist (even though it is a legally registered professional organization) and therefore did not have the legal standing to take PCN to court. Indeed, confusion over what counted as formal and informal and what counted as a market extended to disputes over the actual existence of people facing each other in court. Moreover, one PCN witness insisted that the traders operated in a market and that it was not a legal or proper place for a pharmacist to be operating. But when asked under cross-examination if he had ever been to the market or if he knew where Iga Idunganran Street (the location of the Idumota pharmaceutical market) was, he answered in the negative. As stated in the final ruling, the witness claimed, quite reasonably, that "a market place is what an average person calls a market and that Iga Idunganran Street is a market place" (Felix Ugbojiaku & 2 Ors v Attorney General of the Federation & 4 Ors 2001, 8). Justice Yaya A. O. Jinadu disagreed. In his ruling he concurred with the traders that Idumota is not a market:

> The Plaintiffs [LSMDA] witness testified that where they sell their products is not a market place but a residential area and that in fact the official residence of the Oba of Lagos is situated on that street. However, the 4th defendant's [PCN] witness said that the place, Iga Idunganran Street is a market place. However, under cross-examination, DW1 [Defence Witness 1, PCN] admitted that he did not know where Iga Idunganran Street is located and that he had not been there yet he gave positive evidence that the plaintiffs display their drugs in the open market. This evidence appears to me perverse and malicious. I do not believe any of his evidence. I believe the evidence of PW1 [plaintiff's witness 1, LSMDA] that Iga Idunganran Street is not a market place and also that the plaintiffs do not display their drugs or hawk them. And I hold that the 4th defendant [PCN] has failed to prove its positive assertion that Iga Idunganran Street, is a market place. Having failed to prove the only reasons given by the 4th defen-

dant for his refusal to renew the plaintiffs pharmaceutical premises, those premises ought to be registered since they have satisfied all the conditions laid down by the law (Felix Ugbojiaku & 2 Ors v Attorney General of the Federation & 4 Ors 2001, 16–17).

Justice Jinadu proceeded to list each and every legally designated marketplace in Lagos—all of which had been established before 1960, under colonial rule and long before devaluation had helped to generate a proliferation of open markets. He then declared: "Nothing has been produced to show that Iga Idunganran Street has been established as a market place and the ipse dixit of DW1 [Defence Witness 1, PCN] who . . . has never been to Iga Idunganran *cannot convert a residential street or area to a market place*" (Felix Ugbojiaku & 2 Ors v Attorney General of the Federation & 4 Ors, 2001, 17; my emphasis).

To be sure, Idumota is one of the largest markets in West Africa, but according to this ruling, the market simply did not exist. Moreover, the judge did not acknowledge in his ruling that some residential areas had been highly commercialized and turned into unofficial markets, marking another instance in which interstitial space simultaneously blurs and shores up the boundaries of markets and neighborhoods. Although he was correct to point out that Idumota is not a legally designated market—no market has been designated as such since 1960—he did not comment on the PCN's claim that Idumota is an open market—that is, a residential street (or other interstitial urban space) that has been converted into a marketplace. When I interviewed the president of the LSMDA, he said:

Lagos is a metropolitan village. Lagos is so commercialized that everywhere is now so jam-packed. . . . When I was small, I used to know Iga Idunganran Street as a pure residential area. That's where the men that matter lived [referring to the oba and other traditional Yoruba rulers]. You go to V. I. [Victoria Island, an upscale Lagos neighborhood just west of Lagos Island], the same thing; you go down to Ikoyi [an upscale neighborhood on Lagos Island], the same thing. These areas were marked for residential purpose, but I want to tell you today, Iga Idunganran Street has been commercialized. V. I. is commercialized. Ikoyi is commercialized. Why must Lagos Island be the exception?

Although the other neighborhoods he mentioned are not nearly as commercialized as Idumota, he was right to point out that a distinction between residential areas and the commercial market can no longer be explicitly made; and the law in this case did not capture this indeterminacy.

Actually, the 1992 law did not even define open markets; instead, it set out to elucidate the rationale for the creation of the PCN and to create standards for registering pharmacists as well as for professional conduct. The law appeared to assume that college graduates of good character who followed specific rules would be able to legally prevent traders with no education from working in the wholesale distribution of drugs. Pharmacy premises were only vaguely referred to, with no stipulations pertaining to their standards. In other words, the PCN moved to withhold licenses from traders without identifying precisely what proper premises would look like. However, the 1992 law was revised in 2005. The new law went to great lengths to describe what is not allowed as well as standards for proper premises. The requirements indicated that someone walked through Idumota and then described everything there as illegal. For example:

> 6.-(1) Pharmaceutical premises shall not be located in :
>     (a) motor parks;
>     (b) environment where commercial activities and enterprises are standing and growing very close together, and
>     (c) market places including kiosks and road-side stalls.
> (2) Any pharmaceutical premises surrounded or covered completely by a growing market or standing close to it shall be moved to another suitable location two years after formal notification to do so by Pharmacists Council of Nigeria.
> 6 (3) Pharmaceutical premises within a shopping centre shall not be more than three and they shall be well spaced out,
> 7.-(1) A pharmaceutical premises shall :
>     (a) not be less than 30 square metres; and
>     (b) have a ceiling height of at least 3.05 metres.
> (2) A pharmaceutical premises (sic) shall be made of concrete walls and not in the form of kiosk. . . .
> (3) The floor of a pharmaceutical premises shall be made of concrete, tiles or terrazzo.
> (4) The shop in a pharmaceutical premises (sic) shall :
>     (a) be well painted;
>     (b) have shelves which are well arranged and painted; and
>     (c) have a proper ceiling of the roof.[17]

The PCN (along with other state agencies) used this law as the basis for conducting a market raid in October 2010 that led to the temporary shutting down of 1,253 premises (Ugbodaga 2010). The question of who would move for whom, in order to obey the spatial distance of shops outlined in the new law after hundreds of traders had already set up their businesses, indexed the difficulty of regulating a crowding problem largely brought about by liberalization. The sense that the PCN law was drafted to do away with the market is not only clear to traders—it is explicitly stated in the new law: "Any pharmaceutical premises surrounded or covered completely by a growing market or standing close to it shall be moved to another suitable location, two years after formal notification to do so by Pharmacists Council of Nigeria."[18]

OVER TWENTY YEARS after the case was first heard, its appeal initiated by PCN remains in-progress, and a court injunction prevents the PCN from regulating Idumota. This has presented several problems as far as the registered traders with the LSMDA are concerned. In 1992, when the lawsuit was filed, there were about 200 registered drug shops; in 2010 there were roughly 700 shops. That means that hundreds of traders since 1992 have found their way to Idumota, and they are not registered with the LSMDA, nor does the PCN acknowledge them. As far as the association is concerned, these newly arrived traders have increased the crowding in the market; moreover, it is difficult to keep track of what kinds of drugs they sell. In this case, the LSMDA wants the PCN to regulate Idumota, to keep the number of traders manageable. But as a result, layers of informal and formal practices have become disputed in an unofficial market of indeterminate legal status.

Moreover, traders who arrived in the 1980s and 1990s have sent their children to university to study pharmacy. By the late 2000s some of these second- or third-generation traders had entered the family business as registered pharmacists, which all traders are required to employ. Some traders and pharmacists imagine a future "insider war" within the Pharmaceutical Society of Nigeria, the pharmacists' professional organization that is also pushing to clear out Idumota. Both pharmacists and traders speculate that if a critical mass of younger pharmacists is denied permits to work simply because the family shop is located in Idumota, the fight will proceed between two generations of pharmacists within one professional organization.

The PCN may well want this market shut down, but very few others do. Indeed, the late oba of Lagos, Adeyinka Oyekan, was himself a pharmacist. According to some of the traders I spoke to, at the time of the case the oba spoke on behalf of the traders to the regulatory officials, imploring them to haul away fake drug traders but leave the market alone. Although the oba was used in court to shame the defense, he was only one of several traditional rulers who own most of the property in the neighborhood and have, since the establishment of the market, earned a great deal of rent income as a result. On Iga Idunganran Street, the main road that enters the market and where Ikenna's shop is located, the rent is fairly high, up to 50,000 naira per month (about $330). On narrower side streets, rent is about 10,000 naira (about $60). With more than several hundred shops, this adds up. The people who eke out a living selling drinks, snacks, and credit for mobile phones also do not want to see the market go away; their survival depends on its vibrant commerce. The banks do not want to see millions of dollars' worth of drug money slip out of their hands, either. Customers—especially hospitals and others purchasing drugs in bulk—do not want to see it go away because it is the lowest-priced one-stop shop; maneuvering through Lagos for a diverse array of pharmaceuticals would mean spending all day in traffic and spending much more money than simply visiting the market. The drug companies—both generic and brand-name—have made it quite clear in marketing forums that they do not want to see Idumota closed down because it is the largest site of pharmaceutical sales in Lagos. There is an essential vitality in the market and other remade urban areas that many people depend on, a quality that evades legal definition and bypasses regulatory capacity. It is a vitality that animates how different actors negotiate daily risk and market speculations in the lingering aftermaths of state and market reforms, which I turn to in the next chapter.

# 04

## Derivative Life
### *Nominalization and the Logic of the Hustle*

Uwa bu ahia [The world is a marketplace]. —Igbo saying

Aiye l'oja, oja l'aiye [The world is a market, the market is the world].
—Yoruba saying

We know . . . the general conditions in which what we call, somewhat misleadingly, an equilibrium will establish itself: but we never know what the particular prices or wages are which would exist if the market were to bring about such an equilibrium.
—Friedrich von Hayek, "The Pretence of Knowledge"

## *Market Transformation and Nominalization*

New infrastructures, actors, and pharmaceutical products coalesced into an emerging wholesale and distribution system in Nigeria. Although these shifts provided new buoyancy to the stagnating economy, it nevertheless exacerbated the violence of boom-and-bust cycles, which to this day resonate across official and unofficial economies. The incredible ups and mostly downs in the value of the Nigerian currency, the naira, are the most obvious indicators of such cycles at the macro-economic level. The Central Bank's decision to suddenly devalue the currency as a result of perceived economic crises outside of the country, for example, or even a small price increase on fuel imposed by the Nigerian government, can have strong reverberations in the most minute exchanges or payments. Such economic changes at the national or international level cause increases in the price of tomatoes in the market or the bus fare to another part of town, making it especially difficult for people living on the economic margins of society.

These changes index what Adedotun Phillips (1992) refers to as the nominalization of the economy (see also Falola and Adebayo 2000; Guyer 2004). Phillips's use of the term is restricted to economics, but there is a parallel with its more usual linguistic use. In linguistics, particularly the study of the English language, nominalization refers to the derivative use of verbs and adverbs as nouns.[1] The key link between the use of nominalization in linguistics and Phillips's use of it in economics is the possibility of deriving something out of an economic exchange and giving it a new meaning or material form.[2] To Phillips, nominalization connotes how society's relationship to money began to change: he describes how an intensified pursuit of cash blots out and overwhelms everything else in life. Political instability and the drive to hustle every day for cash and "make it now," as Phillips puts it, leads to desperation as the social body is transformed into new ways of being and opportunities to earn a living are limited (A. Phillips 1992, 22).

This chapter attempts to ethnographically capture hustling the day in the context of new and unfamiliar goods hitting rebuilt markets and new forms of risk that changed alongside these dynamics.[3] I specifically focus on how practices of exchange, pricing, credit, and labor interact with, and indeed often drive, large-scale as well as nuanced, micro-level market dynamics. For example, pricing strategies and price wars not only create uncertainty over a drug's reliability and point of origin, but they also present numerous ways of hedging risks against business practices that allow one to derive additional cash from exchanges in the distribution chain. Moreover, credit practices were tied to labor and high-risk entrepreneurialism.[4] Such practices pass risk through the entire distribution chain, often putting it on the brink of collapse. These forms of speculation, and many others like them in the market, are tied to speculating on life's chances, which I refer to as *derivative life*. I argued in a previous chapter that risky populations needed to be discerned and managed by military governance and corporate practices. Derivative life takes risk out of a population and relocates it in individual pursuits to hustle cash.

I extend individual risk that propels people to "make it now" by exploring the ways that Yoruba, Igbo, and neoliberal (particularly Hayekian nonequilibrium market and Chicago school human capital) theories of the market have converged in the aftermath of brand-name drug market abandonment and the rebuilding of unofficial, spatially interstitial ones. Idumota's wholesaling system is located in Lagos, which is part of Yorubaland and where Igbo traders run the wholesale drug system. Both the Yoruba and Igbo regions—in the southwestern and southeastern parts of Nigeria, respectively—were long involved in both trans-Atlantic and trans-Saharan trade, and extensive markets and market practices had developed in both regions. Prior to structural adjustment, labor, wealth, and principles of investment were key to market formation in Yoruba, Igbo, and (neo) liberal theories of the market, yet there was a real divergence among them in terms of what they imagined market liberalism to be. Nonetheless, they share different notions of individual risk tied to a nonequilibrium theory of the liberal market; and they all generally anticipate volatility and unpredictable social and economic outcomes in ways that make the logic of the hustle legible.

## Derivative Life

Toks lives on a peaceful street reached by several winding roads in a neighborhood located in the middle of Lagos. He shares a three-bedroom apartment with his immediate family and two cousins. Lying on the carpet, I watch the children's show *Hannah Montana* on satellite TV with his children. Toks's wife, Mary, has the day off work from a local nongovernmental organization and has prepared one of my favorite dishes, *amala* with *ewedu* and stew.[5] I gratefully lick up every bit, as the long day I have spent negotiating Lagos traffic with Toks did not involve much eating. We were hustling from one place to the next. While we were sitting in the "go-slow," or traffic jam, near his home, an impromptu market formed, appearing and disappearing with the traffic. As we were moving an inch at a time Toks purchased a Gala Sausage Roll, a mass-processed, packaged, cold corn dog made in Nigeria. I dutifully told him how gross it was. When we reached Lagos Island, we passed a vegetable and fruit market literally situated at the very edge of the road; here passengers make transactions through their car or bus window in the dreadfully slow traffic. I bought groundnuts and bananas that we shared.

Toks tried to make it on his own for a few years after drug industry divestment, but then he decided not to deal so much in pharmaceuticals. He now imports products such as toothpaste, toothbrushes, deodorant, and shampoo. The hallway in his three-bedroom apartment is stacked with boxes filled with U.S. brand-name toothbrushes that were shipped from Dubai, a distribution point for Africa and the Middle East. Although such products compete with other imports, the Nigerian market for items such as toothbrushes is not highly saturated; anyone who has exclusive rights to sell an imported product or who can control some of the market share—even just 5–10 percent—and can market the import well stands to make a lot of money in this populous country. Toks supplies small and large retail outlets, the larger of which are owned and run by expatriates from India, a group that dominates a great deal of the distribution chain for imported products.

Much of the hustle of Toks's life involves "checking on business"—moving through Lagos traffic making several stops: to see someone who "is owing" him; to resolve a contentious, complex, and unpredictable dispute among his workers; or to see how sales are going. One day he discovered that one of his workers had created an elaborate scheme to siphon money off from the business. Dealing with this required several days of work, including visiting all of the people in the distribution chain and letting them know via official documentation that money had been lost and a (now former) employee was responsible. I was with him on these rounds, and at one point we ended up in a part of town where large-scale manufacturing of various products had once taken place. Not only had manufacturing given way to a rise of Pentecostalism and imported products, but the former manufacturing infrastructure had been converted into sites for mega churches as well as larger-scale import wholesalers. We arrived at a warehouse, where Toks met with clients from Bangalore who had had many years of living and business experience in Nigeria. We passed through the gate and saw that the warehouse's site was enormous. We were escorted up the stairs and onto a balcony that had offices on one side and a view of the warehouse below on the other side. It was a stunning sight, because the items that I and so many other people purchase in traffic, in markets, at neighborhood kiosks, and in markets on the roadway were piled up in plain view.

There are no guarantees in this business; Toks must hustle clients, customers, and workers. He makes enough money to send his children to a private school, which is almost a necessity since public education has all but collapsed. He gets loans from friends and acquaintances to purchase goods whose resale could make him financially comfortable. But like the banks, friends and acquaintances charge a great deal of interest, sometimes as high as 30 percent, so much of his profit—that is, all that he had projected to push him into future security—can go away with the loan. So he is always "chasing money," as they say in Nigeria; always trying to make sure that he can make ends meet. This way of living and doing business is chronically tenuous: in both unexpected and calculated ways, one can suddenly make a mint, continue just getting by, or lose everything in an instant. The potential for making it big propels people toward a hoped-for future that most will never reach, but the hope keeps the hustle always in play.

New subjectivities came into formation and new forms of individual risk emerged with changes in the Nigerian economy. Today people must manage all forms of their own security. What has emerged is a subjectivity and a sociality of risk that is mediated by a breakdown in infrastructure. For example, candles are forbidden in the house to reduce the risk of fire in the face of daily power outages; professional drivers are hired for trips on expressways because of the strong possibility of hitting a pothole and getting stuck; people make sure not to look lost when they travel through Lagos; people talk about the trauma of encounters with armed robbers while giving advice on how to handle such terrifying encounters. Individual households, acting in lieu of local governments, must purchase not only health care and education but also create the infrastructure to obtain water and electricity. Life can revolve around hustling security as well as hustling the money needed to ensure that security. These social realities found in devastated infrastructure show how these dynamics "force the features belonging to the realm of warfare and features proper to the conduct of civil society to coexist in a single dynamic" (Achille Mbembe 2001, 74).

In analyzing the breakdown of institutional infrastructures as they are linked to the popular economy and entrepreneurial activity in Kinshasa, AbdouMaliq Simone argues:

> The institutions of mediation no longer provide an adequate anchorage for all the bits and pieces of bodies, experiences, words, objects and memories circulating through the city. Institutions are increasingly incapable of specifying normative practices of planning and transaction enabling actors to work toward a viable future. In these conditions, everyday life becomes intensely experimental, full of hits and misses, but, more importantly, the hits and misses become the

very materials with which to speculate on reorienting valuation to new composites—of actors, goods, services, positions, hopes, feelings, cognitions. (2011, 122–23)

Simone briefly connects life's experimental and speculative practices to the derivative in finance. Derivatives are financial instruments that are linked to an underlying asset. The most common derivatives include futures, options, and swaps. The assets they are attached to include commodities, currencies, stocks, interest rates, and bonds. Rather than trading assets found in the stock market, for example, financial traders enter into derivative contracts, which are agreements to exchange money and assets at some future date based on the value of the underlying asset. The cause of the 2008 financial "global meltdown," as it is perceived and referred to in Nigeria, began with U.S. mortgages. Instead of investing in financial firms and banks that made mortgage loans, finance traders pooled the loans into tranches, or categories. They assigned low, medium, or high risk to these categories. Speculators could bet on the time it would take for homeowners to default (or not) on their mortgages (K. Phillips 2008; Krugman 2009). In this scenario, the derivative is delinked from the integrity of the mortgage as an asset. Instead, it is explicitly connected to borrowers' ability to make monthly payments on home loans, which could prove to become difficult over time—especially for lower-income borrowers. This takes trading out of the realm of investment via the usual stock market, with low-risk, long-term slow growth, and places it squarely in the realm of gambling that bets on quick, often high-risk returns that may have nothing to do with the economic growth of assets in the stock market.

The relationship between money and assets in finance is similar to the association between pursuit of cash and the array of things that constitute the totalities of livelihood.[6] It gives rise to socialities that encourage speculating on life's chances—one of the primary modes of managing an environment of chronic risk. Maneuvering in this arena requires a repertoire of decision-making skills and is entirely separate from the economic rationalities that are hailed by regulation or other forms of governance (Simone 2011). I refer to these speculative acts as *derivative life*, which must embrace economic volatility as the new normal. My use of the term points to the ways in which people must hustle security in the aftermath of a warlike destruction of infrastructure and opportunities. It points to the way that the risk and uncertainty found in systems of exchange and distribution are turned into resources that are often highly creative and experimental (Simone 2011). And although derivative life refers to a form of economic subjectivity, it is not paradigmatic, nor is it the only possible way that life can be lived. Rather, it is the way in which life's chances and speculative practices, especially in the market, come to be inseparable. It connotes not only how the geopolitical reorganization of the economy integrates new goods, actors, and forms of international trade but also how the inclusion of these new components produces various kinds of ontological engagements with the economy, much in the way that Michel Callon (1998), Donald MacKenzie (2009), and Bill Maurer (2005) have imagined it. Thus, derivative life is not about indefinite struggle per se. Instead, it is about a tenacity—one involving agency that negotiates the conditions of infrastructure and that speculates in the hope of attaining well-being and stability, even when economic instabilities chronically underlie life's circumstances.[7]

For example, the mid-2000s saw a boom in Nigerian stock market activity. Many people who had cash on hand, even if it was just their small monthly pension payments, invested it—especially in the oil and gas sector, which promised returns of 500 percent or more. The boom of this particular cycle immediately followed a bank consolidation that was mandated by the International Monetary Fund (IMF) and that attracted foreign capital from European and North American banks and other industries.[8] Additionally, Nigeria had substantial oil revenue as well as a fivefold increase in government securities trading and a fourfold increase in stock market capitalization (May and Baker 2007, 8). But by 2008 the global financial explosion, which resulted from the utter instability of high-volume derivatives trading, drove the European and North American banks to repatriate their investments. Nigeria's boom immediately crashed.

Stock market crashes are not new in Nigeria or elsewhere, but now the boom and bust, whether detected in the Nigerian stock exchange or in unofficial markets, is not only anticipated but is often quite welcome in any sort of investment. The promise and hope of the boom are often viewed as the only available means of security because steady work and the prospect of saving are not consistent, viable options. Because market volatility is anticipated, prospective investors work toward making it big, not over the long-term but rather through limited transactions in which both small and large amounts of money can be made here and there—not at all unlike hedge funds that engage in high risk with the hope of quick returns. No one really wants the boom-and-bust cycles to go away, even when they drive up costs of everything from urban transport to tomatoes.

This is what underlies derivative life—the fact that one can anticipate a market boom and then speculate on it in order to produce further money-making opportunities. Before I describe these quotidian speculations, I discuss how volatility has been supported by various market logics that converged with successive liberalizations.

### Nonequilibrium Theories of the Market

The World Bank began designing structural adjustment programs (SAPS) for Africa in the early 1980s, following the release of what is known as the Berg Report that laid out a new agenda for the continent (World Bank 1981; see also Schoepf et al. 2000; Stein 2008). The Berg Report identified African governance and policies as responsible for stagnated and declining African economies. It did not explore alternative explanations pertaining to U.S. or other monetary policies discussed earlier. Although the IMF had long embraced neoclassical approaches to economic stabilization, this was a relatively new turn for the Bank (Stein 2008). Of principal concern to both the Bank and the IMF is the stabilization of the global economy, a goal that these institutions believed could be achieved through liberalization and privatization.

Howard Stein describes how key economic theories were based on the fixed-exchange system of Bretton Woods,[9] "yet even after the demise of the Bretton Woods system in 1973, the IMF continued to use the same model of stabilization to generate the terms of its loan conditionality" (2008, 57). These models included many assumptions that were not borne out in reality (Stein 2008, 60–63). They can be traced to classical liberal economic theory and include notions that resources (including labor) are fully available and utilized; individuals make rational calculations to maximize their welfare, leading to spontaneous exchanges in markets; people live in a world where the future is certain and entirely visible; the consequences of decision making in rational worlds can be fully understood; and price is the quintessential market signal, which provides the information needed to make decisions about production and purchasing. According to these models, market equilibrium—a state for which economic forces such as supply and demand are balanced—can be achieved because all these factors indicate that the market is always moving toward the most advantageous conditions and therefore maximizes society's welfare: "in short, equilibrium is a natural state" (Stein 2008, 61).[10]

Yet market equilibrium was never achieved in Nigeria. In fact, market volatility became a permanent artifact of structural adjustment. Although many economists saw market equilibrium as natural, there was a substantial split among twentieth-century neoliberal thinkers regarding economic modeling that could purportedly predict market equilibrium, as documented by Philip Mirowski and Dieter Plehwe (2009). For example, the Chicago and Austrian schools respectively disputed that Keynesian economics and socialist state planning provide avenues toward market equilibrium. Milton Friedman of the Chicago school argued that the accuracy of assumptions that undergird market predictions do not matter as long as reliable predictions can be made toward a self-regulating market that tends toward equilibrium (Friedman 1953; see also M. Cooper 2011, 374). In contrast, Ludwig von Mises of the Austrian school took an antipositivist stance and argued that economic knowledge was highly unpredictable, and therefore statistical modeling could not reflect the accuracy of market performance (Mises [1957] 1985; see also M. Cooper 2011, 374).

Friedrich von Hayek, also of the Austrian school, extended these ideas on the uses of limited economic knowledge and critiques of state planning. He explicitly rejected equilibrium theory as characteristic of markets. Instead he argued for a notion of market process that reflects the unpredictable subjective acts of human beings as well as the complexity of social phenomena (Hayek 2007 [1941]). In his later work, he drew on complex systems theory found in the physical sciences for which he argued that spontaneous order arises in market systems (Hayek 1967, 1974, 1988; see also Hodgson 1994). Out of this work, Hayek not only forecasted nonequilibrium as a natural aspect of market dynamics but also saw it as a core value of market systems. In discussing how Hayek and other economists drew on the sciences, Melinda Cooper argues that "complex systems theory reincorporates chaos into the study of systems dynamics. It is interested in how systems adapt, evolve, and self-organize not in spite of crisis but *through the very means of crisis* [her emphasis]. And while it does not abandon the hypothesis of order through feedback mechanisms, it refocuses attention on the possibility of system's evolution toward *multiple stable states and the establishment of order in far from equilibrium conditions*" (2011, 373; my emphasis).

Although the World Bank and the IMF had imagined in the 1980s that they were creating stabilized markets, by the 2000s the IMF had begun to adopt ideas of multiple stable states and new sorts of orders within market volatility. For example, it recognized the impact that market volatility has on households in light of changes in financial markets. It stated that households—"as the 'shareholders' of the public and private financial systems" (IMF 2005, 63) and not governments or the private sector—are increasingly absorbing market risk, which is providing more stability to the financial system. As pensions and insurance are ever more tied to the marketplace, the IMF did not recommend that households be freed of the burden of financial risk; rather it advised that households should become more educated on how to manage unforeseeable future risks (IMF 2005, 89; see also Bryan et al. 2009).

Moreover, the IMF has also described multiple states of equilibrium, in which "good" equilibrium is not about zeroing out the balance of payments (taken as a key indicator of market order) but rather about "low funding costs and affordable debt." And "bad" equilibrium is "where funding becomes very costly or even unavailable, reviving default risk" (IMF 2012, 22). These changes in IMF approaches toward equilibrium not only resonate with Hayek's notion of market systems evolving toward multiple stable states within nonequilibrium conditions. They are also aligned with calls by economists since 2008 to incorporate complex systems theory into economic systems that are chaotic and subject to tremendous and sudden change (M. Cooper 2011).

Financial analysts and the IMF are now embracing market nonequilibrium and volatility, but Yoruba market theories have long anticipated them. In his work on Yoruba markets, Bernard Belasco juxtaposes European classical economics and Yoruba notions of market dynamics (1980, 21–39). Yoruba theories of the market are a microcosm of the larger world: all material and human imperfections are located in the market, where market disequilibrium amounts to the potential for "cosmic, existential and social disaster" (Belasco 1980, 26). Belasco writes:

> Market life is laden with risk and uncertainty not amenable to rational control and scientific prediction because it is fundamentally saturated with a divine irrationality; its disorderliness is an aspect of sacred ambivalence. That is to say, the gods themselves are responsible for the chaos of the market. In that sense the Yoruba anticipate its disorder because the indigenous view is that the market, in contrast to its Western antithesis, is characterized by a natural tendency toward disequilibrium (Belasco 1980, 26).

Belasco traced market uncertainty and risk as indexed by religious and cultural practices such as trading with unknown people or encountering strangers in the market. He also showed how Yoruba gods are viewed as responsible for chaos in the market, making it divinely irrational—all of which he compared to Protestant (divine) representations of the liberal market. But Yoruba experiences with economic ups and downs (Hopkins 1973); war, displacement, and scarcity (Peel 2000); the many times that currencies have changed for new ones; and access to abundance and wealth (Falola 1992), which has come and gone since at least the fifteenth century, in the era of Yoruba-Portuguese trade (Guyer 2004), have also contributed to anticipations of market volatility.

With radical changes in market and state structure as well as in transnational importing patterns since the 1980s, cash may have overwhelmed everything else from this point on. But importantly, it converged with scaled-up pressures to redistribute earnings to extended families and home villages. Here the question of labor is quite critical in terms of how market volatility was managed, especially how Igbo labor practices in commercial exchange converged with neoliberal versions of labor. The Chicago school's theory of human capital and Igbo theories of work and labor share very similar notions of entrepreneurship as central to market liberalization. However, entrepreneurship is imagined in the context of drastically different historical conditions and functions of the state. The convergence of these theories after the implementation of the SAP created the conditions for a unique adaptation to long-term market volatility and helps shed light on how and why the Nigerian pharmaceutical trade thrives and proliferates in the unofficial sector.

Chicago school scholars Gary Becker (1994) and Theodore Schultz (1961) contributed significantly to human capital theory. They argued that education, job training, better health, and so forth should not be thought of as consumable goods; rather, they should be seen as investments that bring returns, especially future higher incomes. For these theorists, economic theory (beginning with the work of the classical economist David Ricardo and continuing to twentieth-century economist John Maynard Keynes) never adequately explicated the role or function of labor. As Michel Foucault (2008) points out, members of the Chicago school did not acknowledge that Karl Marx ([1867] 1992) had foregrounded labor as the focal point in the dynamics of capital. But Foucault speculates what they would say about Marx if pressed.

As Foucault notes, Marx's key concept here is labor power, which is not the actual act of labor but the capacity to do work. The concept means that doing work cannot be detached from the worker's health or from her intellectual and physical ability. Marx sees labor power as a commodity because the worker sells her labor (for a wage), which both is a source of value and creates value because commodity production is not possible without labor. Marx showed that the price of the commodity that the worker produces and the wage she earns are not equivalent. There is a surplus left over from the sale of the commodity after the worker's wage has been paid. The capitalist—the owner of the capital—retains this surplus, which Marx argued amounted to ripping off the worker, since it was her labor that created the commodity. Foucault speculates that the reduction of labor to labor power is for the neoliberals in the Chicago school an abstraction of labor that is not actually produced by capitalism. But rather labor power is an invention of economic theory that cast labor as abstract.

Unsatisfied with the treatment of labor in liberal thought, human capital theorists view labor as a problem of human behavior. These theorists sought to understand how people choose the work they do, and what work means to them. They constructed an active economic subject who was not tied to labor power. The question of value or the price of labor was not relevant here. Rather, the question is about rationality—how the person who labors makes use of what are assumed to be limited resources limited—that are available to her. The worker's wage is not the price at which she sells her labor; instead, wages are referred to as an earnings stream. In this context, both Marx and the neoliberals construct the body and capital as an inseparable unit for the purposes of production. But the interpretive shift is that the neoliberals see the worker as capital invested in an enterprise (Schultz 1961),[11] not a person who is exploited because she sells her labor power at the market price, as Marx saw it. When *earnings stream* is substituted for *wage*, it is launched into a future tense because it is now framed as an indefinite activity that relies on the worker's skills and self-care as germane to her capital and the source of future earnings.[12]

In Igbo market liberalism, the figure of the entrepreneur is seen far more literally than it is in human capital theory. This view can be traced back to precolonial times, when Igbos were organized within stateless societies, where flexibility was inherent in acephalous political and social organizations. Equally important, perhaps, is the fact that land scarcity encouraged migration and nonagricultural entrepreneurial activity, which has now been going on for centuries. Moreover, the Igbos' marginalization within Nigeria after the civil war made them especially interested in returning their profits to Igboland, particularly in pouring capital into public goods such as schools, clinics, roads, and other infrastructure (Chukwuezi 2001). This notion of redistribution is not philanthropy but viewed as an actual exchange in the market, because these public goods serve future entrepreneurial activities.[13] These histories and practices cast entrepreneurship as a necessity.

As it is necessary, entrepreneurship is also valorized, and the market itself holds a great deal of importance to Igbos.[14] Barth Chukwuezi explains that an "elaborate cult of personal achievement called *Aka Ikenga* or 'cult of the right hand' has propelled Igbo people into various fields of achievement, demonstrating how deeply rooted the concept of success is in Igbo social structure and organization" (2001, 57), and this is manifested in market activity under particular historical circumstances. Moreover, Victor Uchendu explains, "the overall objectives of the Igbo 'prestige economy' are to convert tangible, productive assets into intangible, status, and prestige symbols" (Uchendu 2007, 191–92). Apprenticeship in entrepreneurial activity is a key avenue to personal achievement and status because it is tied to the redistribution principle, which invests in human capital by providing labor and, ultimately, sharing new resources between home and diaspora.

But unlike neoliberal theories that see high achievements by workers as made possible by human investments, Igbo notions of market success imagine equality of opportunity but not equality of outcome (Uchendu et al. 1965; see also Agozino and Anyanike 2007). So with the sheer volume of workers in the pharmaceutical trade and the incredible competition, hustling is much more than just getting by. It is about positioning oneself within the drug distribution system in hopes of making it big, coming out on top—not doing so could mean difficulty surviving. Human capital was theorized in the context of the largely stable U.S. economy of the 1950s and 1960s and is now part of standard economic theory. In contrast, derivative life, especially in the Igbo entrepreneurial world of pharmaceuticals, is about calculating the minute risks that are present within quotidian volatility, as Hayek and now the IMF would imagine it. Igbo entrepreneurialism adapted to market volatility by drawing on older forms of apprenticeship labor and multiple forms of credit in order to pass risk laterally through the entire drug wholesale system. But these strategies have the effect of putting individual entrepreneurs and the system itself at constant risk of collapse, rather than establishing new and evolved senses of social and economic order.

With changes in importing patterns and drug products, both Yoruba and Igbo notions of market volatility were brought into a new market paradigm. Systems of exchange that were governed by social norms adapted to the situation. Many scholars have tracked the question of exchange as a systemic phenomenon,[15] but the importance here was rebuilding a market that would incorporate daily adaptations to, or anticipations of, risk in monetary exchange and investment. A critical way to mitigate risk is to use the interface of labor, investment, and entrepreneurship, all of which are embedded in market structures.

Igbo apprenticeship and market structure are dependent on each other, literally shaping each other. The apprenticeship structure is referred to as *imu* [to learn] *ahia* [marketing] and is key to reproducing the exchange principle. After a ceremonial passing of a child from his or her parents to a master, which involves the sharing of kola nuts and palm wine (Agozino and Anyanike 2007), an apprentice just out of primary or secondary school can serve between five and nine years.[16] Apprentices are usually young men, but sometimes young women are matched to older relatives in various artisanal trades. Apprentices do not receive a salary, but the master is responsible for their room and board, transportation, and health care.[17]

After an apprenticeship in Idumota, the young man or woman is given a severance pay by the boss, amounting to 20,000–50,000 naira ($125–$330), which is enough to rent a very small shop in Idumota for three to five months.[18] Occasionally, the amount is substantially more than this, and at times a boss may provide a small market stall for the former apprentice. But for the most part, apprentices usually do not receive enough money to invest in drug products. The severance pay is the only money that apprentices are technically allowed to make because they are discouraged from earning money outside of the apprenticeship.

Newly released apprentices with little capital take their money and start doing *baranda*.[19] *Baranda* means "buying for a quick resale" in Hausa, the language spoken in Niger and northern Nigeria and a lingua franca of trading in West Africa. Its use is interesting in this context because most of the distributors of drugs speak Igbo and English, although the multilingual world they work in is dominated by Yoruba and Pidgin English. Newly released apprentices will take the little money they have been given, go to another trader in the market, get pharmaceuticals (often on credit), and resell them for a profit of as little as 50–200 naira ($0.30–$1.30), what Jane

Guyer (2004) refers to as "marginal gains." When the product is sold, hopefully by the end of the day or the week, the former apprentice pays back the money owed. Over time, increased credit may be extended, and the money needed to make larger sales becomes available. Two or more apprentices may pool their resources and rent or buy a very small shop. They often need more than $5,000–$10,000 to purchase drugs from companies that sell wholesale, and of course they also need customers to buy from them.

The market is a continuously revolving door for apprentices: once one is released from an apprenticeship, he takes on apprentices himself. Although this system has long been in place and is used in other forms of manufacturing in the popular economy (like the manufacture of spare parts and textiles), it was actually invigorated by the financial constraints produced by SAP, the lack of cash on hand, and the loosened regulations on pharmacy premises. All these factors worked together to greatly increase the number of apprentices, the level of capital volume, and the physical market space of Idumota. As a result, drug products themselves do not simply move from company to distributor to the end user. Instead, they often make their way through several layers of lateral wholesale distribution that create a particular flow in the market. Products slightly increase in value with each move before they reach the end user.

For example, a nurse may come to the market to buy saline solution for her clinic. She approaches a cash-strapped seller. If she does not have a regular supplier or if she does but, for some reason, that supplier cannot help her, the cash-strapped seller may search for what she is looking for. If a trader typically sells antibiotics and antimalarials in tablet form, for example, he may know very little about saline solution. But he might go to a neighboring trader who sells liquids. If the cash-strapped trader can find a saline supplier, that supplier will give him saline on credit, and the trader will sell to the buyer he found in the market. He will sell the saline for a higher price than he paid for it and pocket the small profit. Depending upon the repayment arrangement, he may not pay the saline supplier everything that was credited to him right away; instead, he might put that money to other uses, such as paying the rent or purchasing a new supply of drugs.

In the case of these micro exchanges, several scenarios could take place. One is an exchange or barter of goods. Two traders may simply trade goods without payment but keep track of the price of each of the traded goods. They take pains to have a good memo of understanding in place, because between the moment of exchange and the moment of paying up, one or both may change their price (or there could be a sudden devaluation), which usually means the value of the initial exchange goes down. Another scenario is a two-way exchange, in which goods and money are exchanged simultaneously. But the exchange is unequal, with one trader credited 1,500 naira and the other 1,000 naira, so that the latter owes the former 500 naira. Both of these types of small exchanges are usually a one-time borrowing or trading mechanism, where the money due is expected at the end of the day or week, and where everything is tabulated in a side accounting book, which traders refer to as a credit book. If the repayment period is longer, perhaps a month, then the amount will be invoiced. Exchanges at the macro level happen between traders and the companies, which orchestrate different types of exchange—cash and carry, supply goods on credit, or payment due in two weeks—or one month depending on the relationship that has been established over time.

Within this system, debt does not simply accrue via loans; it is also generated by a culture of repayment, creating individual debt and a chronic generalized instability of debt throughout the entire system. Repayment is linked to the accounting practices of traders, such that *profit is built into credit transactions* even if repayment is lingering and profit is not there.[20] Specifically, they use sales agreements to indicate what has been credited, as well as what has actually been paid. Accounting for profit as both credit and money earned is similar to notions of protonumber described by Jean Lave (1986) and Helen Verran (2001) such that numbers and accounting can be both multiple and informal depending upon their purpose and use. As Helen Verran (2001) points out, there is a politics to working with numbers in particular ways. In this instance, accounting procedures represent both an actual transaction as well as a future promise. But, building profit into credit transactions is also a speculative practice that can generate new forms of risk in the supply chain when goods are not paid for. The worry involved in waiting for repayment or coming up with the cash to repay someone else is familiar to everyone working in the market, which is characterized by both being owed and owing money. The responses and meanings that people make of these practices are a shared sociality throughout the market. When one trader demands payment from someone else in the market, one of the most common explanations for not being able to comply is that someone else owes you or that other social and economic entanglements are involved.

One day when I was sitting in Ikenna's stall, in walked a medical representative working for a company that had supplied Ikenna with a large supply of drugs on credit. In fact, just about all of the drugs in his very large shop had been obtained entirely on credit. The marketer demanded repayment, but Ikenna did not have the money. The exchange between Ikenna and the marketer grew heated and angry, with the marketer yelling that he would call people who had witnessed Ikenna committing to pay up. Ikenna sat against a drug-filled wall cabinet saying nothing, clearly stressed out, with his head buried in his hand, knowing full well that the responsibility for ultimate repayment could fall on the marketer. Ikenna returned the unsold goods, which by now were closer to their expiration date and thus more difficult to sell. More than likely, the marketer had recorded these credited goods in his books as an actual sale that had generated profit. He would have to reverse those accounting numbers, which could certainly affect his job.

The intense day-to-day stress involved in these common exchanges can have dire consequences. For example, Temi, an academic pharmacist, used to work in the private sector for a pharmaceutical distributor that imported large bulk drug orders. She told me that one day she received a large supply of ciprofloxacin (an antibiotic) from an Indian manufacturing company that had been ordered for a customer by her distribution company, based in Lagos. When she opened the package, the contents appeared to be discolored. She had them tested for chemical content and found that the drugs were barely within the low end of the pharmacochemical range. She felt that the low level of active ingredients would mean a sooner-than-later expiration date, so she decided to send the stock back to the company. Shortly thereafter the Indian company folded, partly due to the return of these drugs; her company went bankrupt, mostly because of the loss of the Indian Company, which was her largest supplier.

There are unexpected, complex calculations in which debt may include labor or redistributive logics as part of a borrower's debt scheme. Toks told me about how a client had owed him money for over two years. According to Toks, the client would not pay because he was paying only for the "more important drugs" that he obtained from multiple suppliers. (A buyer might be keeping up his payments with one wholesaler and not another.) Toks had credited the client with a large stock of multivitamins, but it was a product that had been recently introduced on the Nigerian market. The client claimed that because it was new, he had to spend a great deal of time marketing it, meaning that it would take time for the product to gain recognition among consumers, and therefore sales would initially be low. The client asserted that he had the burden of introducing the drug, and therefore he argued that he did not need to pay for them. But he later bought more of the same multivitamins from Toks's affiliate and paid in full. In the context of simultaneously owing and being owed, it is not always possible to eject anyone from the selling and buying circuit through gossiping or blacklisting. If, like Toks's client, someone repays one debt but not another, it is not likely that traders will all agree to boycott the person.

At a larger scale, traders in Idumota attempt to spread the risk throughout the supply system. Unlike those in other markets in Nigeria, they buy directly from the manufacturing companies, making them the top of the distribution chain within the country and beyond. Most manufacturing companies supply drugs on credit to their long-established clients. But because this point of the supply chain is where the bulk of the drugs accumulate before they pass through several more layers of distribution, the risk of a general collapse is at its peak here. That is, in these exchanges, goods moving on credit are plentiful, while cash can be very scarce. The end-user cash floating back up through distribution networks is crucial. One of the main reasons that cash can flow slowly in this system is due to pressure on some Lagos-based sellers to return to their village with signs of success; and such signs might include driving a luxury car or "dashing" cash to elderly relatives and other family members (Chukwuezi 2001), which constitutes the cultural circulation of the redistribution principle.

As unpredictable repayment is floating through these critical points of risk, it becomes impossible to know whether a client could actually ever pay up, or to know the financial buoyancy of any business in the supply chain. In fact, one of the biggest distributors in Idumota nearly went under in 2005, shocking everyone. These dynamics are animated by pricing dynamics, which provides room to create derivative cash extractions out of market transactions, practices that are intertwined with social exchange and cash obligations.

### The Sociality of Price

Price, as conceptualized by neoclassical economics, provides immediate signals to indicate the health of production, supply, and demand within markets.[21] But what can price indicate in the context of extreme market volatility? And what happens when productive capacity is replaced with imported products that represent labor and value generated in faraway places? Price in Idumota reflects visible and unmarked socialities, such as hustling, multiple lateral exchanges that materialize marginal gains, personal allegiances, and social obligations across place (including outside the market), and labor built into credit systems.

Price for similar products radically varies for several reasons. First, price is not regulated in Nigeria (Aduloju 2000).[22] I was repeatedly told by traders and some pharmacists that this posed an enormous problem for the drug distribution system that does not establish a price range for drug products as the price difference between similar generic products can vary as much as 3000 percent. As Ikenna put it to me, "[NAFDAC] is not interested in regulating prices. *They cannot control fake drugs without price because it is price that drive fakes* [my emphasis]. But NAFDAC will tell you that it is an open [free] market. It is demand and supply; it is a competitive market." In addition to fakes, he described further consequences: "You know that there are people over-profiteering. That is why everybody wants to be a drug manufacturer, that is why everybody wants to register products, that is why everybody wants to come and dump. People are over-profiteering and the money they are making is too much. Why wouldn't I want to go and manufacture? Why wouldn't I go and produce and dump my product? Because I know there's Nigeria [where one can always dump drugs]."

Second, the manufacturers set drug prices and drive price variation. Typically, they establish selling targets for the same drug products (upwards of thousands of boxes of drugs per month) to multiple traders that spark a chronic price war and intense competition. This has the tendency to consolidate the wealthier traders at the top and squeeze out those making very marginal gains at the bottom. Deregulated price and severe price variation mean that price arbitrage is the primary way to move products through unofficial markets. That is, once pharmaceuticals enter the market, they are traded by taking advantage of price differentials. In this case, a trader buys as low as possible and sells as high as possible with every exchange. As Sara Berry (1985) has pointed out, price does not indicate precise, definitive transactions. Yet price can mark the routes that drugs travel. Although not always obvious, people working in the market can predict what price might mean or what it will do, even when the visiting consumer cannot.

Although drug prices are not regulated in Nigeria, there are many commonly understood incremental costs that apply to pharmaceuticals in general. First are the added costs of marketing, especially for imported drugs, which make up most of the market. Second is the markup at every point of distribution. And third are the multiple ways of acquiring gains through various practices of speculation on the distribution chain itself. This last incremental cost is hard to trace, which means that the history of a drug's movements can become illegible to traders, pharmacists, and regulators alike.[23]

At the level of marketing, price depends on a number of things. One must ascertain what it will take to market a product. This is important because people selling items on the street are linked to a distribution network, at the top of which importers decide whether or not a product is marketable and profitable. For example, on a trip to Nigeria in 2005, I carried packets of a powdered multivitamin that contained 1,000 milligrams of vitamin C. I was in the car with Abiodun when I poured my packet into a plastic bottle of water that I had bought from the market that spontaneously formed around our car in what was a significant traffic jam. Like many other pharmacists who deal in pharmaceuticals, Abiodun also markets fast-selling nutritional supplements. He liked my vitamin powder and thought its fizzing capability would appeal to Nigerian consumers, so I gave him a few packets.

When I saw him again a few days later, Abiodun told me that he had done some market research, which for him meant bypassing the actual company that markets the vitamin powder and instead finding the factory in Malaysia where the vitamin powder is made. He had called the factory to discuss an export price. A Nigerian importer has to bargain the export price down to a rock-bottom figure because after all other costs have been factored in, the retail cost must be appealing to people living on very small incomes. The export price is different from the manufacturer's price, which is the standard wholesale price to retailers; the former, usually lower than the latter, takes into account the fact that the product must travel through nodes in a transnational system of commodity flow, accumulating not just markups at each stage but also payments (Maurer 2007), all of which drive up the cost. An importer must calculate the total "landing price," including value-added taxes on imports, the cost of the shipping container, shipping costs, and the cost of getting the product through customs. Ideally for Abiodun, the landing price and the retail price had to differ by 30 percent in order to make the deal not just profitable but worth his while; in the end, my vitamin powder was not. The marketing process also has to figure in the number of products to be sold over time. Much has to be calculated, including the fluctuating valuation of the naira as well as how fast a product can be expected to move over time once the marketing is in place.

Within the distribution chain there is a common markup system that involves "trade price," "chemist price," "hospital price," and "institutional price," all of which have built-in discounts that generate confusion over drugs' ontology. The trade price is the general and usually lowest price for which medicines are sold to distributors and wholesalers. After that price come three higher prices: the chemist price, usually paid by pharmaceutical retailers that sell smaller quantities of a product; the hospital price, which is especially for clinics and hospitals and is generally higher than the chemist price; and institutional prices, for supplying large companies like those in the oil industry. This is generally the most expensive price, amounting to a markup on the trade price of 35–50 percent.

If a trader orders a very large volume of drugs directly from a drug company, worth well over $10,000, he or she can get a discount.[24] However, depending on the volume of the distributor or wholesaler's order, this base price attracts different discounts. If a trader buys 100 cartons of a drug product, the distributor might take 5 percent off the trade price. If a trader orders 1,000 cartons, the reduction may be 10 percent. Another person buying just ten cartons will most likely not get any discount, unless he or she has a previous history of discounts with the company. Obtaining a deep discount is one reason why traders pool their resources; in turn, that allows them to charge a lower price, win buyers, and generally outcompete their neighbors in the market. Another way to get a discount (of about 5 percent) is if one is buying a new product that has yet to be marketed. Again, the labor involved in marketing is recognized as a deterrent to purchasing a new product, which is why there is a discount. At times the discount price can actually be lower than the trade price—the cheapest price that one can get officially get—due to large bulk discounting. The discount is important here because it obscures value and ontology. As Ikenna indicated above, when the retail price is below the trade price, it raises questions about whether the product is genuine, since fakes are sold for lower prices than the trade and retail prices in the market.

Local manufacturers have a different sort of calculation to make. The cost of drug manufacturing in Nigeria is very high due to the fact that basic infrastructure such as electricity is simply not available to manufacturers, and they have to generate their own. This requires obtaining fuel for the massive generators, which can take up the bulk of overhead depending on how much power the state decides to provide day to day, which is never predictable. It also depends on the price of fuel, which itself depends not simply on world market prices but on fuel shortages, which are common in this oil-producing country.

Products' price variations are compounded by general changes in the economy, including devaluation, slight price increases, and national strikes. The markets and the infrastructure supporting it, including transport, respond immediately by also shifting prices upward. That is, the entire popular economy raises prices in the absence of credit and monetary security. In 2010 Nigeria increased the legal minimum wage, and although it is not widely honored, actors in the popular sphere such as private bus operators, taxi drivers, petrol sellers, traders, and others increased their prices. Price raising calls into being an entire sociality of networks and resourcing that copes with even the slightest changes.

Even with varying pricing baselines, markup strategies, and unpredictable yet anticipated price fluctuations, there are a number of ways that someone working in this business can speculate on changes in prices. For example, consider a company that is based in Lagos and that has a retail distributor in the northern city of Kano. A worker for the company in Lagos places an order with the company on behalf of the retailer in Kano for 10 million naira worth of drugs. Once the drugs come through, the worker takes half of that order (5 million naira worth of drug stock), sells it to the retailer in Kano, and then sells the other half to an oil company for 7.5 million naira, which represents the institutional price, garnering a larger markup. Because the worker placed the order for the retailer in Kano in the amount of 10 million naira, he is required to deposit only that amount into the company's account, keeping the extra 2.5 million naira for himself. This strategy mutigates risks of currency devaluation in between exchanges and the risk of other credit exchanges falling apart. Yet it creates the added risk of being criminally exposed.

Price is the fundamental marker of confusion because there is no way to know whether the drugs moving through derivative price scaling or lateral exchange actually got their start from narcotics dealers who dumped "licit" drugs into the market, from direct imports from a distributor, or from "fakes" that are priced to outsell all others. Nevertheless, drugs of all chemical compositions travel along the same speculative interstices of formalized incremental costs and markups as well as the same lateral pathways of exchange. Important here is that traders, money launderers, and drug companies are all essentially using the same markets and the same sites of transit and means—cash and discounts—to do business.

The three-point distribution chain during the oil boom gave way to multiple private forms of distribution in which informality was built into formal or commonly understood systems of exchange. As these systems were reshaped to meet the needs of those hustling cash, calculations of risk and anticipated volatilities were built into labor, credit, and price scaling. Indeed, hustling the day in Igbo entrepreneurship was not that different from the practices employed by the brand-name manufacturers to stay afloat under difficult circumstances dictated by Wall Street. The volatility of both neoliberal and indigenous Nigerian market liberalism adapted through coexisting in a single space. Their dynamics point to capital's impetus to chronically reproduce itself under now normalized and accepted terms of market volatility.

In this context, cash and the market are not simply nodes at which exchanges take place; rather, they are profoundly socialized through their important derivative forms. Hustling these derivative forms and the speculation it takes to discern potential success in market exchange are precisely what derivative life is all about.

How these practices materialize within the commodity chain that stretches across continents is the subject of chapter 5.

## Chemical Arbitrage
### *A Social Life of Bioequivalence*

We don see plenty shit for Africa / We carry am sotey / We don see plenty shit for Africa / We carry am sotey / We carry am sotey / A gbe gbe gbe o su wa / A je je je o su wa / Political shit, economic shit for Africa / A gbe gbe gbe o su wa / A je je je o su wa / A mu mu mu o su wa / A gbe gbe gbe o su wa

Oyinbo come Africa give us shit / Africans come dey give demselves bullshit for Africa

The shit don cause trouble o in Africa here / The shit don cause trouble o

Don't bring that shit to me—My brothers and sisters / Don't bring that bullshit to Africa—As you dey hear am.

—Seun Kuti, "Don't Give That Shit to Me"

### *Chemical Arbitrage and Downward Pricing*

Post-1980s market volatility gave rise to a derivative life whose activities tied risky speculation to credit, labor, and life chances. It also led to a vast influx of pharmaceuticals from around the world. In contrast to the previous, brand-name drugs, whose prices were on the high end, these new generic drugs were priced in alignment with the relative impoverishment of the population brought on by structural adjustment (SAP). The switch from a majority brand-name to a majority generic market did make it easier for poor people to purchase drugs. It also became easier to manufacture and transport them—multitudes of them—to West Africa. In addition to being generic, a large proportion of them are of low quality or entirely inefficacious. While Nigerians became increasingly concerned about fake drugs circulating on the national market since SAP, both Anglophone and Francophone West Africans also became wary because Nigerian markets supply most of the wholesale drugs to the region (Isute 1989).

A number of factors made drugs cheap and accessible on the private market. The 1990s speculative wave of consolidations and asset dumping in the pharmaceutical industry converged with the creation of new sites of offshored manufacturing in response to increased pressures to reduce costs. Opportunities to outsource and offshore pharmaceutical manufacturing and raw material production (materials that are either unprocessed or minimally processed, such as chemicals) became available in the Chinese and Indian economies, both of which were growing rapidly. Since the 1990s, lucrative "contract manufacturing organizations" (CMOs) have proliferated. CMOs are industry brokers that facilitate offshore manufacturing at every level of the drug development process.[1] A CMO industry report lists China as the favored site for outsourcing because manufacturing costs can amount to 40 percent below typical U.S. and European costs (Mueller and Mintz 2012). The rise of these markets and drug economies was key to the survival of brand-name drug manufacturers. They were also important to the development of a new Nigerian drug market. Since the 1990s, Chinese companies manufacture and export nearly all of the raw materials used in the Nigerian drug industry. Indian companies manufacture and export over 50 percent of drug products sold in Nigeria. Over 80 percent of Nigeria's drugs are imported from abroad (Emeto 1986, 10); see table 5.1 for a breakdown by country.

The process of moving these products from Asia to West Africa depends on several intertwined factors: price, national regulation, consumer capacity to buy, and drug quality. Like the multiple lateral forms of product movement that take place in Idumota's drug market, the drug supply chain that includes Asian, European, and West African companies involved in raw material production, pharmaceutical manufacturing, and transcontinental distribution relies on a number of arbitrage strategies. Arbitrage is a form of trading that capitalizes on the price differentials as was seen in Idumota market in the previous chapter. This kind of buying low in one market and selling high in another is a typical strategy in many finance (see Miyazaki 2013; MacKenzie 2006) and commodity markets, including pharmaceuticals. Arbitrage eventually comes to an end because the price of a product

TABLE 5.1. Finished pharmaceutical products imported into Nigeria, by country

| Country | Number of products | Percent of total |
|---|---|---|
| 1. India | 3,012 | 52.79 |
| 2. China | 730 | 12.79 |
| 3. United Kingdom | 228 | 3.99 |
| 4. Pakistan | 165 | 2.89 |
| 5. Indonesia | 142 | 2.48 |
| 6. Holland | 117 | 2.05 |
| 7. Switzerland | 114 | 1.99 |
| 8. Malaysia | 112 | 1.96 |
| 9. Slovenia | 107 | 1.87 |
| 10. United States | 105 | 1.84 |
| 11. Germany | 102 | 1.78 |
| 12. France | 94 | 1.64 |
| 13. Korea | 87 | 1.52 |
| 14. Belgium | 52 | 0.91 |
| 15. Spain | 35 | 0.61 |
| 16. Vietnam | 30 | 0.52 |
| 17. All others | 473 | 8.29 |
| Total | 5,705 | 100 |

Source: Obileye 2008, based on data from the National Agency for Food and Drug Administration and Control.

increases as it moves between markets or traders; ultimately the price hits the upper end of the product's value and there is nothing left to arbitrage.

But for pharmaceuticals that are meant for a large, low-income, and a highly difficult-to-regulate regional market, arbitrage has remarkably movable end points. Price differentials of similar drugs ultimately disappear after just a few rounds of arbitrage due to the already low price designed to appeal to poor consumers. The next end point after price is drug chemistry, which means changing the chemistry or lowering the composition of a drug's active pharmaceutical ingredients so that it becomes cheaper and more competitive. I refer to this as *chemical arbitrage.*

In this chapter, I discuss how downward pricing pressures, large-scale offshoring and outsourcing, and arbitrage strategies produce dynamics that necessarily work across continents to generate huge amounts of chemically varied drugs destined for West African markets. I relate stories told to me by pharmacists, traders, regulators, and officials on counterfeit drug task forces.

They must deal with what is partially a shadow economy that produces real-world effects, including low drug quality, drug resistance, and a skewed market structure. These professionals were able to describe how arbitrage dynamics work within Nigeria; yet although many of them understood the way that raw materials and drugs were manufactured in Asia and moved across the world to West Africa, some of the details they gave me were hazy.

I am interested in a "phantom epistemology" (Peterson 2009), or an empirical elusiveness that is both familiar and unknowable, when it comes to reformatting the chemical compositions of drugs. But elusiveness can be easily connected to both popular and policy discourses that pronounce fake drug traders as evil and criminal. Certainly this discourse of evil people selling fake drugs speaks to regulators' and consumers' concerns over drug safety. But they bypass understanding the geopolitics and political economies that drive the fake drug trade in the first place. And so in addition to my fieldwork, I draw on academic research and media and policy reports that have gathered excellent data on the making and movement of drugs, especially fake ones. But very few of these reports actually analyze pricing structure and arbitrage, which are important dynamics that became quite apparent to me as I witnessed the activities and listened to the analyses of my informants.

I begin by describing the relationship between local human and microbial biologies and the structure of the Nigerian drug market. The same nonevolving drug classes that have been marketed since the 1970s are mismatched with changing microbial and human biologies in Nigeria. That is, existing therapeutics are hardly efficacious for existing diseases. The disparity between disease burden and available drugs that Mr. Adebayo faced (described in chapter 2) was dramatically exacerbated in the aftermath of drug market abandonment. High levels of drug resistance have been one of the worst outcomes. I show how drug resistance is driven by Nigeria's market structure and, in turn, how market structure is shaped by the search for ever-depressed offshored manufacturing and distribution costs.

These dynamics of drug resistance and market structure are not separate articulations or discrete events but rather a dynamic continuum, or a *social life of bioequivalence*. Bioequivalence is a regulatory standard in pharmaceutical quality control. It compares a generic drug and its brand-name model by analyzing two forms of equivalence: how close the generic drug's chemistry is to that of the model and whether the generic drug is absorbed by the body in the same manner and amount of time as the brand-name drug.[2]

I connect antibiotic control as "open-ended experiment" (Landecker 2013), "open systems" (Bensuade-Vincent and Stengers 1996, 249; Barry 2005, 53) in chemical molecules discussed by social science scholars of chemistry, and concerns about the flexible and volatile nature of African "open economies" (Seers [1963] 1970, 166–68). Bioequivalence has a dynamic social life in the way that Arjun Appadurai (1988) understood it, where the fluctuating life of drug chemistry is shaped by economic and political encounters.[3] Here the nonstatic "open systems" of chemistry meet the volatility of markets, producing a chronically unpredictable landscape that raises constant concerns and social anxiety over national drug safety.

## Local Biologies and Drug Resistance

In July 2010 I was walking with a friend from an Idumota trader's market stall to Iga Idunganran Street. Just as we were finishing our conversation, a young man walked by us with five very large boxes neatly stacked on top of his head. This was not at all an unusual sight: there were always many men and women hustling boxes of drugs that had just arrived by boat or plane or carrying boxes to vehicles headed to retail establishments. What caught our attention in this case was the label on the boxes: "chloroquine injection." Up until 2010, chloroquine was the standard treatment for malaria, but now is largely ineffective against most malaria parasites in Nigeria. We surmised that the man hauling these drugs was not headed to another West African country, where the chloroquine could possibly still be effective. Rather, we suspected that he was headed somewhere else in Lagos. He had Lagos State license plates and was parked not in the West African transport lot but right in front of our car. Where the boxes were headed and what they were intended for were unclear to us.

This encounter occurred at an interesting political moment. Although numerous Nigerian drug-trading companies were still importing this highly profitable drug, debates were raging among clinicians about whether chloroquine should be taken off the World Health Organization's Essential Drugs List, a regularly updated list of affordable medications recommended to treat high-priority local diseases. Part of these debates revolved around the question of drug resistance. For example, in southwest Nigeria, *Plasmodium falciparum*, one of the species of the parasite that causes malaria, was found to be 97 percent resistant to chloroquine. In the northwest, however, it was found to be only 33 percent resistant, and at that rate chloroquine is still considered efficacious (Adagu et al. 1995). These "local biologies" (Lock 1995, xxi) account for the ways "biological and social processes are separately entangled over time" (Lock and Nguyen 2010, 90). In Nigeria, varying biologies are also marked by changes over time, including how they are entangled in social discourse and technological, regulatory, and market dynamics.

To illustrate, I describe a clinical case presentation I had the privilege to hear. The patient in the case was an eight-year-old girl with a severe bacterial infection that was resistant to treatment. The case was presented by Oladipo Aboderin, a medical microbiologist based at Obafemi Awolowo University (OAU), and it was subsequently published in *African Journal of Laboratory Medicine* (Aboderin et al. 2012). The girl came to the university teaching hospital after being sick for two weeks with a fever, abdominal pain, watery stool, and recurrent vomiting. She had been hospitalized previously at a private teaching hospital and had been given antibiotics, including amoxicillin (widely ineffective in Nigeria), ciprofloxacin (more effective), and artesunate (one of the drugs on the Essential Drugs List used to treat malaria, but only in combination with other malaria drugs).

The clinicians at OAU performed five blood cultures and found species of *Klebsiella* in three cases. *Klebsiella* can cause bronchitis, pneumonia, urinary tract infections, and diarrhea. It is considered a nosocomial pathogen—that is, people can be infected with it during a stay in a hospital. It belongs to the same family as the well-known bacteria *Escherichia coli* (or *E. coli*) and *Salmonella*. Two antibiotics successfully treated one of the cultured *Klebsiella* isolates, but none of the antibiotics worked on the other two. While the girl was in the hospital and her fever could not be controlled, she received three transfusions of whole blood and two transfusions of exchange blood (the patient's blood is removed and replaced with fresh donor blood or plasma), and multiple courses of antibiotics were administered. When none of these therapies worked, clinicians suspected that they were dealing with a highly resistant strain of *Klebsiella*, one that produces extended-spectrum beta-lactamases (ESBL)—which, to the clinicians' knowledge, had never been reported in Africa. The production of ESBL is a resistance mechanism in this family of bacteria. It is rapidly evolving, and new therapies are having trouble keeping pace. Cephalosporins, antibiotics that are structurally similar to penicillin, were introduced in the 1980s and were used "for treatment of severe conditions such as bloodstream infections, pneumonia and intra-abdominal infections, until ESBLs started compromising [cephalosporins'] usefulness in response to overuse and selective pressure. Organisms that produce ESBLs are an important reason for therapy failure with cephalosporins and have serious consequences for infection control" (Aboderin et al. 2012, 1).

The OAU researchers sent the specimens to Iruka Okeke, a microbiologist and a professor at Haverford College in the United States, who confirmed that the clinicians were working with an ESBL-producing strain of *Klebsiella pneumoniae*. The one antibiotic that had been found to be effective against this strain was imipenem, and when it was administered to the girl, it cured her within a week. This strain was found to be resistant to many other older- and newer-generation antibiotics.[4] Imipenem is not routinely available in the OAU teaching hospital, a fact emphasized by the clinicians (Aboderin et al. 2012). Nor is this drug, to my knowledge, registered with the regulatory authority in Nigeria. This means that it is not routinely manufactured in or imported into Nigeria.

The details of the girl's previous admission at the private hospital are not known; indeed, the dearth of referral information when patients move from one institution to another in seeking care is a widespread problem in Nigeria (Okeke 2011). So it is difficult to know whether she was given both antibiotics and antimalaria medication before arriving at the OAU teaching hospital because she had malaria and another infection at the same time or because the clinicians at the other hospital were following the widespread practice of using a broad-spectrum treatment in the absence of diagnostic technologies. In the presentation I attended, Aboderin mentioned that several weeks of antibiotic therapy may have exacerbated drug resistance.

As Okeke discusses in her remarkable book on the dearth of diagnostic technology in Africa (2011), clinicians assume their patients have malaria because it is widespread and endemic, regardless of the fact that fever can indicate not just malaria but multiple other infections. Indeed, the first time I had a severe cerebral malaria infection, I was sitting at home with a friend in Lagos. While we were eating dinner, I told her that I felt a little light-headed (I was not yet feverish). She took one look at me and said: "You have malaria!" There is an undercurrent of "knowing" when it comes to malaria, and people have various folk strategies they employ when they suspect that they may be getting a bout of it (for example, getting extra exercise, not sitting still, and taking high doses of vitamin B12—all of which I tried myself with future illnesses, although I had no diagnostic confirmation that I even had malaria). Even if snap diagnoses like my friend's are incorrect, most people often bypass diagnostics and simply seek antimalarial drugs. Pharmacists are likely to ask about symptoms and sell the drugs even if those symptoms might be caused by other illnesses, such as typhoid fever (Okeke 2011).

A remarkable thing that the clinicians did in the case of the eight-year-old girl was to track the amount of unnecessary funds that were spent in the absence of adequate diagnostic technologies. During her sixth hospitalization, the girl received inefficacious antibiotics, blood transfusions, and diagnostic tests, and her hospital costs amounted to the equivalent of $583.77, which is about half the annual per capita income in Nigeria. The authors assert that had there been adequate diagnostic capacity, the girl would have been hospitalized no longer than one week, and the hospital costs would have been one-tenth of the actual figure. This may be the first ESBL *Klebsiella pneumoniae* reported in Africa. However, Aboderin and colleagues (2012) note that other researchers have found ESBL in other bacterial species, but the lack of diagnostics makes it unclear just how widespread a problem clinicians are actually facing.

In fact, the literature produced by bench scientists in Nigeria indicates that malaria parasites and many species of bacteria are proving to be increasingly and highly resistant to older-generation drugs and even some newer-generation ones. In the 1980s and early 1990s there were reports of extremely high resistance to tetracycline, ampicillin, chloramphenicol, and streptomycin (Eko and Utsalo 1991; Oboho 1984; Idigbe et al. 1992). Okeke and colleagues (2000) and Lamikanra and coauthors (2011) tracked microbial resistance to these drugs over time and found increasing resistance to strains of *E. coli*. By the 2000s and 2010s, researchers were recording extremely high resistance (90–100 percent) to older-generation drugs as well as existing and rising resistance to the newer generations of antibiotics known as cephalosporins and quinolones in all parts of the country (Habib et al. 2003; Aboderin et al. 2009; Daini et al. 2006; Ozumba 2007; Omoregie and Eghafona 2009). More recently, others reported high levels of multiple drug resistance (even to cephalosporins and quinolones) to cases of bacterial infections, including typhoid and tuberculosis (Akinyemi et al. 2000; Idia et al. 2006; O. Olowe et al. 2008; Okesola and Aroundegbe 2011; Chigor et al. 2010; Lawson et al. 2010; Dada-Adegbola and Muili 2010).

What are the reasons for such high levels of drug resistance? Hannah Landecker (2013) describes two models of drug resistance. The first, long-understood model is referred to as microbial adaptation, where some mutant bacteria survive antibiotic therapy and then quickly reproduce new populations of resistant organisms. Nigerian researchers have provided several reasons for the problem of pervasive drug resistance, which include widespread self-medication (Montefiore et al. 1989; Adeleye 1992; Obaseiki-Ebor et al. 1985; Idigbe et al. 1992; Dada-Adegbola and Muili 2010), lack of diagnostic technologies (Montefiore et al. 1989; Okeke 2011), over-prescribing of top-market earners (Ohaju-Obobo et al. 1998), and the high cost of newer-generation antibiotics, which pushes patients to buy cheaper, older-generation products (Oyelese and Oyewo 1995).

These are not the only problems. The second model of drug resistance describes when microbes, regardless of species, regularly exchange genetic material as a means of survival (Landecker 2013). For example, if one person residing in a household with others is taking antibiotics, the medication triggers signals for microbes to exchange genetic material with all the other microbes inhabiting all humans in the household. In short order, patients can incur resistance to drugs that they have never taken. The implications are huge according to the World Health Organization and the Centers for Disease Control, which characterize antibiotic resistance in completely catastrophic terms (Landecker 2013).[5] Critically, Landecker shows that in this scenario, the presence of antibiotics set the stage for a competitive microbe advantage. She states that "all this brings into focus a view of the antibiotic era as a massive rearrangement of an existing biology, which will never again be as it was. . . . [A]ntibiotic control begins to look like one large *open-ended* and under-designed experiment in new microbial genomes" (Landecker 2013, 15; my emphasis).

Certainly, infinite microbial genomic variation has a relationship to antibiotic usage and diagnostic technologies in Nigeria. But also critical to this "open-endedness" are the peculiarities of a market structure made possible in the aftermath of 1980s structural adjustment reforms and 1990s drug-industry speculation and consolidation. This context has produced dynamics in the market that further explain why disease burdens do not match up with treatment availability.


*Market Constitution and Market Reproduction*

Largely inefficacious antibiotics such as ampicillin, ampliclox, tetracycline, cotrimoxazole, and streptomycin—used in the clinical case discussed above—are the most commonly used officially registered drugs in Nigeria. In fact, antibiotics are by far the largest class of drugs selling on the private

TABLE 5.2. Locally manufactured drugs' estimated market share, by drug class*

| Drug class | Percent of market |
| --- | --- |
| Analgesics, antiheumatics, and antipyretics | 25 |
| Antibiotics and antibacterials | 15 |
| Multivitamins and hematinics | 15 |
| Antimalarials | 14 |
| Antihypertensives | 8 |
| Antiretroviral medications | 6 |
| Cough and cold preparations | 5 |
| External and topical preparations | 5 |
| Antituberculosis medications | 4 |
| All others | 3 |
| Total | 100 |

Source: Wambebe and Ochekpe (2011, 38).

*It should be noted that locally manufactured drugs constitute roughly 20 percent of the market share. Imported drugs make up the rest and skew these results.

drug market (tables 5.2 and 5.3). The National Agency for Food and Drug Administration and Control (NAFDAC) listed a total of 1,876 different antibiotic products, most of which are different generic versions of older-generation drugs that are not at all efficacious throughout the country.[6] Over-the-counter (mostly) analgesics, nutritional supplements, and antimalarials take the largest share. In contrast, the class with some of the fewest registered products is anthelmintics, used to treat hundreds of millions of worm infections that occur each year in Nigeria.[7]

I juxtapose these two different classes of drugs and their treatment landscapes to pose questions about how the private market has developed in such skewed ways. In the 1970s, many drugs found in the Nigerian market were simple antibiotics, antimalarials, and analgesics. But though these drugs were simple, many of them were also effective and widely sold in North American and European markets. However, as the biologies of numerous bacteria species and malaria-causing parasites changed over time, the imported drugs meant to tackle these infections did not change to meet new medical needs. Instead, an intensive competition for market share had and still has a tendency to encourage the manufacturing, importation, and sale of nonefficacious and often low-quality 1970s pharmaceuticals, many of which encounter widespread resistance.

TABLE 5.3. Locally manufactured and imported pharmaceutical products registered with the National Agency for Food and Drug Administration and Control

| Product class | Number of products | Percent of registered products |
|---|---|---|
| Antibiotics | 1,885 | 26.23 |
| Nutritional supplements, hematinics, herbal products | 1,420 | 19.76 |
| Over-the-counter (antacids, antihistamines, nasal drops, inhalants, cough syrups, hemorrhoid treatments, mouthwashes, antiseptics, determatologicals, anti-spasmodics, antinauseants, and ear, nose, and throat treatments) | 1,234 | 17.17 |
| Analgesics and anti-inflammants | 745 | 10.36 |
| Antimalarials | 484 | 6.73 |
| Antihypertensives and cardiovascular treatments | 201 | 2.79 |
| Antifungals | 181 | 2.51 |
| Antivirals and antiretrovirals | 153 | 2.12 |
| Synthetic hormones (noncontraceptive) and steroids | 125 | 1.73 |
| Electrolytes, saline, anesthetics, and other surgical instruments | 122 | 1.69 |
| Anthelmintics | 108 | 1.50 |
| Vaccines, vaccine raw materials, biologicals | 106 | 1.47 |
| Antidepressants, antianxiety treatments, tranquilizers, sedatives, antipsychotics, relaxants, barbiturates | 84 | 1.16 |
| Antiasthmatics and bronchodilators | 67 | 0.93 |
| Antidiarrheals | 46 | 0.64 |
| Antidiabetes | 40 | 0.55 |
| Contraceptives | 14 | 0.19 |
| Treatments for kidney and liver disease | 4 | 0.05 |
| Not classified* | 167 | 2.32 |
| Total | 7,186 | 100 |

Source: Derived from National Agency for Food and Drug Administration and Control (2011).

*These drugs were not classified because their chemical names could not be determined.

How does one make sense of the skewed relationship between market structure and local biologies? In the 1970s and 1980s, a great deal of literature was published on what was referred to as drug dumping in the Third World. The pharmaceuticals that were dumped were product surpluses unloaded on black markets. Or they were drugs that had been deemed dangerous for human consumption in the United States and Europe but could nonetheless be marketed in the Third World because of the lax regulatory laws in those countries.[8] Although dumping is considered to be unethical or outright fraud, the disconnect between the drug-market structure and local biologies indicates that more attention should be given to other forms of drug dumping. For example, Mr. Kumar, a CEO of an Indian drug importation company, explains how dumping played out in Nigeria:

> [The multinational drug companies] looked at Nigeria only as an exploitation ground. . . . Let us take the antibiotics. Today in this country if you go ask for antibiotics, the best you will get is ampicillin, coaxillin, which are very, very old generation antibiotics. . . . These are the products that multinationals are continuously manufacturing, and if they were bringing the higher antibiotics and the new molecules from abroad at a higher price, the normal man will not able to afford it. Like, for example, let us take a product like this cefalexin sodium [an antibiotic], which is manufactured by the multinational. That was costing around 5,000 naira [about $35] for one injection. How many Nigerians can afford 5,000 naira for an injection? For a course of seven injections, they will be spending 35,000 naira [about $245]. None of them [consumers] could afford it. [So they] go to a pharmacy nearby, buy some sort of a clone of ampiclox or amoxicillin and be happy with it.

The market structure that accommodates huge amounts of ineffective antibiotics while bypassing needed antiworm, anticancer, antihypertensive, and cardiovascular medication is accelerating the changes in population biologies of both humans and microbes.[9] Although elements of this structure were in place at the inception of Nigeria's pharmaceutical market, market divestment and devaluation enforced that structure. Specifically, when global drug markets were restructured in the 1980s and 1990s, two critical events took place. The first is that manufacturing sites were reorganized. The brand-name drug industry was already well established outside of the markets of middle- and high-income countries, but with market crashes and currency fluctuations, many companies relocated to—or consolidated their operations in—Asia, especially South Korea, Singapore, Taiwan, India, and China (Virk 2008).[10]

A former Nigerian worker for Abbott Laboratories, a U.S.-based company, illustrated the 1990s situation for me. He invoked the example of erythromycin, an antibiotic that remains relatively effective in parts of Nigeria. Abbott manufactures erythromycin not in the United States but in Pakistan, among other places. The lower labor costs involved in doing so give the company higher profit margins. Abbott then sells the product in Nigeria at rather inflated U.S. prices because the company can claim that it is a U.S. drug. This pricing strategy recognizes the buying-and-selling culture in Nigeria. Abbott was one of the first companies to bring erythromycin to Nigeria, and theirs was the only brand in the market. It was years before any generic drug manufacturer began to market erythromycin, and as of 2010 there were no more than five small companies distributing generic erythromycin in Nigeria. Product recognition and prescribing patterns that do not often substitute high-quality generic drugs for brand-name products mean that the original version of the drug can still command high sales.

The second critical event was that while markets were restructuring, labor was rendered cheap; but at the same time manufacturing became too costly in Nigeria. Moreover, an array of long-term SAP imposed taxes on imports, and the state's retreat from providing very basic infrastructure (like electricity) needed for industrial manufacturing made it far more lucrative to import and trade drugs rather than to make them. One of the key differences between trading and manufacturing are the business commitments they involve. Local manufacturing requires the long-term investment of capital and time. Manufacturers' business calculations must assess the health profiles and purchasing capacity of Nigerians as well as fast-moving products, company profit margins, and technological capacities. In contrast, trading is completely geared toward the price movement of the market and not the long-term drug needs of the population.

For example, Nigerian pharmaceutical importers and distributors who do not work in the market, but distribute to retailers or clinics, gave me several different scenarios for ideal importation strategies. Most important is that if an importer wants to distribute several drug products, she must first establish a product line that always maintains high sales, such as antimalarials, antibiotics, and painkillers. If she is in business for the long term, she looks to smaller but possibly emerging markets, such as statins (anticholesterol products) or antihypertensives, where there are fewer competitors because these markets cater to consumers with higher purchasing power. If she works with a U.S. or European company that manufactures brand-name drugs offshore, she may assume that drug quality will remain high, which ensures that she will have a steady income stream based on the company's reputation and willingness to pay for imagined drug safety.

One of the wealthier Idumota traders is very reluctant to buy products that are new in the market because they are not a sure thing in terms of sales. He always waits to see how such a new product initially performs—allowing others, usually distributors, working outside Idumota, to take the risk first. If he thinks a product is doing well, then he will consider a partnership of sorts with retail clients. Traders pay very close attention to how fast products move in the market. If, for instance, customers—especially those who buy in bulk—come to the market asking for a product that is not available there, traders are known to drop everything, figure out where the drug is selling in West Africa, and travel all night long to a market outside Nigeria to buy the product. Or if the price of one over-the-counter generic drug crashes, traders in the market seek out new high-earning products instead; they may alter what stock they carry according to the market's boom-and-bust dynamics. Because the vast majority of drugs are imported via trading networks, the future of drug products is located not in anthelmintics, cardiovascular drugs, or new drug product breakthroughs but in market price fluctuations and, certainly, the public's recognition of and ability to pay for certain drugs. Thus, existing market practices and market structure are continually reinforced as massive numbers of cheaply priced and largely ineffective antibiotics and analgesics outpace pharmaceutical needs geared toward other diseases.

These pricing logics not only drive the proliferation of older and inefficacious drugs for the West African market, they also drive chemical arbitrage practices leading to fake drugs. Instead of capitalizing on price differentials, chemical arbitrage means that drug chemistry and drug dosages are intentionally deviated from standard ranges; these practices provide a wider markup margin and further arbitraging activities. For example, instead of the usual 200-milligram dose for paracetamol, a trader or distributor can negotiate with a manufacturer to make pills containing only 100 milligrams but label them as containing 200. Or drugs that may not sell well in one market (such as an anti-inflammatories) can be renamed and relabeled to sound like a high-selling drug (like an antibiotic) that is then exported to the Nigerian market, usually at very high price markups (Oparah 2005). One of the first ways that this began to appear in Idumota was through multiple layers of drug distribution in unofficial Nigerian markets, specifically one known as subdistributorship, which represents both a marketing

economic motives behind faking — Chemical arbitrage // — market dynamics practice as well as various levels of pharmaceutical distribution. Subdistributorship occurs when traders and distributor companies bypass the multinational importation company, going straight to the factories, where they negotiate new prices and create their own products. These practices evolved such that price, drug chemistry, and distribution become simultaneous sites of arbitrage and have since resulted in the production of millions of drugs that can deviate from bioequivalent and chemical standard ranges.

These arbitrage dynamics in Idumota market are not isolated. They represent one point of many in the drug manufacturing and distribution processes. They rely on similar arbitrage strategies that move pharmaceuticals of all qualities across continents. The imported drugs that travel to Nigerian markets, and indeed all others, are conceptualized, manufactured, and distributed based on the competition emerging from ever-downward pricing pressures, the regulatory regimes of nation-states, and the porousness of borders around the world through which pharmaceuticals must travel.

### Drug Chemistry and Regulation after Market Restructuring

When I first encountered the problem of fake and substandard drugs in Nigeria, the people producing these products were portrayed as operating in the shadows, and their identities remained largely unknown. This never made much sense to me, especially since the majority of drugs on the market during the 1990s were considered fake or substandard. How could anyone responsible for producing this enormous supply of drugs remain unknown? Moreover, it was hard to imagine pharmaceutical plants manufacturing fake drugs remaining concealed for very long, evading state authorities.

But there are several avenues that enable local and transnational operations to remain veiled. Perhaps the most important factor driving the hidden nature of fake drugs is not illicit activity but the more transparent activity of manufacturing offshoring. In the 1990s, countries such as Pakistan served as sites for offshoring Abbott's erythromycin. Since the early 2000s, the brand-name drug industry has increasingly turned to two sites: India and China (Pore et al. 2008).[11] Outsourcing is the procurement of goods or services under contract with an outside supplier, and offshoring is the practice of moving or basing a business operation abroad. Both outsourcing and offshoring are increasingly utilized in manufacturing processes. For example, brand-name companies offshore research and production to prominent Chinese and Indian national companies, which in turn outsource to smaller, local manufacturers. There is a great deal of licensing activity and partial merging—up and down the pharmaceutical value chain—from preclinical chemistry to clinical trials (Pore et al. 2008).

The promise of a therapeutic revolution that gave rise to the 1990s drug industry consolidation did not produce many hoped-for new products; now there are even fewer drug pipelines, upcoming expiring patents, and rising R&D costs (Pore et al. 2008). As European- and North American-based companies move to Asia, they are closing down plants or asset dumping in both their home and foreign markets where costs are higher.[12] They are also acquiring or licensing to a number of national firms based in Chinese and Indian home markets,[13] which helps to grow these industries.[14]

In addition to outsourcing and offshoring, the implementation of World Trade Organization (WTO)-mandated intellectual property laws in both India and China (as well as national changes in good manufacturing practice standards) was very effective in reorganizing national industries.[15] These changes meant that medium-sized companies began to consolidate and grow bigger, while many, but not all, smaller companies were squeezed out. Driving costs down even further, India and China have become each other's preferred trading partners; for example, Indian drug imports in China amounted to $58 billion in 2005 as opposed to U.S. imports that were valued at nearly $30 million (Pore et al. 2008, 113). One outcome of increased industry consolidation is that the wealthiest Indian and Chinese companies have been acquiring American and European firms; the industry literature refers to this as "reverse offshoring" (Pore et al. 2008), a misnomer if we understand these activities through the impetus of capital rather than via U.S. and European hegemonic trading power.

Merging and acquisition landscapes differ slightly from 1990s strategies. At that time, drug-industry consolidation led to dumping less-productive assets while strengthening existing product lines and adding already well-earning products to a company's profile. In this more recent scenario of Chinese and Indian companies acquiring American and European firms and vice versa, the focus of expansion is on reduced or abstracted stages of manufacturing. For example, active pharmaceutical ingredients (API)— the key chemical or biological ingredients in drugs—are made in the primary manufacturing stage. China and India are the world's first and third highest producers of API, which is a multibillion-dollar industry. They produce API for drug companies around the world, including Nigeria.[16]

*Taking due to market dynamics of 1980s/90s but also using same strategies as "legit" industry*

Then comes secondary manufacturing, which is the production of pharmaceuticals in their final form. The third stage is tableting and packing drugs for distribution to wholesalers. An intermediary step within these stages is also possible, which could include outsourcing a fragment of these manufacturing stages to a local company that makes API, for example, within the offshored site.

These activities are further complicated in China, which has a large chemical industry with over 80,000 companies (Bate 2012, 177). Chemical companies can make API or completely cross over into drug production itself. But China's drug regulatory agency, the Food and Drug Administration, has no jurisdiction to inspect chemical companies (Bogdanich et al. 2007). If it did, it would be especially difficult to regulate simply due to the sheer size of both chemical and pharmaceutical industries—a problem that all national regulatory agencies face. Regulation in any country in the world is designed to oversee manufacturing based on national regulatory laws.[17] But regulatory bodies and their legal mandates are not well designed to oversee the crisscrossing of prolific offshored and outsourced manufacturing, making it nearly impossible to inspect, and sometimes even trace, manufacturing premises (Bate 2012; U.S. Food and Drug Administration 2013). Even though Nigerian, U.S., European, and other regulatory authorities have offices in overseas markets like China, none of those countries, including China, have the capacity to actually inspect and regulate all of these facilities in any rigorous way. Indeed, Bogdanich quotes Congressional Representative John D. Dingell as saying that "China alone has more than 700 firms making drug products for the U.S., yet the FDA has resources to conduct only about 20 inspections a year in China" (2007, A1; see also Harris and Bogdanich 2008). It is, therefore, difficult for any drug regulatory agency to guarantee the safety of the national drug supply.

The fake-drug industry relies on offshoring to Asia, outsourcing within offshored sites, and the impossibilities of regulation. For example, a major fake-drug scandal involved Scientific Protein Laboratories (SPL), a U.S. company based in Wisconsin. It is the primary owner of a Chinese company, Changzhou SPL, which manufactures heparin, an anti-coagulant (blood thinner) derived from pig intestines. In March 2008, the FDA claimed that 81 deaths and 785 adverse effects occurred across eleven countries due to heparin contaminated with a much cheaper raw material (Harris 2008). The *New York Times* investigators David Barboza and Walt Bogdanich report that the Changzhou plant "was certified by American officials to export to the United States even though neither government [Chinese or U.S.] had inspected it. The plant has been exporting heparin to [the American health care company] Baxter [International] since 2004.... Some experts say as much as 70 percent of China's crude heparin—for domestic use and for export—comes from small factories in poor villages. One of the biggest areas for these workshops is ... in coastal Jiangsu Province, north of Shanghai, where entire villages have become heparin production centers" (2008; see also Bogdanich and Hooker 2008).

The heparin case shows how chemical arbitrage opportunities have become available in offshoring activities as well as in the outsourcing that occurs in offshored sites. These manufacturing processes feed into distribution channels as well. When producers and distributers work together (more often in ways that do not draw attention to themselves as in the heparin case), they first ascertain the regulatory capacity of a drug's destination. Different regulatory regimes have different capacities to monitor the various aspects of fake drugs (from drug chemistry to packaging) and fake drug producers and distributors take this into account. Once the regulatory constraints are ascertained, they calculate the lowest amount of API and the cheapest amount of inactive ingredients to create a drug that will make it into the destined market without raising the suspicions of regulators. There is often far more deviation outside of the standard API range in difficult-to-regulate markets versus those markets that are better regulated (Bate 2012).

Finished drug products as well as raw materials for pharmaceutical ingredients that are manufactured in Asia move laterally among multiple distributors. At this stage, they can pass through as many as six trading companies before they reach the pharmaceutical manufacturer or wholesaler. As the journalist Katherine Eban (2005) has discussed, the lateral moves at this stage are made within an extensive network in the wholesale drug trade. The network includes distributors, intermediaries, secondary wholesalers, and a vast array of businesses that run the gamut between the official and unofficial, the licit and the illicit. Just as is the case with arbitrage conducted in Idumota, where multiple lateral exchanges make gains in sales, global pharmaceutical distribution chains are driven by price differentials set by the manufacturers. These traders—diverters, or arbs, as they are commonly called—take advantage of the price differences by buying discounted drugs and reselling them at marked-up prices to other distributors and wholesalers (Eban 2005; Yankus 2006). The distribution chain constitutes many people and companies across global regions; with each link in the chain there are a new price markups. In Europe, arbitraging pharmaceuticals is allowable via parallel import laws, making it an especially pervasive practice there (Maskus and Ganslandt 1999).

It might help to briefly illustrate the drug distribution system in the United States, where three major wholesalers—AmerisourceBergen, Cardinal Health, and McKesson—procure drug stock directly from manufacturers; these three companies handle over 80 percent of the drugs distributed in the United States. But in recent years, these wholesalers have purchased from secondary wholesalers, who themselves often purchase from sources other than the manufacturers. The reason for these small diversions is, again, price. The secondary wholesalers search out discounted products because they do not necessarily have a price advantage over the larger wholesalers. Donald DeKieffer points out that "the major distributors operate at very thin profit margins, rarely exceeding five percent. If, however, they can purchase inventory at 10% or more below the price offered by the manufacturer, the result goes directly to the bottom line. This has traditionally been too tempting to resist for even the most ethical of companies" (2006, 329).

Moreover, the same drugs are priced differently across countries due to their varying regulatory policies. For example, Europe has fairly strict pricing caps on drugs, while drug prices are not regulated in the United States or Nigeria.[18] Intermediary companies or drug arbitrageurs rely on these price differentials to move products.[19] The multiple lateral movements, many of which take place in Europe, do the work of obscuring manufacturing origins. One may never know that drugs or raw materials came from an unregulated or unregistered company, or from a company that is registered but only part of whose manufacturing chain is regulated (Bate 2012).

The secondary wholesaling tactics that take place in the United States are not unlike the multiple wholesaling diversions of fake drugs in other parts of the world. That is, distributors draw almost entirely on the regulatory gaps, price differentials, and gray trade links to facilitate the global fake-drug trade, which uses the same distribution routes as trade in legitimate pharmaceuticals. The distribution chain for both intentionally faked and legitimate products relies on free-trade zones around the world, like those in Dubai or the Panama Canal, which are not subject to rigorous inspection and moves on quickly to sites of sale or manufacture (Bogdanich et al. 2007). Indeed, counterfeiters use free-trade zones to hide pharmaceuticals' and chemicals' origins as well as to make, resell, market, or relabel fake drugs (Bogdanich et al. 2007; UN Office on Drugs and Crime 2009; Loewy 2007). In Dubai, where many fake drugs stop in transit to West Africa, the usual requirement for local ownership of companies is waived, and there are no import and export fees or income tax (Bogdanich et al. 2007). As authorities catch on to the regular use of one free-trade zone, counterfeiters simply move on to new sites that are not well surveilled.

These examples from the global distribution chain highlight a number of gray areas in which breakdowns in regulation are driven by global drug economies. The massive dispersals in the production and distribution chains make it difficult to discern the difference between intentionally faked or unintentionally substandard drugs because regulatory inspection—of everything from raw materials to finished products—has difficulty distinguishing between them. Once they reach markets like Idumota, they are lost to regulatory oversight.

## Routing Drugs into West Africa

How do fake and substandard drugs enter Nigeria? Mr. Kumar, who has been importing Indian pharmaceuticals since 1980, asserted in an interview over dinner that:

> There is one basic community from Nigeria, and most of the Indian third-grade companies export all sorts from India where they may not even have a pharmaceutical factory. So these are the two people who are involved in bringing this fake and substandard products. If you ask me of any such companies, I will not be able [to] name any such companies because any of those such companies without a name to contend with or a reputation to be worried about, will not enter into this [discussion]. There have been some good Indian companies which have been here, like Ranbaxy has been here for now twenty, twenty-five years. They have put up a manufacturing unit here. Vitabiotics, this is another good company here. May Organics, another good company here. There are good companies which are here, but the point is there are also these trading ulcers.

I always encountered cagey language like this when either Nigerians or expatriates talked to me about who produces fake drugs and who facilitates their entry into Nigeria. India and China have both been stereotyped as centers for industrial piracy. In the case of China, Laikwan Pang (2008) points out that the image of the pirate cannot be separated from the real or imagined industrial power that China possesses. China can produce any kind of product, and as such it "is tied to today's global capitalism in all senses" (Pang 2008, 120). Because the bulk of both legitimate and illicit drug products come from China and India, many diverse actors in Nigeria may encounter each other. From their perspective, it becomes necessary to sort out who is legitimate and who is illegitimate based on chemical deviancies. Making assumptions about people based on their ethnicity and national origin could mean including oneself in these categories.

The transnational alliances that Mr. Kumar spoke about can come into being in several ways. Tony—a former officer of the Pharmaceutical Society of Nigeria, the main Nigerian professional organization for pharmacists—told me that he had received an e-mail message from a company in China informing him that the firm took orders for any specifications, which includes not only drug chemistries, but also tablet coloring and packaging. Manufacturers such as this are largely small- to medium-scale companies that are linked to the entire supply and distribution chains across continents. As Yi-Chieh Jessica Lin (2011) points out, the distribution of fake products out of China entails first moving these products by boat or air to neighboring Southeast Asian ports, where they are then shipped to intermediary countries in places like Europe, where new documents or relabeling can take place. Given that parallel importation is legal in Europe as mentioned above, much of the actual faking can take place there. Critically, like the money laundering strategies of Nigerian businessmen who created and relied upon capillary networks, the total embedding of local networks to move fake goods out of China is equally important (Lin 2011). Certainly, they employ or draw on key actors in customs and transport to facilitate fake products across borders.

After fake drugs travel out of Asia by sea or over land, they pass through free-trade zones or other porous regulatory depots and arrive in West Africa. As both Tony and regulatory officials explained to me, drugs entering Nigeria can be smuggled directly into the country. But more often they are first directed to neighboring West African countries. If they are traveling by boat, they are usually shipped to the Republic of Benin, whose main port is in the city of Cotonou, only 100 kilometers west of Lagos. The port authority in Benin inspects only shipments that are to remain in Benin, which is a major hub for used-car imports and sales. Goods that are simply passing through Cotonou and in transit to other West African countries are not inspected (although cargo may be scanned for explosives or searched for narcotics). Rather, the "acquits" system, which allows transporters to cross borders within the region without global customs clearance (Baxerres and Le Hesran 2011), provides documentation that certifies inspection at the point of embarkation and is enough to pass goods through customs. As Baxerres and Le Hesran note, "Consequently, trade of specific goods, such as pharmaceuticals, can escape customs statistics" (2011, 1252). Smugglers take advantage of these gaps in the regulatory apparatus by packing fake drug products in the middle of a shipping container and surrounding them with legitimate products. Once the drugs have cleared customs in Cotonou, they are loaded onto a truck and move to their final destination in Nigeria. When the truck reaches the Nigerian border, it is up to the border officials to decide what to do about the cargo. A driver may insist that only NAFDAC can inspect it; and payments made to officials can ease the truck's way across the border.

Once fake drugs leave manufacturing premises destined for local or foreign markets, there are a number of ways they can escape attention while generating profits through arbitrage. Several pharmacists told me about manufacturers and their distributors who place real and fake drugs in the same package, to increase the profit margin. For example, if a fake drug costs just 10 naira per tablet to make, and the real product costs 250 naira, the extra profit in selling a fake is 240 naira (about $1.60). If a customer comes to the market or a pharmacy shop and buys several products, and a trader or a salesperson throws one or two fakes in, the gain in profit may seem extremely small, but it can add up over time.

Much of what is known about fake drugs results from the joint work among national, regional, and international agencies. Those include members of the United Nations, federal governments, non-governmental organizations, and brand-name drug companies. While there are regional task forces that cooperate across the fifteen West African states, there are no harmonized laws. One reason for this is that the term *counterfeit drugs* has no similar juridical definition within the region. Moreover, coordination among the police, courts, legislators, and regulatory bodies is not well executed (West African Health Organization 2011). However, regional coordination is nascent and has been preceded by recent joint statements and actions plans.[20] Their analysis of fake drugs always acknowledges problems with consumer safety and public education, but solutions to these problems mostly involve appeals to commercial interests that match war-on-drugs strategies, discussed in chapter 3. These include developing punishment mechanisms such as stringent jail time rather than coming up with policy to prevent fake drugs, such as price regulation.

Nigeria's Narcotics and Counterfeiting Federal Task Force is responsible for surveilling these drugs in the country. It also cooperates with other West African agencies to surveil the West African region due to pervasive fake drug smuggling over West African borders. A high-ranking member of the task force explained to me that it provides extensive coordination among West African state drug regulatory authorities to identify and stop transnational business chains that are facilitating the movement of products into West Africa. For example, the same official told me about the arrest of a Nigerian businessman who was discovered with a drug product that he claimed was manufactured in India. However, the airport manifest stated that the businessman's load had come from China. The official took the matter to Interpol, which notified the police in China. The police located the Chinese company, which had faked an Indian company's drugs (something that may be increasingly common given the trading relationships between China and India). The Chinese police retrieved the phone number of the Nigerian importer from whom the arrested Nigerian businessman purchased the drugs, and the importer turned out to be a clearing agent at the Lagos airport. The task force official was informed that the fake drug manufacturers in China were executed. I sensed that the official was slightly horrified but also pleased that some punishment had been implemented.

Idumota market has its own unofficial drug task force. Chidi is one of the members. With other members who are also pharmaceutical traders, he goes on daily sweeps checking for fake drugs in market stalls. He told me:

> [Fake drugs] will give us a bad image. If we catch you selling fake drugs firstly, the union [Lagos State Medicines Dealers Association] will first of all apprehend you . . . the union will now alert the police. You will be in police custody before we now [tell] NAFDAC, [which] will now go and pick you up. NAFDAC will subject [your products] to a chemical test. You pay heavily—105,000 naira for the test, for each product. Then after the test, you will pay if you didn't pass the test, and you will go to court and from there go to jail. . . . During the time of investigation and resigation, the shop will remain closed. . . . So we don't tolerate any type of fake drugs in this market.

Drug traders like Ikenna and Chidi, among others, make it very clear that if there is even a rumor of fake drugs, much less their actual presence in Idumota, it is bad for everyone's business. Regardless of whether the actions Chidi described go as smoothly as he reported, he and others claimed to me that the internal market surveillance has actually prevented the dumping of fake drugs in Idumota. Like global distribution networks that seek out porous transit sites, fake drugs dealers turn to new destinations in Nigeria if a market like Idumota applies strict internal control mechanisms.

Opinions about what drives and fuels the distribution of low-quality drugs vary widely. Tony, the former Pharmaceutical Society of Nigeria official, said:

> It is only the [fake drug importers] that have been put in place by these market people, and they have their businesses dotted all around. If you put a continual load of fake drugs in Idumota this evening, by tomorrow morning you wouldn't see it because they would have distributed it, put it on the buses that are doing night travels, [and] they are off! The one going to Kano [a city in the northern part of the country] has gone [snaps fingers], the one going to [the airport after they] land, someone picks it [snaps fingers] [and] dispatches it to the north. It goes off like that! That is why we are saying, the society is saying, "No to drug market," because if you have well organized drug distribution you don't allow them to prosper together because when they prosper they are able to do more evil. . . . So what I am saying in essence is that the drug market is the bedrock of fake drug distribution. So things should be taken off and because of that you can't do a recall. So the recall system is not there because they are not bothered, they are all interested in the money.

Ikenna insisted to me: "It is the system. It is the system. There are people working [to facilitate the sale of fake drugs] at the airport. There are people working at the seaport. Even this 100 percent inspection for drugs is still implied, but these things [fakes] still come in even up till today. Who is deceiving who? It's a system thing, my sister."

Ikenna pointed out that fake drugs are rooted in a systemic network tied across regions, while Tony connected it to the unofficial drug markets. Both viewpoints are valid. Tony is right to indicate that open markets are the primary site of fake drugs' distribution. But it is not simply that thousands of private wholesalers have helped to open up channels for fake rugs. Idumota is only one nodal point in a very complex transcontinental supply system.

The speculative marketplace has encouraged the search for ever-depressed manufacturing costs. As a result, new forms of abstracted manufacturing and multiple routes of distribution have provided a veiled means for fake drugs to be produced and distributed. Even before these drugs make it to Nigeria, the pricing and arbitrage strategies that tie drug manufacturing and distribution together ultimately make it difficult to tackle the enormous amount of fake and substandard drugs entering the country. Nonetheless, the Nigerian public has a great desire for the drugs they purchase and consume to one day meet much higher standards.

### Social Life of Bioequivalence

I was at home one day with Toks while his son was recovering from what he suspected was fake worm expellant. When the child had a bad reaction to the medicine, he took a closer look at the label and discovered that there were at least six different things wrong with the packaging, which can include an absent or not-well-copied NAFDAC approval seal, the wrong font used on the package, wrong labeling of ingredients, wrong labeling of dosage, and so forth. It was disturbing to him that as a pharmacist—someone with expertise in the matter—he did not avert the problem much sooner.

A great many of my friends and the people I met in passing had personal stories to tell me about fake drugs once they knew my research was about pharmaceuticals.

"My sister almost died. . . ."

"I myself am a pharmacist, and I couldn't tell that I gave my daughter fake cough syrup."

"I was sick for a week after I took ACT [artemisinin combination therapies, for malaria], which I'm sure was fake."

"They're talking now that the reason for HIV-drug resistance is because there are fakes in the government program."

"I lost my father to fake drugs—that man was in his prime—oh!"

Fake drugs are one of the many hazards of Nigerian life, and people never seem to tire of debating the ills, risks, and dangers of these drugs. They want something much better than this. In all these stories that people shared with me, there was little sense that anything could be done. Not only is there no appropriate or workable mechanism to recall drugs, but the regulatory focus is mostly on fake drugs. As a result, it is difficult to discern whether the problem with adverse reactions to drugs stems from allergic reactions to high-quality drugs, from the fact that limited regulation of local manufacturers has led to the production of substandard drugs, or from chemical arbitrage that has resulted in the sale of drugs with low levels of their active pharmaceutical ingredients or with dangerous added ingredients.

During the 1980s, especially, pharmacists often bore the brunt of the blame because they were viewed as the gatekeepers of pharmaceutical quality ("The Minister of Health and Fake Drugs" 1988; Atueyi 1988). But they themselves are victims of circumstance: lack of good infrastructure in the universities; difficulties securing constant and adequate drug supplies in the public health sector; and pricing structures that force pharmacists to choose between stocking higher-priced and higher-quality drugs or importing cheaper and less certain ones (Kehinde 1993). In addressing these widespread public concerns, I use bioequivalence as a way to think through the politics of drug chemistry shaped by market volatility and by the public desire for a safe drug supply.

In their discussion on the origins of this term, Daniel Carpenter and Dominique Tobbell note that "'bioequivalence' gives legitimacy and reality to generic drugs. It implies that one pharmaceutical commodity can substitute for another in most (if not all) critical therapeutic respects, and by so doing bioequivalence establishes a framework for market transactions based upon price. It is a joint regulatory and scientific creation, not purely a technical construct, and not purely a legal concept. Bioequivalence developed at the interstices of state, commerce, professional and academic medicine, professional and academic pharmacy, administrative law, and even the politics of federalism" (2011, 94).

Carpenter and Tobbell analyze the twentieth-century history of bioequivalence, which amounted to a struggle in the United States over precisely which aspects of a drug need to be regulated when generic versions emerge in the market. One critical question was whether both the mimicry of drug chemistry and a drug's bioavailability—the rate of a drug's absorption and manner in which it is processed in the human body—should be regulated. Both are now overseen in the regulatory process.[21]

But standardized drugs can vary in terms of the inactive ingredients they contain and their bioequivalence to other drugs as well as vary from one batch to another (Hayden 2012). Two drugs are considered *similar* because they fall within a standard chemical range, but they are not precisely the *same* simply because their chemistry can vary within this range. NAFDAC requires only that a generic imitator be chemically equivalent—not necessarily bioequivalent—to the brand-name original. The problem for NAFDAC, and even consumers, is not that drugs vary in standard chemical ranges, but that it is difficult to identify high-quality drugs and potentially dangerous substances among the extraordinary multitude of products on the market. What happens when many products of varying chemical potential are for sale in markets that are affected by speculation and downward pricing pressures? Like Kim Fortun (2001), Michelle Murphy (2006), and Cori Hayden (2012), I am interested in how we understand chemical dynamics outside of laboratories and within human concerns.

Bernadette Bensaude-Vincent and Isabelle Stengers argue that research and development in industrial chemistry is not merely about discovering or creating new molecules. Rather, it is about the creation of "informed materials," meaning that chemical structure becomes highly enriched in information as it is adapted to ever-evolving industrial needs (1996, 206). Alfred N. Whitehead (1978) treated chemical molecules not necessarily as discrete entities but as relational and historical events. Rather than bounded, he viewed them as extensions into and parts of other entities comprising new notions of matter, which is a theoretical concept that is prominent in quantum chemistry. Here, chemical composition comes into being based on molecular and environmental associations (such as temperature and the presence of other molecules and impurities) to which Andrew Barry (2005) emphasizes the constantly changing properties and contingent nature of chemical compounds. Barry (2005) and Bensaude-Vincent and Stengers (1996) address what happens when chemistry is translated into pharmaceutical research and drug production. For Bensaude-Vincent and Stengers, the problem is that there is a difference between the purified chemical in the laboratory and the dynamics of its molecules once it encounters the human body. For Barry, the problem is more complicated and also involves regulation, decisions regarding costs, clinical trial results, intellectual property, and a number of other political issues that mediate drug production (2005, 57–59).

The idea of the molecule's relationship to its environment, either chemical or political, is important here. The encounter that molecules have with their environments—or "open systems," as Barry (2005, 53) calls them—is understood by these authors as operating within controlled atmospheres such as the private research laboratory that is subject to regulatory oversight. Hayden (2012) takes these politics of numerous informational and relational forms a step further by drawing attention to the copied (not brand-name) drug and its chemical constituents. In her work on drug copies in Mexico, Hayden demonstrates the political nature of equivalence that echoes both older and current versions of Mexican nationalism. Drawing on histories of Latin American populism and musing on how these histories resonate with current politics about generic drug substitution, Hayden probes the Mexican-made discourse exploited by the generic companies she studies. She explains that there is another side to this quasi-nationalist resonance: "the strong association of the domestic copy and the 'popular masses' with the specter of uncertain authenticity (the same but ... ?), national identities marked by an ambivalently 'imitative' relation to the metropole, and the uncanny powers accruing to the proliferative copy. It also, of course, draws our attention to race, ethnicity, and indigeneity as the modes through which the tensions between sameness and difference within these 'national' projects have long been mediated" (2012, 178; ellipsis in original).

The uncertainty of authenticity, the ambivalent "'imitative' relation to the metropole," and the "proliferative copy" (Hayden 2012, 178) are especially pronounced when the open systems of chemistry encounter "open economies" in Africa. Dudley Seers ([1963] 1970, 166–68) defined open economies as markets that were highly amenable to external influences, especially in the context of colonial economies that were completely integrated within larger imperial ones.[22] But my concern here is with the way that external influences of market volatility, now considered standard dynamics in African economies, significantly shape drug chemistry and "informed materials." Both Bensaude-Vincent and Stengers (1996) and Friedrich von Hayek (1967) are key figures in biology, physics, and physical chemistry, whose work is concerned with nonequilibrium dynamics—the former to explain the contingent nature of chemistry and the configuration of informed materials; the latter to explain new orders arising out of nonequilibrium and chronically volatile markets. All these scholars bypass or reject positivist laws and models as explanations for the dynamics of chemistry and markets.

When the open systems of drug chemistry meet the volatility of open African economies, price and chemical arbitrage are the primary strategies that people employ in order to make it in the system. This inherent flexibility of chemistry and markets poses several implications for dreams of bioequivalence. As a new and highly volatile pathway that links Lagos and Jiangsu far more closely than the U.S. and Chinese Food and Drug Administrations, the unbounded molecule encounters numerous changing chemical associations such as talc, dangerous inactive ingredients, and impurities mediated by free-trade zones; chemical and distribution arbitrage; and diffuse unregulated sites of manufacture. These dynamics must cope with downward pricing pressures, low national per capita incomes, consumer product recognition, and regulatory regimes that must contend with Nigerian factors. A dream of bioequivalence is the desire to live with chemical certainty—a certainty that Nigerians imagine to exist in the pharmaceutical metropole. This is not necessarily a biosocial appeal (Rabinow 1992), for which entitlements to drug safety are driven by common health burdens. Rather, it is postcolonial, tied to questions of equity in an unequal world.

So, in rejecting the discourse of evil fake drug traders and concomitantly India and China as paradigmatic sites of drug faking, perhaps we can look to the ways that poverty drives fakes in the face of limited price arbitrage that gives way to chemical arbitrage. Perhaps we can see how arbitrage shapes the contours of the West African drug market—a market that is necessarily intertwined with activities driven by downward pricing pressures such as offshoring. Perhaps we can see just how fake drugs are the outcome of the speculative nature of the drug industry. Indeed, the pressures of the speculative marketplace tie the motives of the poorest people in the world struggling to keep afloat with the wealthiest global companies whose primary options in this highly competitive industry are to survive by being the highest earners and the most strategic mergers.

The social life of bioequivalence does not simply refer to how all these dynamics reverberate across continents, bringing disparate people into unexpected commercial and social relationships. It also refers to a longing to live with a little less market chaos, a little more security in the drug supply, fewer medicines that are mismatched with disease burdens, a little less strain involved in hustling the day, and—as Seun Kuti puts it in this chapter's epigraph—a little less shit dumped in Africa.

## Marketing Indefinite Monopolies
### Intellectual Property, Debt, and Drug Geopolitics

Perhaps, never since the Berlin Conference of 1884 during which various European countries shared Africa among themselves has any single event had a more pervasive impact on the continent as the debt crisis. Never since independence has sovereignty in Africa been more impugned upon or subverted.

—S. Ogoh Alubo, "Debt Crisis, Health and Health Services in Africa"

Competition is a sin.  —John D. Rockefeller

*Intellectual Property, Debt, and Monopoly*

When nonefficacious, fake, and substandard drugs flooded the Nigerian market in the aftermath of liberalization, more advanced, expensive, and patented therapies made by brand-name manufacturers were confined to North American and European markets. The brand-name companies began to rely increasingly on blockbuster drugs that garnered majority sales in these markets, where higher consumer incomes and national insurance schemes support sales. The brand-name manufacturers still receive income from drug markets outside of North America and Europe.[1] But they market over-the-counter and older-generation drugs in Africa because of the limited purchasing power of very low-income people. This international division of drug sales was in place during the 1970s, but it became even more pronounced once pharmaceuticals got connected to the speculative market in the 1980s. Speculation required an infrastructure to ensure that the new dynamics of pharmaceutical capital could operate and thrive. Specifically, new debt, intellectual property (IP), and drug marketing regimes were implemented. These events and activities provided the framework for the industry's speculative practices and its subsequent withdrawal from the African drug market. In the process, new types of monopolies arose in the international pharmaceutical industry.

Debates about drug industry monopolies largely revolve around the capacity to access drugs for people living with HIV or other diseases that require treatment with expensive and patented drugs. Industry consolidation is important here: only a handful of brand-name firms now produce the majority of the world's drug supply.[2] These manufacturers conduct the vast majority of drug development across the globe, and—unlike companies in the generic drug industry that produce pharmaceutical copies—they manufacture new and patented drugs. International AIDS activism, especially since the 1990s, has made very visible the incredible difficulties of accessing HIV treatment outside of North American and European markets, especially for poor people. The question of monopoly arises because when these drugs are still under patent protection, generic drug companies are forbidden from manufacturing them, making treatment nearly impossible to secure.

In this chapter, I explore how debt regimes, IP law, and marketing practices in Nigeria after structural adjustment shaped pharmaceutical monopolies in fundamental ways, concentrating the supply of patented drugs in places in North America and Europe while there is a sheer absence of them in Nigeria and most of Africa. I begin with pharmaceutical marketing strategies, which profoundly shape how drugs are distributed in West Africa. Building on the last chapter's discussion of the reproduction of the national drug market, I first explain how medical representatives—the term for drug marketers in Nigeria—select and distribute drugs in this region. Marketing inefficacious yet well-known and popular drugs is an outcome of debt regimes. And it is clear that the remarkably low average household income in West Africa helps determine the kinds of drugs that are marketed there.

I next turn to IP law, which is governed by global trade rules, specifically those of the World Trade Organization. AIDS activists, legal scholars, and policy makers have rightly argued that the patent is largely responsible for the lack of access to drugs for poor people, mostly because it gives drug companies exclusive rights to research, price, and distribute drugs in markets of their choice. The patent does not work this way in Nigeria, nor in most of Africa, because patented drugs are not marketed in any widespread way there. Brand-name manufacturers are not after the patent per se, but they do desire securing a monopoly across markets, which can be achieved by means other than the patent. In Nigeria, the monopoly is mediated by very specific marketing practices conducted by brand-name manufacturers that deliberately keep life-saving, patented pharmaceuticals off the national market in order to protect high drug prices outside of Africa.

Last, I discuss the role of debt regimes, which enables the patent to restrict sales to certain markets. I highlight the making of the U.S. debt regime that was launched rather inadvertently in the aftermath of President Richard Nixon's taking the dollar off the gold standard and the debt that materialized in Africa in the aftermath of structural adjustment programs (SAPs). These different debt regimes not only helped reorganize capital flows and concentrations, but they also effectively set indefinite and unequal terms of competition in the drug industry. Debt and the patent are important because they undergird how pharmaceuticals are both valued and circulate in drug markets around the world.

## Drug Companies' Marketing Strategies

I first met Obi in 2005, when he was working for a high-powered brand-name pharmaceutical company. As a trained pharmacist and a highly successful and experienced marketer, he was responsible for a number of drug products. He marketed these drugs in Nigeria and throughout West Africa. For a marketer, it is important to establish a product line especially in the Nigerian market because the population of Nigeria is equal to that of all other West African countries combined. Marketing to a critical mass of potential consumers is something that a marketer considers when going through the arduous process of marketing a drug in the region. Over the years that I have known him, Obi has held different jobs, sometimes with the multinational brand-name drug manufacturers, sometimes with Nigerian firms, sometimes working on his own. Much of this moving around has to do with his reputation as a marketer (he has been wooed away from existing jobs) or with his dislike of various drug company politics.

All marketers have their own methods of marketing, and Obi has a calculated approach to the business. If his existing product profile is doing well and his company wants him to introduce a drug that is new to the market, he approaches medical specialists who could potentially use the drug and conducts what he calls a "product introduction." This first stage can happen over an informal lunch. The goal is to recruit what are known as key opinion leaders in the field—specific physicians and clinicians who are well known and well respected and who can be influential in the next stages of marketing. Obi told me:

> When it is a brand-new molecule—that is, [one] probably never used here before—the best strategy is to get the key opinion leaders to buy them first because for a new molecule, most doctors on their own cannot start writing [prescriptions for] the products. They need to know that, "oh, there is a specialist that is using it." So, for example, let's say you are talking to cardiologists. You have an informal dinner or a lunch to officially present the product to them. You understand? And that way, these people, they will be critics of the product; they will analyze [it] and tell you whether [it is] good or bad, whether it will be successful in this environment, what are the shortfalls, what are the problems you are likely to encounter.

If the new product is a competitor to—or the manufacturer claims that it is an improvement on—another molecule that is already widely known among practitioners, the same users are approached and told that this is a different and better brand of the same product. Reasons given for why it is better could include a lower price, fewer side effects, or a reduction in the required frequency of use. As Obi puts it, in this case one is selling a new benefit of a molecule that is already known; he effectively finesses a way of marketing a me-too product among various versions of the same drug in a crowded market. At these informal lunches and dinners, the marketer attempts to convince the clinician or the key opinion leader of the product's efficacy. Clinicians at this stage may either be convinced or ask for further studies.

Once they are convinced, clinicians are then enrolled to work with the marketer to take the product to the next stage, which is to give a formal clinical presentation at a major teaching hospital. This is referred to as a *clinical meeting* and Obi uses the key opinion leader as the keynote speaker. Clinical meetings are conducted by marketers. They are essentially public relations meetings that are the first critical stage for most marketers in establishing the product's presence. Mr. Kumar, marketing for his own India-based company, had this to say about the clinical meeting:

> The best part is when you go and organize for this clinical meeting, you will get all the interns who will be attending there. There will be none of the heads of departments or the consultants who will come and sit there, coordinate with you, talk to you, and know more about the products. It will be most of the student intern doctors who will be clamoring for the free giveaways. It is really sad. . . . For heaven's sake, what products are we talking of? We are talking of products which are already there in the other countries for HIV and other diseases. We are not talking of new research molecules that are here, so what is the purpose of a clinical meeting?

Obi's strategy is slightly different. He makes sure that the senior clinicians are ready to back up the product at the clinical meeting. Key to a marketer's survival and success is understanding the hierarchies of status and rank and then strategizing the marketing stages from there. Obi described his approach to me:

> First, you take care of those top guys. What they do most times is wait for the junior ones to ask questions . . . because they [the senior clinicians] are already well informed—which adds to their ego [laughs]—they respond to those questions. But if you notice that you cannot convince that group, you reconvince, or you ask them what can I do to convince you. "Oh, we need more data, oh we need this, we need samples to test." [I respond,] "Okay, okay, we'll get this for you and we will come back again in one month."

The clinical meeting is the most important early step in marketing products. For Obi, having the key opinion leaders present ensures that his message is delivered with extra credibility. So the leaders back him up, especially since some doctors or other clinicians may claim that they never heard of the presented products in medical school or elsewhere. Without a key leader in place, other senior physicians in the meeting can, in the eyes of marketers, derail the entire process by simply resisting a new product on the grounds that it is too expensive, has too many side effects, or is another unnecessary me-too drug. According to Obi, junior physicians or clinicians do not normally contradict what the senior ones have to say about the product.

In my observation clinical meetings are accompanied by disease and therapeutic awareness lectures. Often knowledge of therapeutics is initially provided by drug company marketers, as clinicians who meet with fifty or more patients each day do not have time to read medical journals, or they may have limited or little access to them. Obi told me:

> I remember when we introduced lipid-lowering drugs, we had to do a disease awareness campaign to create an awareness in the environment that . . . a high level of lipid concentration is a complication of hypertension, high blood pressure, all that stuff. So if you are [dealing with] that, it is easily achievable, but when looking at genetic engineering products and all those new products, it will take a long time before Nigeria can come to that stage [of widespread consumption] because the purchasing power is low.

Because the purchasing power for more advanced therapies is low, marketing these or other drugs can be very costly. In the early 2000s Mr. Kumar attempted to introduce intraveneous fluconazole, which was not available in liquid form in the Nigerian market. Fluconazole is a powerful antifungal drug that is used to treat opportunistic fungal infections commonly occuring in patients living with HIV.

> We had a case in [a teaching hospital], a nine-year-old girl who was an HIV-positive patient and who had severe fungal infection of the throat. This girl was dying. I had to literally go to the doctor and tell him, "sir, here we have a product. . . ." [It] worked magic, and the girl was up in the bed after three continuous doses of this flucanazole. . . . When we launched [intraveneous] flucanozole, we ran it in various teaching hospitals. Some of the doctors were very, very happy about this product. They wanted the product, but the so-called bureaucracy can't allow us to launch this product. When I'm talking of the bureaucracy, they will first tell me, "go and do your clinical meeting." . . . For what? If I have a person who doesn't have the funds to do the clinical meeting—well, yes, I have to do my marketing, I understand. . . . [Then they will say], "you have to go into this committee, that committee, you will have to be registered, for which you will pay so much." Then after that, you will have to hold a clinical meeting. I will have to do twenty-five clinical meetings, and each clinical meeting is at the cost of around 200,000 naira [about $1,600], and

so I should have another 2.5 milllion naira [about $20,000] for one hospital, one teaching hospital. Then I will have to go and sit down with a group of pharmacists to discuss [the product]. Then there are various other "Nigerian factors" that will come to play before I push this product. Yeah, I mean for what? So if I am a person who has not got enough funds, my product is killed. Today [July 2009] there are no fluconazole IV fluids available in this market and today we are talking of five million registered Nigerians who are [living] with HIV. That supplementary infection is a fungal infection. The best is fluconazole. . . . What will they treat these HIV cases with?

Once the key opinion leaders and doctors begin to order a new product for their hospitals to purchase, a marketer will then proceed with pharmacy promotion by getting products to different pharmacies and hospitals. Products have to be in place before widespread comprehensive marketing takes place—that is, before the prescriptions start going out. This provides immediate sales because of the concentrated and immediate distribution that hospitals in particular can provide. Professional networks can greatly influence how this plays out. For example, marketers and hospital pharmacists may previously know each other from pharmacy school or professional organizations. An academic pharmacist, Temi, explained to me that pharmacists working in hospitals and clinics often attend university with those marketing for drug companies. Such relationships can also influence which drugs get purchased and stocked in bulk amounts. Indeed, a study conducted by Obehi A. Akoria and Ambrose O. Isah (2009) found that drug representatives were by far the most popular source of drug information available to hospital pharmacists.

Unofficial markets such as Idumota are not important at this point in the marketing strategy. Without the promotion of the drug product by key opinion leaders and the jump start that hospitals provide, selling to distributors in Idumota can amount to drug dumping. Idumota works strictly in the context of customer demand. As mentioned in an earlier chapter, traders will chase down products—even traveling outside Nigeria—as soon as drug products start to move or as soon as customers, especially wholesalers or large institutions like hospitals, begin asking for them. So the marketing process must begin with clinical experts before it moves into the large bulk sales that take place mostly in the unofficial markets.

Once the marketing process has passed these key points, marketers have to ensure that the packaging of the product is in order. There are two issues here, especially for new brands of existing marketed products. The first is that packaging is key to a marketing strategy because if Nigerians become accustomed to buying a certain product and suddenly its packaging changes—using different language, trademarks, logo colors, required regulatory labeling germane to a particular country, and so forth—customers immediately suspect the product is fake. As Mr. Kumar told me, "If you have to [market] ampicillin, cloxacillin here, you will have to do it in pink color and black color capsules. You must change the color, [otherwise] your product will not sell. Amoxycillin, red color. Paracetamol, of a particular size, white color. It is real nonsense. You know as pharmacists, we are used to now think of color, shape, size, price. Nobody was looking at what is inside the product!"

The second issue is how well the packaging appeals to customers. The traders are extremely adept at knowing right away what kind of packaging will help to sell a product. For example, I was asked by a friend in Lagos who is an AIDS activist to bring samples of condoms and lubricants from the United States when I traveled to Nigeria in 2009. The World Health Organization had just promoted the use of lubricants with safe-sex strategies, and my friend was looking for ways to launch them in Nigeria, where only a small supply was available. I took the samples of condoms and personal lubricants to Chidi and Nweke to get their advice on which products would sell well. To them the ingredients and textures of the lubricants and condoms made no difference: all that mattered was the packaging. I was unable to discern what packaging might be more appealing than others, but they described what kinds of artistic work and logos would travel well for nonpharmaceutical medical devices.

When both brand-name and generic drug companies look to global markets to distribute their products, the first thing that they think about is the relationship between product pricing and average household incomes. They all recognize that there are only a few drugs available for many unacknowledged diseases such as cancer. But instead of focusing on disease burdens, companies' product porfolios only reflect the potential for drug sales in the West African market. Whenever I brought up the potential to market patented drugs in Nigeria with marketers for brand-name drug companies, they immediately dismissed the idea: "No, no, not for this market." Brand-name manufacturers distribute their drugs in South Africa and

Egypt, but they see West Africa as a place where simpler molecules can be easily unloaded on a mass scale—a conceptual distinction like that made by the distributors of fake drugs.

A company will introduce a new drug to the West African market only if it is already selling fast-moving products there. In other words, it must keep its own economic survival in mind. The known products can guarantee the current cash flow if the marketing is good, but a marketer has to work hard to make the unknown product generate future earnings, as the investment in the new product over the first five years may yield little economic return. Product recognition and drug education among the public and medical professionals in particular are important. There are many different brands of drugs on the market, but capturing even a minute share of Nigeria's anti-malaria market, for example, pays off because upward of 150 million people in the country get malaria at least once a year. These marketing strategies are not simply about international divisons between the haves and the have-nots. Rather, they are part of IP regimes that became structurally linked to global trade rules and thereby produce these divisions.

## The Market, New Property Forms, and Indefinite Monopolistic Effects

The pharmaceutical patent has long been analyzed in terms of its ability to monopolize drug markets throughout the world. Certainly, debates among AIDS activists, policy makers, academics, and drug companies have paid attention to IP law and its impact on drug accessibility in poor countries since the launch of the World Trade Organization in 1995 and especially the Trade-Related Aspects of Intellectual Property Rights (TRIPS) Agreement, which govern patents and IP rights on a global scale.[3] TRIPS provides twenty-year exclusive rights to develop, manufacture, price, and sell drugs in competition-free markets. This is especially important in the context of offsetting the pressures of the speculative marketplace because brand-name companies can recoup millions and sometimes billions of dollars in sales per year. As a result, they will not undertake research and development without the patent in place. Hence, patents and the return on investment are mutually dependent.

A number of significant historical convergences occurred between the 1970s and 1990s that gave rise to the contemporary drug monopoly, which I have discussed in previous chapters. These included late 1970s drug industry profit decline, upcoming patent expirations, and few products in the research pipeline, which greatly threatened future industry innovation and profits. The Reagan administration responded by budgeting more money for life sciences. In 1980, the U.S. Congress also passed the Bayh-Dole Act, which enabled smoother technology transfers between research-based academia and biotechnology companies (M. Cooper 2008; Greene 2011). That same year, the U.S. Supreme Court ruled in *Diamond v. Chakrabarty* that patent rights could be applied to genetically modified organisms (Jasanoff 1995).

But also important was the 1980s drug industry turn to market speculation in the wake of global recessions, which created an impetus to transform the very meaning and criteria of property. Karl Marx emphasized that capital becomes mobile only when it breaks through its own limits and contradictions ([1857–58] 1973 and [1894] 1974). Through the crisis of overproduction, the impetus of capitalism is to derive continuous surplus value despite markets' limitations on distribution. This creates a tension between increasing the exploitation of labor and the pressure on markets. The one limitation that capitalism must carry with it in order to mobilize itself is that it must invent and deploy new aspects and definitions of existing property forms (M. Cooper 2008). In other words, 1970s notions of patents and ownership could no longer support capital's new impulse toward speculation, so definitions of ownership had to be expanded to accommodate this speculative turn.[4]

As a result, IP was newly transformed on two levels via the TRIPS Agreement.[5] First, the criteria for obtaining a patent changed.[6] In order to be awarded a patent in the life sciences, an inventor must demonstrate that an invention, process, or composition of matter is "novel," nonobvious (for example, a molecule cannot simply be found in nature), have specific uses, and must involve an innovative step. By 1980 patent law was counting cell lines and microorganisms as novel[7] if they had been altered by molecular technologies, which counted as innovative steps.[8] These legal reforms were ultimately incorporated into the WTO's TRIPS Agreement in 1995, which linked these changes in intellectual property law to global trade governance (Drahos and Braithwaite 2002; Raghavan 1990). These changes were essential to the birth and growth of the biotechnology industry.

Indeed, the TRIPS Agreement was strategically important to the brand-name manufacturers, who used it to strengthen intellectual property rights to regain control of global drug markets (Drahos and Braithwaite 2002; Raghavan 1990). They lobbied the U.S. government to pressure the rest of the world for a new patent regime with an enforcement mechanism that restricts generic competition through the threat or outright implementation of international trade sanctions (Drahos and Braithwaite 2002; Raghavan 1990). The threat of sanctions serves as a protectionist measure for drug research and development that takes place within global brand-name companies or within public research institutions that transfer patent rights to brand-name manufacturers for marketing purposes. This arrangement gives brand-name companies (vs. generic ones) a clear advantage in securing "legitimate" intellectual property rights.[9]

A patent technically governs legal exchanges between consumers and inventors of patent-protected products. The law conceptualizes such transactions as based on a notion of "fair exchange" or as "bargains," as Mario Biagioli (2011) has pointed out. Patents are designed to facilitate scientific development by disclosing the invention, process, or composition of matter and, at the same time, protecting that development as the inventor's property rights for a limited amount of time. Under the fairness premise, the inventor gets exclusive monopoly rights and has access to the product, a transaction that is meant, under patent law, to encourage the public good and scientific development.[10]

Notions of economic exchange in patent law are related to the principle of fair exchange, which connotes an inventor's right to recuperate costs in exchange for public access to her or his product. Critically, only the market can serve as the exchange mechanism between an owner's IP rights and the public's access to the owner's product. However, the market never does a good job of ensuring access to either generic or patented medicines, even under conditions of universal health care.[11] That is, how the market should work to facilitate fair exchange is not defined in patent law, which propels legal fictions of fair exchange. Given that the market is black-boxed in patent law, what happens when the market for patented products *ceases to exist* as it did in Nigeria?

The disappearance of the brand-name Nigerian drug market has serious implications for drug access and patent law. Patent law assumes the presence of the market as the primary facilitator of (at least a fictitious) fair exchange between owners and consumers of patent-governed products. With the brand-name market gone, the mechanism that bridges exchanges between owners and consumers no longer exists. Therefore, fair exchange can no longer serve as the rationale for the patent law. The disappearance of the patent law's primary premise, when it comes to African consumers, poses questions about the actual purpose of the law and the legitimacy of patent rights when fair exchange cannot exist.

The question of fairness is connected to infrastructures needed for patent rights enforcement. While intellectual property rights holders must seek out those who infringe on their products, the law assumes that a certain infrastructure is in place to assist the surveillance and policing of pirated products. Several state agencies are required to do the actual surveillance, policing, and punishing, meaning that the patent office, drug regulatory agencies, drug enforcement agencies, and courts must work in concert to make this happen. The problem with this scenario in Africa is that when countries implemented structural adjustment in the 1980s, state deregulation was required, which incapacitated existing or future regulatory functions. Specifically, structural adjustment policies reduced the capacity to curtail perceived infringement of brand-name products. Yet, just ten years later, the WTO mandated that Nigeria and other African states perform the robust task of protecting transnational capital by regulating counterfeit capital within the scope of the TRIPs Agreement.

In Nigeria, protecting pharmaceutical capital in this manner happens via NAFDAC, the regulatory agency's market raids, rather than actual patent enforcement. And moreover, what is being protected in these raids are usually generic and over-the-counter drugs and not patented ones. Nigerian workers in the patent office have indicated to me that they are more often preoccupied with electrical outages and interrupted salary payments. A lawyer who works closely with the office told me:

> We don't have substantive examination in the Nigerian Patent Office. All they do is make sure that the forms are correctly filled and they grant a patent. So you can get a patent for almost anything in Nigeria today, even if it is expired. I mean it could fall into public domain in some other place and they may not scrutinize it. The reason for this is that there is no infrastructure in place: we need pharmacists, researchers, and so forth to do the examination.

The lack of infrastructure was also an issue in the 1970s and 1980s, but it did not pose a problem for patent enforcement per se. According to Owen Adikibi (1988), the lack of infrastructure in the patent office contradicted a very good Nigerian national intellectual property law that encourages local innovation, and it partly contributed to multinational corporations' dominance as patent owners. He traces how multinational corporations' monopoly on patents is a direct outcome of colonial patent law used by the British to protect against other foreign national interests in Nigeria. When the postcolonial state implemented a new law in 1971, it essentially broke the British monopoly hold on Nigeria but encouraged competition among multinationals around the world rather than opening up room for local innovation.

Adikibi found that the "majority of the patents in the country are either protecting a globally 'standardized process' or, even, processes that are obsolete in the home countries" (1988, 517). In the Nigerian pharmaceutical industry, where the brand-name companies controlled the market at that time, Adikibi found that "67% of the patented processes were standardized and widely available while 22% were obsolete" (1988, 517). He argues that these statistics represent strategies to monopolize markets and preempt future competition between multinationals. The period he studies (1972–84) is worth examining. In that interim, between 327 and 664 mostly multinational patent applications were annually filed in Nigeria, representing a moment of competitive if not nascent industrialization among multinational corporations. But, according to the World Intellectual Property Organization (2013), in the post–structural adjustment period, between 2003 and 2008, six or fewer patent applications were filed annually with the Nigerian Patent Office; the numbers climbed to between 17 and 44 between 2009 and 2011. The numbers demonstrate how patents have become far less significant in the context of post–structural adjustment deindustrialization.

Despite this history of the patent's use for securing monopolies, notions of fair exchange still persist. But fair exchange appears to have been overwhelmed by industry logics that rely on intellectual property as a form of security in research and marketing pursuits. Indeed, no company will do drug research on promising leads unless intellectual property protection is in place (Jasanoff 1995); and, certainly, changes in patent law that I just described have accommodated these industry needs. These dynamics are especially underscored by the industry's survivor mentality, fueled by investment community expectations. Moreover, existing marketed products completely rely on patent law situated within global trade governance because the law is the main mechanism for generating high earnings needed to cope with extreme financial risk.

In this sense, the patent moves away from facilitating fair exchange and, instead, buttresses the speculative pursuits of the brand-name manufacturers. The drug patent's legal life technically represents the terms of a social relationship between consumers and owners, which expires twenty years after the patent is first awarded. But in the absence of a market that facilitates social and economic exchange, this relationship cannot exist. The patent's twenty-year life is, thus, not relevant in this context. Rather, the monopolistic effect is indefinite as long as no market exists to facilitate fair exchange and as long as the Nigerian drug industry cannot produce its own novel pharmaceuticals or generic equivalents of patented products.[12]

While I have analyzed a legal fiction (fair exchange) as well as its underlying basis (the market), there is a real-world effect here. In the aftermath of these histories of patent-trade transformations, drug industry consolidation, and brand-name Nigerian market abandonment, brand-name manufacturers have achieved freedom to strategically eliminate patented drugs in very low-income markets as a way to protect drug prices in high-earning markets. Before I turn to the marketing practices that facilitate surplus in high-earning markets and dispossession in low-earning markets, I explain how debt regimes undergirded these dynamics.

## Market Value and Endless Imperial and Subservient Debt

The industry's turn to speculative capital meant to survive its own inability to produce profit was greatly facilitated by the existing reconstitution of the debt form in the global economy (Hudson 2003 and 2005). Debt transformed nation-states' relations when the collapse of the Bretton Woods system ended global fixed exchange rates. In 1971 President Nixon delinked the dollar from gold, and the U.S. Treasury bill replaced the gold standard. Prior to these actions, the United States had been the major source of world liquidity as well as the world's main creditor country. But following these actions, the United States "became the world's main debtor nation and by far the largest recipient of foreign capital" (Arrighi 2002, 22).

Under the gold standard, like any other country the United States could exchange its currency for gold. This in effect kept its balance of payments in order because debts demanded repayment. But once the gold standard was abandoned, the United States's relationship to debt changed. As Michael Hudson explains (2005), the Treasury bill was converted into an international monetary standard. This meant that it came to function as a debt issued by the U.S. government because banks outside the United States were unable to exchange dollars for gold, and the only option available to them was purchasing U.S. Treasury bills. Melinda Cooper has described this scenario as "a promissory note to U.S. power in which all other national banks are more or less obliged to invest" (2008, 29). An unchecked loan was created that did not require U.S. government repayment (Hudson 2005; M. Cooper 2008). This allowed the United States to amass a limitless and unpaid debt that the rest of the world essentially finances—what Hudson (2003) refers to as "super imperialism."

Debt has long been accepted as a way to finance investment gaps, a logic that was applied to bilateral and multinational loans that were administered for early 1960s postcolonial infrastructure building and human development initiatives in Nigeria. By 1970, just as the civil war ended, Nigeria's debt was relatively low at N488 million (about US $341.6 million) and consisted of long-term repayment, up to fifty years, at low interest (Sanusi 1987, 6). While the naira was strong against the U.S. dollar throughout the 1970s, peaking at 0.54 equivalent (Obi et al. 2010), things began to rapidly change by the early 1980s when what is known as "world debt crisis" ensued.

The story begins with Mexico, which in 1982 announced that it was defaulting on its external debt of US $85 billion. In the 1970s, western banks had received huge petro-dollar deposits from the Organization of Petroleum Exporting Countries (OPEC) in the face of few investment outlets. Large, growing economies such as Mexico, Brazil, Argentina, and Nigeria as well as cash strapped non-oil producing low-income countries were the targets for recycling petro-dollars in the form of loans. But once Mexico defaulted, U.S. banks also went into crisis because much of their loans were extended especially to Latin American countries. The worst of these was Citicorp, which had loaned a total of $9.8 billion to Brazil, Mexico, Argentina, and Venezuela; the loans amounted to 25 percent of these countries' sovereign debt (Dalil 1987, 15) and 128 percent of Citicorp's capital (Monteagudo 1994, 61).[13] In Nigeria, the total outstanding loans administered by the top nine banks amounted to two-thirds its total debt, specifically US $667 million out of a total of US $903 million (Sachs and Huizinga 1987, 4). After the oil bust, Nigeria was identified as one of the fifteen most highly indebted countries by the 1980s U.S. Reagan administration and thus targeted for new reforms.

With the banking industry and "Third World" debt completely intertwined, a strategy initiated by both the banks and the Reagan Administration aimed to protect the bank industry and the U.S. financial system from completely collapsing (Sachs and Huizinga 1987; Monteagudo 1994). Banks needed time to rebuild capital reserves, which meant that the loans that were quickly turning bad had to remain as current as possible. In other words, banks had to find ways to keep loans continually serviced as well as keep countries from defaulting on loans even if that meant extending new loans in order to keep up with interest payments (Sachs and Huizinga 1987, 2).

Knowing that full repayment was not possible, banks attempted to transform these loans into better workable assets (Monteagudo 1994). Facilitated by the Reagan Administration's Baker and Brady Plans and encouraged by regulators, the banks avoided debt reduction and debt forgiveness in favor of increasing loan-loss reserves (under the Baker Plan), and debt rescheduling and debt-equity swaps (under the Brady Plan). In this way, bank reserves were secured.[14] For example, loan loss reserves were sold on the secondary market at deeply discounted prices (Dalil 1987), for which banks can take capital losses on the books without further risking a decline in the market value of the bank itself (Sachs and Huizinga 1987). In fact, banks' outstanding loans were counted as assets (Monteagudo 1994). Banks were able to pay out large dividends to shareholders because they were essentially allowed to overstate their incomes.

These policies afforded Africa's creditors a new hedging power via the International Monetary Fund that forced structural adjustment programs on African states. The negative effects on African economies were enormous as S. Ogoh Alubo (1990) dramatically points out in the opening epigraph. Nigeria was accumulating an unsustainable debt, which had gone from about $18 billion at the beginning of the debt crisis in 1982 to $32 billion by 1990 (Okonjo-Iweala et al. 2003). Gloria Emeagwali (2011) shows how the U.S. Treasury, U.S. State Department, and Public Action Committees (corporate donors who fund election campaigns) designed SAPs to be directly linked to new financial markets and the rise of speculative capital. As in the Nigerian case, African debt payments provided an explosion of finance capital for Wall Street investment banks, pension funds, and insurance companies. At that time, African control over capital movement in and out of African countries effectively ended (Caffentzis 2004).

The issue here was not only about how much money Nigeria and the rest of Africa owed to its creditors—some who had also been its former colonial occupiers—but also the conditions of repayment. While African debt demanded interest and payment, U.S. debt did not demand repayment, effectively securing its global economic power by constituting a new form of debt imperialism. These terms eventually led to the political restructuring of debtee countries, which sent their economies plummeting and resulted in long-term debt servitude.

Debt was transformed into both a speculative object and a platform for further speculative practices. That is, the reformulation of debt on an international scale helped reduce much of the risk of speculation at an industry level because when faced with potential collapse or failure, two possibilities would be available to the pharmaceutical industry. First, the rise of a U.S. imperial debt hampered prospects for immediate future African competition in global trade. For example, it became too expensive to manufacture drugs and far more lucrative to import and trade them, which supports manufacturing endeavors outside of Nigeria and other African countries. And second, with a superior competitive edge, brand-name drug companies simultaneously were positioned to engage in other risky and speculative activities in hopes of generating promising new breakthrough products. This also meant that the brand-name companies could focus on meeting the dictates of the investment industry, utilizing acquisition strategies and developing further patent protection to secure market-segment monopolies throughout the world.

The logics of imperial and subservient debt are linked to both drug and market values. In his work on U.S. drug markets and consumption, Joseph Dumit (2012a) demonstrates that in order to create value for drug company investors, pharmaceutical markets have to be grown. The goal is to maximize indefinite treatment by getting patients to consume more drugs. Certainly, drugs for prophylaxis or those that treat chronic diseases command the largest U.S. market shares. Dumit refers to this phenomenon as "surplus health," which is the "capacity to add medications to our life by lowering the level of risk required to be at risk" (2012a, 17). As he notes, "health" is no longer about illness and disease in these logics but rather about the treatment of *health risk*. For example, the threshold of "high" cholesterol, indicating risk for heart disease, has been lowered over time to expand the number of people who are at risk, which potentially increases prescriptions. The clinical trial is put to work in order to produce facts about health risks. Analyzing industry reports, Dumit points out how clinical trials are viewed as investments that are designed to identify increasing numbers of health risks. The abstraction of health into health risk is key here because it essentially allows for the infinite expansion of treatment, and thus the infinite expansion of markets.

Kaushik Sunder Rajan has pointed out (2012) that the logics of surplus health essentially highlight contradictions that the industry perpetually faces. One fundamental contradiction identified by at least the 1960s (Greene 2007) is that the industry necessity to grow meant that treatments to cure sick people would mean the end of revenue. Turning disease into chronically managed conditions could sustain revenue over the long term. Indeed, Dumit (2012b) argues that the logics of pharmaceutical value are analogous to the logics of wage labor in industrial capitalism elucidated by Marx. For example, once clinical trials, which grow drug markets and maximize the consumption of therapeutic products, are employed, they are reconceptualized to help generate surplus value instead of addressing disease burden. "Surplus health" should be seen as a simultaneous process where growing high-income markets without limits necessarily occurs alongside abandoning or disabling low-income ones. In the next section, I show how drug marketing works to accommodate debt, property, and valuation regimes that together create the conditions for the making of drug monopolies.

### Drug Monopolies via Circulation

Multinational brand-name drug manufacturers recognize the enormous Nigerian generic market and tap into the incredible amount of money to be made there. Like their generic competitors, they primarily market fast- and high-selling products, referred to as "branded generics." These products include vitamins, cough syrup, aspirin, antibiotics, and so on; they are considered "branded" because they are made by brand-name manufacturers. GlaxoSmithKline, for example, a British-based brand-name pharmaceutical company, has a manufacturing plant in Lagos that chiefly produces paracetamol, thus competing with Nigerian manufacturers. It is also the highest traded pharmaceutical company on the Nigerian stock market (Wambebe and Ochekpe 2011, 36). Companies like GlaxoSmithKline rely on the high reputations they have retained since the oil boom to sell more expensive generics. Criticizing this situation, Mr. Kumar said to me, "Every multinational [drug company] makes blood tonic, paracetamol, and antimalarials. Why does a multinational need to produce bloody paracetamol, for god sake?"

Despite the proliferation of branded generics, Nigerian drug marketers working for multinational companies are charged with creating what they refer to as "specialty markets." A specialty market is rare and small; it is designated for so-called more advanced or more expensive, patented therapies. Such market niches are not difficult to create because a marketer is obliged to establish only a small number of clients, which the marketer usually sells to a few retail outlets at high prices. But creating specialty markets in West Africa involves figuring out how to protect the dynamics and integrity of European markets. The following excerpt from an interview illustrates these complexities. The conversation happened when I was having lunch with Obi, who at the time was working for a global company. We were with a friend of his, Wole, a wholesale pharmacist who had worked as a marketer for several multinational drug companies. It was the first time that the strategy of specialized West African drug markets had been explained to me. As we sat down to enjoy some amala together, the conversation went something like this:[15]

"You would be shocked if I told you the difference between production costs in places like Asia and Africa versus the U.S. and Europe.

"What are the costs?" I asked.

Obi looked at me and began to laugh.

"What?"

"I can't tell you that."

"Well, what are you telling me?" I asked, clearly thinking that his opening to this conversation was going somewhere.

"We only source from the most expensive places [of production] for the West African [drug] market."

"You're kidding! Why?" I was stunned.

While Obi continued to laugh—probably at my naiveté and the situation he finds himself in—his friend Wole explained. "If you have drugs shipped from a plant in the UK to Nigeria, it will be really expensive on the Nigerian market. This is good because if they are somehow bought and smuggled across West African borders then at least the price of the drugs have to start higher than when they are sourced from manufacturing plants in, say, Morocco or Egypt, which produce those same drugs much more cheaply."

Slight confused by the geography and all the moving parts, I asked, "So keeping drug prices high on the West African market is another way of ensuring that parallel importation [smuggling] is restricted?"

Wole continued, "Yes, exactly, but . . ." Obi then interrupts and explains to me. "Yes, but you have to understand, the problem is not the West African market, the problem is that if those drugs [which are cheaply produced in] Morocco or Egypt somehow get into the European market through Nigeria, then it will undercut profits in Europe . . ."

Obi's friend finishes by stating ". . . and they will do anything to protect their European and U.S. markets even if it means making drugs prices higher in Nigeria than in Europe."[16]

I looked at both of them completely dumbfounded and said, "I need to absorb this for a second." There was a long pause in the conversation because it did not occur to me that ensuring the highest possible price of drugs on the West African market was a primary strategy of marketing. I then looked at Obi and asked, "What is it like for you to know all this while at the same time creating the West African market for [your company]?"

In a more or less tongue and cheek manner he declared, "If I had a gun, I would kill them; I hate them, I would kill them all." Now the three of us were laughing and I reverted to Pidgin and said to him, "Da head no correct o [You're crazy]!

As was explained to me by several marketers working for brand-name drug manufacturers, the primary reason for keeping brand-name drugs out of the Nigerian market has to do with fears of smuggling such drugs from West Africa into Europe—and not the reverse. The cost of supplying drugs from different production sites is key to preventing smuggling. As Obi's friend Wole indicated, and I later came to learn more about, companies produce the same product across different sites at very different costs. For example, it costs much more to manufacture a drug in England than it does in Morocco, usually due to the difference in labor and infrastructure costs. If drug companies have to choose between England and Morocco as the place to manufacture drugs for the Nigerian market, the companies choose England because the cost is much higher. They add this higher cost to the export price, taxes, shipping costs, customs clearance fees, and so forth and come up with what is called a "landing price" (as discussed in chapter 4). The landing price must be the equivalent to or higher than the European market price to deter the smuggling of drugs into one of the industry's highest-earning markets.

Revealing this point, Médecins Sans Frontières (Doctors Without Borders) conducted a survey on the cost of antiretroviral medication for HIV/AIDS in Lagos retail pharmacies. The survey was conducted in 2001, before these medications became widely available in free drug programs; hence, the survey represents a sampling of a specialty market for antiretroviral therapy. The survey found that six of eight available anti-HIV drugs were priced higher than the regulated price in both the United Kingdom and Spain (de la Torre 2001, 2). The other two drugs were cheaper than, but closely approximated, the UK and Spanish prices.

These marketing practices fall on a continuum of price-protection strategies found across national markets, which are essential to maintaining the indefinite monopoly. Stefan Ecks (2008) and Kaushik Sunder Rajan (2011) use the example of the cancer drug Gleevec, manufactured by Novartis and marketed in India, to illustrate pricing and monopoly politics. While Novartis attempted to patent Gleevec in India (Sunder Rajan 2011), it did not expect that country would be a lucrative market for the drug because persons of average income there cannot afford it. Rather, its real interest was to protect markets in the United States and Europe. Novartis feared the potential for cheaper versions of generic Gleevec to be imported into the United States and Europe, which could potentially undercut its price in these high-earning markets (Ecks 2008; Sunder Rajan 2011). Additionally, Novartis started a free drug program in India for those who cannot afford Gleevec. Both Sunder Rajan and Ecks argue that providing free drugs in India protects high drug prices outside India and placates demands for lower prices in Indian markets.[17]

Unlike their Indian counterparts, Nigerian companies pose no competitive threat to brand-name manufacturers because they do not have the capacity to formulate and manufacture more-advanced, patented drug products, like cancer drugs (Wambebe and Ochekpe 2011). However, as in India, price remains critical because the one threat Nigeria poses to brand-name companies is the possibility of smuggling patented drugs to Europe if they can be sold there below European market prices. In addition to price, patents are critical but play a much different role in sub-Saharan Africa than they do in India and other middle-income countries with strong generic industry competition. That is, there are exceptionally few pharmaceutical patents because there are exceptionally few patented products sold in private markets. Likewise, very few patent applications are submitted to the Nigerian patent office per year (World Intellectual Property Organization 2013). So the drug industry does not need the patent in Nigeria, nor in much of Africa, to ensure the existence of market-segmented monopolies. Rather, the absence of marketing patented products in Nigeria secures price-protected monopolies elsewhere.

The patent successfully facilitates corporate capital's access to the Indian market. Certainly, it is debt that secures corporate capital's access to the Nigerian market. That is, instead of outright control or domination of a market that is characteristic of the patent, debt's vital task for corporate capital is not to disable, but to wipe out the competition over the long-term in order to stay on top of the pricing wars. The infrastructure for this objective is important here. While Wall Street relies upon debt payments flowing out of Africa for fresh injections of capital, the drug industry relies upon Wall Street financing, the dual nature of debt, and an indefinite monopoly in order to survive and thrive. In this sense, surplus health, as a logic of drug industry market growth, is possible largely in the context of African dispossessions. It is one marketing strategy that occurs alongside current West African marketing practices—both are undergirded by the monopoly, which is more or less guaranteed.

But the monopoly also encounters its own contradictions. It comes to rely upon simultaneous strategies of dispossession and ever-increasing accumulation. These two contrasting pressures propel price, chemical, and distribution arbitrage as well as concerns over drug safety across continents. This tension between infinite growth in high-earning markets and an absence of critically needed drugs in low-earning ones illustrates Eric Cazdyn's (2012) assertion that crisis is what happens when capitalism goes right.

Certainly, these politics are a far cry from Joseph Schumpeter's (2008) description of the monopoly as producing a low-risk environment for business innovation. Schumpeter argued that innovation was the endgame of monopoly when in fact the monopoly itself is the endgame. The ultimate result is that a politics of valuation is dissociated from the actual health needs of a population and, instead, connected to the primacy of pharmaceutical markets situated within the dictates of the speculative marketplace.

## Old Specters, New Dreams

In July 2010 I was having lunch with a pharmacist friend, Olu, at a mom-and-pop restaurant in Ikeja, a suburb of Lagos. After some great food, talk of family, and invigorating conversation about Nigerian pharmaceuticals, Olu decided to call an old college friend of his, Femi, who is the managing director of one of Nigeria's biggest drug companies, Zenrex Laboratories (not the real name)—which before the 1970s had been the subsidiary of a formidable multinational manufacturer of brand-name drugs. On the spot, Femi invited us to come visit him at his company's manufacturing plant. We hustled through Lagos traffic, and when we reached the plant we entered the main gate. I immediately noticed the security guards' friendliness and their unusual lightheartedness. There seemed to be something far different going on besides the usual drudgery of signing people in and out of the premises. After one guard put in a call announcing our arrival, we were escorted upstairs, where we met Femi. Dressed in an impeccable suit and tie, he was extremely affable.

About a year before our arrival, the entire factory had been shut down for eight months in order to be rebuilt from the ground up. The company survived the shutdown by selling imported products. A six-month supply of drugs sold out in two months, and, according to Femi, the company "really suffered" during the next four months without production. But the sacrifice was made because the plant was being transformed in order to become eligible for the World Health Organization's prequalification status. This means that a manufacturing plant must be in world-class condition and meet all global standards for quality production and assurance. With that stamp of approval, the company would be able to legally manufacture high-end drugs like antiretrovirals in Nigeria and distribute them in the country and beyond. This would be highly significant because it would enable a Nigerian company, for the first time, to compete with European and Indian multinational companies in the sale of more advanced pharmaceutical products on the West African market.

When Femi offered to give us a tour, we jumped at the chance. We walked first through the administrative areas, and Femi explained that Zenrex had invited a company from Europe to do a full audit of the newly built premises. When the auditors had finished, they presented their findings to the company staff. One of the more banal things that the European team emphasized was that in the administrative areas books were tattered, offices were cluttered, dusty documents were stacked in the hallways, and roomy public areas were being used for storage—not an unusual sight in civil-service or private-sector offices in Nigeria. But the Zenrex management decided to ask its custodial team to conduct a premises-wide audit geared toward a thorough clean-up. As Femi tells it, the head custodian, Austine, showed up not in his custodial uniform but in a dark suit with freshly shined shoes and announced to Femi that he was on official business. Austine went through Femi's office with a fine-tooth comb and insisted that many things needed to be cleaned up or thrown out. He even insisted that the outdated calendar on the wall had to go. Femi protested at first, because the calendar had a picture of one of the company's products. Austine compromised. Femi could keep the picture, but the calendar had to be thrown away.

I felt slightly off balance, listening to Femi tell this story with great affection. Not only were status and work hierarchies completely inverted, but low-level workers were given a remarkable sense of ownership. People who do menial jobs for a living in Nigeria are often completely invisible to others in the workplace. It would normally not occur to managers to do things like recognize the role that staff members such as Austine play, much less elevate that role to a greater level of importance. So when Femi told us that the custodial staff and the security personnel who greeted us outside the building have seats at monthly company meetings, we were taken aback. But just as I was thinking that all this might be nothing more than an interesting corporate moment, Austine walked by, and Femi said with great enthusiasm, "Ah, this is the man right here!" I had never been introduced to the janitor, nor the gatekeeper, nor the house help or other low-level workers in such a way, if indeed I had ever been introduced to anyone in such a position at all.

We moved on to the manufacturing premises. As we passed through areas for mixing raw materials, making pills, and quality control, Femi introduced us to people who generously stopped their work and told us many "before and after" stories of the old plant and the new plant, and what had been learned along the way. As someone who had worked as a microbiologist in the biotechnology industry in the early 1990s, I had been through audits conducted by the U.S. Food and Drug Administration and was fully aware of the standard operating procedures for moving in and out of labs and keeping them and their surrounding areas up to par. Indeed, the rooms dedicated to various manufacturing purposes were big and spacious, practically glistening. Both Olu and I were surprised to see that workers were genuinely happy. When I relayed this story to other Lagos friends, they were also surprised by what I described. One friend, who in his boisterous way is never short of words, quite unusually paused then smiled and said, "Oh! I just love to hear this!"

All of this may sound like a celebration of corporate togetherness, but I read the all-around enthusiasm as an opening to future possibilities. In the midst of dire conditions for industrial expansion, including the lack of local raw materials and steady electricity, making pharmaceuticals is far more of a risk and a much bigger investment and commitment than is importing and trading them. I could not help think that what we experienced at Zenrex resonated with "when Nigeria was Nigeria," a nostalgic adage that invokes the memory of 1970s prosperity, when the country enjoyed its second decade of independence.

IN THIS BOOK, I have endeavored to analyze social and economic turbulence, not just as neoliberal reverberations across continents and over time but as dramatic changes in markets, drugs, and people's lives. When the drug industry feared it might be unable to maintain its earnings stream into the 1980s, it took several measures to keep afloat in a decolonized and increasingly competitive world. The industry tied itself to the NASDAQ, connected intellectual property law protection to global trade, and made it easier to transfer knowledge from public universities to the private sector.

In Marxist terms, it circumvented its crisis of reproduction through finan-cialization. But the crisis never went away—expected high rates of annual return can never be accomplished, because not enough drugs can be made and approved for the market quickly enough. The internal structural con-tradictions require the industry to cope by means of never-ending mergers, acquisitions, and asset dumping.

These events in the pharmaceutical industry never occurred in isolation. It was caught up in the same economic problems faced by many industries and countries, for which cutting back on the welfare state and economic financialization appeared to be reasonable responses. When the United States took measures to repatriate capital in the 1970s, a massive reversal of fortune and structural adjustment programs essentially emptied out Af-rican coffers, helping produce newly "risky populations" via a militarized austerity. Once widely abundant brand-name pharmaceuticals followed the flow of capital out of Africa and into consolidated and subsidized mar-kets. Some Nigerian commentators did not find the manufacturing crash that surprising. Indeed, Nigeria had its own industrial contradictions, such as import-substitution policies that kept the country from developing as an industrial powerhouse, a structural problem inherited from colonialism. Yet at the same time, even those who saw the writing on the wall did not expect the crash to be as radical and dramatic as it was. In this context, I have attempted to demonstrate ethnographically that structural adjust-ment and drug industry speculation were not simply events that cruelly co-incided: they were entirely inseparable. The actions taken to avert crisis—financialization of the drug industry and austerity in Africa—had profound and direct consequences that reverberated across markets and continents. In the process, new forms of capital took root and grew, and national and international trading networks have been remade. This book is not about quotidian coping strategies in Nigeria but about the ways daily market life—labor, price, credit, and other social practices—is linked to transna-tional and financial capital as well as policy changes in North America and Nigeria that are mutually constitutive, as well as localized, in significant Lagos markets.

In writing about the drug industry, I have avoided the usual discourse of corporate greed. My intention has been to focus on the structural log-ics of pharmaceutical capital through which corporate practices can be un-derstood. Chronic crisis conditions induce pharmaceutical capital to travel from site to site, embedding and abandoning, from Nigeria to India and China. In pursuing investment demands, corporate strategies adjust their accumulation and dispossession cycles by responding to downward pricing pressures—processes that simultaneously encourage fake drug flow into West Africa. If anything, greed is not particularly the capitalist's perversion, but rather built into the system itself.

In writing about Nigerians' attempts to reorient their lives in the aftermath of market and state reforms, I have paid relatively little attention to notions of criminality and corruption. These I set aside not because of Nigeria's notoriety but because of the ways criminality and corruption have taken on a cultural life and logic of their own, increasingly since the end of the oil boom. Instead, I have focused on the speculative practices found in the pharmaceutical market to emphasize the ways actors must negotiate structural constraints and market conditions. But in the process, it has been my aim to characterize the system itself ethnographically as it appears to these actors.

Indeed, speculative practices thrive whether they happen through company mergers and acquisitions driven by investors' expectations or through market traders aiming to make the smallest or greatest of gains; and derivative life is fueled just as much by market dispossessions as by the pressures on the drug industry to produce earnings that are impossible to maintain. I do not imply that the stakes of speculation are the same across sites, nor that those who deploy speculative strategies are equal actors in the world of pharmaceuticals. Rather, speculation has been a necessary tool that is used in all locations to dodge the fallout from massive market volatility.

Although the stakes and the practices of speculation are different among actors and across spaces, there are several reasons for focusing on how they play out in Nigeria. I have taken a cue from Nigerians working in pharmaceuticals and followed their analysis of tangled local politics, whether it is regulation practices or "Nigerian factors," that can be traced back to transcontinental drug circulation. I have attempted to use ethnography to give us a new viewpoint on drugs by making Nigeria the geographical center of the pharmaceutical universe in this story. I hope I have managed to change the way we see how the world works and how we understand globalization.

As many Africanist scholars have asserted over the years, Africa is often imagined as delinked from the global economy, completely separated from the worlds of consumption, modernity, and certainly finance. In fact, Africa is anything but disconnected: it is connected to Asia and the Middle East via commodity markets and connected to Europe and North America via debt, aid, secondhand goods, and extracted materials. Moreover, theories of globalization have often emphasized consumption, accumulation, and, importantly, some semblance of industrialization and state infrastructure as fundamental backdrops or objects of analysis. Although pharmaceutical consumption and various forms of accumulation are obviously very important to this story, they take place in the context of brand-name drug market dispossession.

They also take place in a country that lacks widespread industry and state infrastructure. The kind of adaptations that form neoliberal subjects in places where things like industry and state institutions are fairly robust—what can be characterized as late capitalist flexibility—is very different from the flexibility, hustling, and speculation characteristic of derivative life situated within the absence of state infrastructures. And so, accumulation or flexibility in the context of these absences, transcontinental drug movements in the face of uncertain regulation, and drug manufacturing in the absence of widely available electricity are the kinds of dynamics that need to be brought further into analyses that seek to understand terms of the global.

A critical example is that there was never a permanent rift or disconnection between consolidated drug markets and eviscerated ones. Rather, such markets constitute points within global drug circuits that help us understand monopoly politics. The practices of different actors working with either brand-name drugs or generic products reveal that monopolies are not simply made by patent law, which is governed by the World Trade Organization. Rather, the monopoly is also mediated by market dispossession, debt, and marketing practices. It produces drug geographies such that the infinite growth of high earning markets can exist alongside the absence of patented druge in low earning ones.

The question is what can a company like Zenrex do to change or at least ease these constraints on people's lives? Every obstacle remains in place, yet there are plenty of fluctuations at work. Zenrex's visions of pharmaceutical futures emerge at the same time as the highly touted rise of new African capital markets and wealthy business elites. It is not clear just where fresh capital will be invested. What role will vibrant economies in India and China play, in the aftermath of an already long presence in West Africa? And what role will the "former colonial masters," as they are referred to, and the United States play? Drug capital could go through its usual recycling once again. But new forms of speculation and contestation are likely to emerge.

# NOTES

*Introduction: Chemical Multitudes*

1  Alubo quotes a government report, which states the symptoms begin "with fever, vomiting and diarhoea which were usually treated for malaria at the OPD (Out Patients Department) or at home and in most cases, the patient has a period of convalescence with a relapse of fever, this time with Anuria (complete suppression of urinary secretion) . . . just before the children die they would swell up (particularly abdomen, face and the limbs) bleed from the mouth and anus, become dyspnoic (laboured breathing)" (qtd. in Alubo 1994, 99, parentheses in original, ellipsis in original).

2  Although the federal government considered the possibility of hemorrhagic fever, it decided it would also test the drugs that had been administered to the children. Samples were sent to university teaching hospitals located in the cities of Jos (Plateau State) and Ibadan (Oyo State) and also to the U.S. Centers for Disease Control and Prevention, in Atlanta, Georgia.

3  Thanks to Jeremy Greene for directing and helping me think through these histories alongside *The Third Man*.

4  In a publication of the United Nations Industrial Development Organization, Charles Wambebe and Nelson Ochekpe indicate that these figures vary widely: "The estimated market for prescription ethical pharmaceuticals is US$ 500 million and that for over the counter (OTC) pharmaceuticals about US$ 900 million. Furthermore, The Pharmaceutical Manufacturers Group of the Manufacturers Association of Nigeria estimates the Nigerian market for biological products (including vaccines, insulin, interferon, etc.) to be worth about US$ 100 million. In addition, related health care and lifestyle products account for about US$ 500 million" (2011, 11). The authors contrast this data with the following: "Business intelligence services estimate the pharmaceutical market in Nigeria at US$ 600 million . . . for 2009. Out of this figure, BMI [Business Monitor International] attributes the largest share of US $418 million to generic medicines, US$ 121 million to over the counter (OTC) products and US$ 61 million to patented products. Frost & Sullivan estimated a pharmaceutical market value of US$ 740 million in 2009. Out of this figure, US$ 266.4 million were attributed to generic medicines, US$ 177.6 million to branded products and US$ 296 million to OTC products" (2007, 11).

5 Important works on the histories and current social politics of markets in Lagos and neighboring markets include but are not limited to Ngozi G. Egbue (2006), Toyin Falola (1984), Laurent Fourchard and Ayodeji Olukoju (2007); Faith Ossy Ikioda (2013); Niara Sudarkasa (1973). Other important works on markets outside of Nigeria include and that I draw on: Michel Callon (1998); Julia Elyachar (2005); Karen Ho (2009); Donald MacKenzie (2006, 2009).

6 West African countries are some of the poorest in the world. Yet for almost each country in this region, consumer markets rank much higher than national poverty indexes. That is, collectively West Africa is a relatively big consumer with Nigeria as the biggest consumer on the continent, and the West African market is therefore highly desirable to those who sell cheap products, including fake drugs (The World Bank 2005).

7 Very important book-length ethnographies and edited volumes link drugs as technological objects to other important issues in the postcolony that include questions of biopolitics and access to medicines, interfaces with traditional medicine, the making of absent medication and obscured disease in relation to political economy, and the link between colonialism and modernity: Adriana Petryna (2002); Petryna et al. (2006); João Biehl (2009); Vinh-Kim Nguyen (2010); Andrew Lakoff (2005); Nancy Rose Hunt (1999); Steve Feierman and John Janzen (1992); Julie Livingston (2012); Kaushik Sunder Rajan (2006); Sean Brotherton (2012); Cori Hayden (2010); and Stacey Langwick (2011) to name a few. Other researchers investigating pharmaceuticals in the U.S., such as Joe Dumit (2012a), Jeremy Greene (2007), and David Healy (2004), among others think about pharmaceuticals via questions of markets, risk, and consumption.

8 With the exception of public figures, those who appear in the book have been given pseudonyms. For some who are a generation older than me, I use the prefix "Mr." or "Mrs." to represent my relationship to them while conducting field research. All others who are my age or younger, I only use first name pseudonyms.

9 Beecham was a British pharmaceutical company that after several mergers became GlaxoSmithKline. The new entity still uses the Beecham brand name for over-the-counter products sold in Nigeria, England, and other countries.

10 As Alubo (1994) points out, these regulatory politics have to be measured against the fact that the health care system does not extend in any widespread way to rural Nigerians, who often turn to unregulated private pharmaceutical sellers.

11 Quality assurance, that is, regulation of the different manufacturing stages, was an expressed concern in the industry literature by at least the 1980s ("Absence of Quality Assurance Aids Faking" 1988).

12 The UN Office of Drugs and Crime (2009) estimates that up to half of all malaria infections are treated with fake drugs in West Africa. This amounts to about forty-three million malaria cases per year, with the fake drugs involved worth roughly half a billion dollars.

13 Other kinds of overseas authentication were included. Nigerian banks are now required to have clearance permits before processing financial documents for drug

importers. Certificates of sale must be signed by a minister of trade from the exporting country, and they must also be authenticated by a Nigerian embassy or a Commonwealth mission (Bate 2012).

14  More conservative estimates put this at about $1 million per day (see Okelola 2009).

15  Portuguese and Arab trade with Africa, trans-Atlantic slavery, and European colonialism were precedents for this new era.

16  For Nigeria, see especially the work of Obafemi Awolowo (1967). Other prominent African thinkers involved in the nationalist project, pan-Africanism, and independence include Kwame Nkrumah (1970), Julius Nyerere (1974), Thomas Sankara (2007), and Amilcar Cabral (1979).

17  Anthropologists who have focused on the social effects of neoliberalism within and outside of Africa include but are not limited to Brenda Chalfin (2010); Jean and John Comaroff (2001 and 2011); Mark Edelman and Angelique Haugerud (2005); James Ferguson (2006); Carol Greenhouse (2010); Aihwa Ong (2006); and; Anna Tsing (2005). Especially noteworthy among the Africanists, Edelman and Haugerud (2005) argue that anthropologists lean more toward theorizing globalization and development rather than political economy. James Ferguson (2006) has argued that Africa is largely an inconvenient case when it comes to theories of globalization. Inconvenient because it does not satisfy proponents of state-to-market transitions, as most of the continent still poorly manages the blow of 1980s structural adjustment programs. Africa is also inconvenient for theorists whose critiques of globalization largely imagine wealth accumulation achieved via expanding capital markets in search of both cheap labor and consumer goods, which does not easily map onto African realities. More recently, Jean and John Comaroff (2011) have asserted the need to think more rigorously about a "theory from the south," where new capital frontiers are opening up and where the "practical workings of neoliberalism have been tried and tested" (Comaroff and Comaroff 2011, 14).

18  Pharmaceuticals and pharmaceutical markets found outside of North America and Europe have been widely studied. The early foundations of this research was influenced by the work of Charles Leslie (1976), John Janzen (1978), and others who elucidated the concept of medical pluralism as the co-existence of multiple healing systems, both religious and secular, that people draw upon when seeking various kinds of medical care. Scholars who turned to the study of pharmaceuticals were interested in accounting for a theoretical gap in the medical anthropology literature. Anthropological works by Didier Fassin (1988), Anne Ferguson (1981), Mark Nichter (1980), Sjaak van der Geest (1988), Sjaak van der Geest et al. (1996), and Susan Reynolds Whyte et al. (2003), to name a few, asserted that little attention was paid to how people come to desire and seek out Western pharmaceuticals (and not necessarily Western biomedicine). Beyond studies in shamanism, spirit possession, and indigenous medicine, they were interested in how pharmaceuticals play a significant part in health and healing. They asked who purchases drugs and who provides them, and they attempted to elucidate how people perceive what drugs actually do. But beyond quotidian practices, these scholars linked the complex

ways that drug distribution systems, government and private health care, and poverty as well as urban and rural divides ground the conditions of drug use.


## Chapter 1: Idumota

1  I do not use the term *informal economy*, mostly because it suggests a clear break from the state and its regulatory interventions, or a break from the private sector, whose commerce is officially taxed or otherwise accounted for. The popular economy includes a mix of official and unofficial forms of exchange and interaction. See Guyer (1994).

2  Agudas, also known as Amaros, first reached the Nigerian coast in the 1830s and settled in Olowogbowo, on the west side of Lagos Island. Other returnees who were liberated shortly after capture, such as the Saro from Sierra Leone, helped settle the island during this period. The Saro were captured people destined for the Americas in the aftermath of the abolition of slave trading. They were recaptured by the British before arriving at American shores and were resettled in Freetown, Sierra Leone. Many of them were Yorubas. Olabiyi Yai (2001) describes how the Agudas retained both their language and cultural identification, unlike the Saro and the former American slaves who migrated to Liberia. The Agudas, Saro, British citizens, and indigenes made up the entire population of Lagos Island in the late precolonial period. The period between the end of slavery and the Conference of Berlin in 1885 is rich in trans-Atlantic exchanges between the Americas and the West Coast of Africa (see especially Clarke 2004; Matory 2005; Verger 1976).

3  For a remarkable book on the history of Brazilian architecture in Lagos and Yorubaland, see Manuella da Cunha and Marianno Carneiro da Cunha (1985).

4  The MSF Access Campaign's "purpose has been to push for access to, and the development of life-saving and life prolonging medicines, diagnostic tests and vaccines for patients in MSF programmes and beyond" (Médecins Sans Frontières n.d.). One key aspect of the campaign is to ensure that states implement the Trade Related Intellectual Property Agreement of the World Trade Organization in ways that favor easy access to generic drugs.

5  In referring to the formal and informal distribution system for pharmaceuticals in South Cameroon, Sjaak van der Geest has suggested that "what appears chaotic and formless (in-formal) at first sight proves fairly structured when one looks more closely and starts to understand the commercial logic of the whole" (1988, 131).

6  The figure is an estimate. Another estimate is that the volume of drug sales in the market grows at a rate of 10–15 percent every year (Wambebe and Ochekpe 2011). Kunle Okelola (2009), executive secretary of the Pharmaceutical Manufacturers Group of the Manufacturers Association of Nigeria estimated that the size of the total pharmaceuticals and health care products market in Nigeria was more than $2 billion in 2009. Okelola told me that about 30 percent of the pharmaceuticals in Nigeria pass through unofficial markets. Ezeanya (2000, 11) estimated that it was as high as 70 percent. Others in the industry told me that it is more like 50 percent. If the higher figure

is correct, 50 percent of $2 billion—or $1.4 billion—flows through the drug markets annually. I estimate that Idumota handles about one-quarter of that flow ($350 million); the markets in Kano and especially Onitsha are bigger and probably handle more of the flow, even though Idumota is the major off-loading point for drugs that enter the country. If the lower figure—30 percent—is correct, the total is $600 million instead of $1 billion. Another unofficial figure came from a pharmacist who had conducted a study on Idumota when it was shut down for several weeks as a result of riot in the early 2000s. He estimated to me that the equivalent of $5.6 millions' worth of drugs passes through Idumota every day.

7  Needless to say, slavery and the colonial encounter did similar work of transformation, but I do not go into that here. Rather, I am interested in late-capitalist incorporation, which could be said to begin around 1970.

8  It should be noted that Igbos run the national wholesale trade and the Lagos market. However, others may control Nigerian community and regional markets. For example, according to Gernot Klantschnig, Yoruba women run some of the drug markets in Ibadan (personal communication, November 22, 2013).

9  A number of historical, journalistic, and personal accounts have appeared that support different sides and present various perspectives on the war (see, for example, Ademoyega 1981; Forsyth 1969; Saro Wiwa 1989). Several works of fiction and poetry have also depicted the conflict (see, for example, Abani 2003; Achebe 2010; Adichie 2007).

10  I did not conduct extensive surveys, but others in Idumota confirmed this range, some providing higher estimates. The traders I met over the course of this research, who were from other parts of Igboland, also believed that most of the traders were from Orlu. No official figure confirms these estimates.

11  Community-based and larger-scale institutions that operated across dispersed Igbo villages were the basis for local economic systems between the ninth and the nineteenth centuries (see Northrup 1978; Onwuejeogwu 1981). They were also the basis for market infrastructure, including roads and multi-currency, credit systems, and credit suppliers (see Austen 1993; Northrup 1978; Onwuejeogwu 1981). For example, institutions such as marriage and inheritance facilitated extended commercialization. Traditionally an Igbo may marry outside of his or her village, and the oldest son inherited the father's land, forcing others to work in commerce (Meagher 2010). Several scholars have described the history of land pressures and migration patterns from the precolonial period to that after structural adjustment (see Afigbo 1981; Dike [1956] 1981; Isichei 1978; Onwuejeogwu 1981). See Berry (1985) on similar developments in western Nigeria.

12  Chukwuezi writes: "In some areas of the country, Igbo properties were seized under the infamous Abandoned Property Decree on the grounds that the Igbo were not indigenes of these areas. Believing that the only secure place was their rural home, many Igbo started investing in their home villages, while continuing to pursue outward-directed trade" (2001, 56).

13  In her fascinating study, Meagher (2009) shows how in spite of ethnic violence across the country, these business networks forged very strong interethnic trade

and business alliances. For example, she describes how an "ethnic" riot in the market in Aba (in eastern Nigeria) united traders from the north and south—with business people of varying ethnicities in both regions (including Igbos in the north) bringing a sense of normalcy back to the market.

14 As a result of OPEC's very sharp increase in the price of oil, a number of events were set in motion. First, high-income countries in North America and Europe were faced with an abrupt rise in energy costs that effectively reduced consumption. Second, non-oil-producing low-income countries suddenly had huge energy bills and often had to choose between investments in infrastructure or equally essential energy supplies (Dalil 1987). Third, in OPEC oil-producing states, the oil booms managed to command enough capital to expand infrastructure and improve social welfare and domestic economies. However, inflation was high, and while new imports skyrocketed there was also underemployment because the new income was not equitably distributed, creating further class divisions (Dalil 1987). See also Apter 2005; Watts 1984.

15 Bill Freund calculates that after 1973 "there was a dramatic increase in government reserves acquired and held abroad, at first primarily in pounds sterling but with a big shift to US dollars from 9% of reserves in 1970 to 42% in 1976. In 1974, these reserves seemed to be almost incalculably high, sufficient at a go to pay for twenty-four months of imports; they totalled N [naira] 4.187 millions at peak in April, 1975" (1978, 93).

16 It also exacerbated existing social inequalities that had existed before the oil boom. Prior to this period, the territory now known as Nigeria had been well integrated into the Atlantic economy, where merchant capital surplus had been accumulated by ruling elites. Expanding cash crops served local ruling elites and the external markets of the British Empire, while most peasant households had enough only to survive. By the 1960s, foreign-owned manufacturing based upon import-substitution created a pool of newly waged laborers while enriching the industrial class. A great many more urban workers found employment in petty commercial activities.

17 For example, imported cars outpaced finished roads and expressways. Existing capacity to generate electricity could not keep up with expanding demand, and industrial manufacturing was continually faced with power cuts (Freund 1978, 95–96).

18 At the same time, new pharmacy schools at major universities were opening beyond Lagos. Pharmacists, not traders, completely dominated the drug supply and distribution system in Nigeria at that time. When the country became independent, there were only three pharmacy schools in existence—Yaba-Lagos, Zaria, and Ibadan—and Ibadan was not yet well established (Adenika 1998; Egboh 1971).

19 The relevant law—the Nigerian Enterprises Promotion Decree of 1972, which was amended in 1977—is often referred to as the Indigenization Decree.

20 These subsidiaries included Biode, Rajrab, and Leady Pharma (all founded in 1980) and Biomedical Services (founded in 1981).

21 The results of three relevant studies were reported by Adenika (1998). The first study, from 1971, found that all ten manufacturers in Nigeria imported all their inputs. A

follow-up study in 1976 found that 5 percent of Nigeria's total drug supply was produced locally. There were then fifteen local drug manufacturing companies, very few of which were indigenous firms, out of nearly 100 firms importing and marketing drugs. Half of the manufacturers had substantial production capacities, but production was still limited to tableting and liquid-mixing operations. A second follow-up study, conducted in 1984, found that tablets and liquids constituted 62 percent of local production. In terms of drug classes, analgesics, hematinics, antimalarials, and cough or cold medicines constituted 71.2 percent of the number of drugs produced.

22  See also David Harvey (2007), who has argued that these monetary policies were designed to transfer massive amounts of wealth to elites, carving out concentrations of wealth in particular geographical regions. Under President Nixon, these events may have created the impetus to expand federal welfare programs and agencies (such as Social Security, food stamps, the Occupational Safety and Health Administration, new laws on access for people with disabilities, and block grants to states) in order to offset the economic crisis. Similarly, domestic and international events (such as the 1970s Nelson hearings on the effects of "the pill" and the World Health Organization's Essential Drug Program) greatly influenced the future formation of U.S. drug policy (Greene forthcoming). But all these changes ultimately led to the financialization of the U.S. economy, which became entrenched under President Ronald Reagan's administration and has continued into the present era.

23  Bill Freund (1978, 98) argues that Nigeria was "financing the additional payments for exploration and drilling, [had] reduced profit taxes and royalties, and [had] increased tax credits and annual allowances, at a time when oil production and prices [were] falling."

24  On corruption in Nigeria, see Daniel Smith (2008) and Kristin Peterson (2009).

25  Vin Ujumadu (1986) argues that no pharmacist was appointed to represent the Ministry of Health on the import licensing panel, and thus the panel had no expert knowledge about how the industry would fare.

26  According to an industry report, dilapidated infrastructure means that it costs a Nigerian firm about six to seven times more than an international competitor to produce drugs (May and Baker 2007, 6).

27  Round-tripping became institutionalized with the advent of black-market currency trading in the aftermath of structural adjustment programs. The phrase is now often used to refer to what the public perceives as the unethical currency arbitrage performed by Nigerian banks (Uche 2004).

28  Trading within different tiers of exchange was enabled by the Second-Tier Foreign Exchange Market, which was established in 1986. In 1987 the government tier was merged with the second private tier (Hashim and Meagher 1999) to form the Autonomous Foreign Exchange Market. For a full history of these exchange markets, see Olaniyan and Nwoke (1990). See also Abebanjo (1987).

29  The *Nigerian Journal of Pharmacy* noted the following percentages of locally produced drugs that were consumed in the Nigerian national market: 21.8 percent in

1973, 22.8 percent in 1974, 29.1 percent in 1975, and 31.6 percent in 1976 ("Percentages of Locally Produced Drugs" 1979, 4).

30 Drug companies that were given a fraction of their required import license could only cater to 20 percent of the nation's drug requirements ("PSN Wades in Import License Crisis" 1984). Ninety percent of drugs in Nigeria in 1990 were imported. Foreign exchange was used to buy expensive advertisements to promote "unnecessary" drugs ("Mrs. Okoli Pleads for Indigenous Producers" 1990).

31 College graduates are required to serve two years in the National Youth Service Corps.

*Chapter 2: Risky Populations*

1 Creditors of African nations included the Paris and London Clubs, the International Monetary Fund, and the World Bank.

2 Structural adjustment programs were insisted on by the IMF and the World Bank yet resisted by the public and several state leaders. General Ibrahim Babangida, who took over the government in a coup d'état, implemented a home-grown austerity policy that in some instances was more extreme and detrimental than the IMF's original prescriptions (Olukoshi 1992).

3. See especially Ferguson (1999); Guyer (1994); Nyang'oro and Shaw (1992); Okome (1998); Olukoshi (1993); Thomas-Emeagwali (1995); Turshen(1999).

4 David Harvey (1991, 147) first characterized "flexible accumulation" as the primary mode of post-Fordist capitalism. Anthropologists have tried to understand the micro and local dynamics through which capital embeds itself in social, cultural, and economic processes (see especially Appadurai 1996; Ong 1999; Tsing 2005).

5 In other parts of Africa, household incomes and nascent industrialization were also crashing (see especially Ferguson 1999; Schoepf et al. 2000; Bayart [1993] 2009).

6 I qualify this statement by noting that even though these investments included expanding universities and the health care system, for example, much of the rather substantial World Bank loans that Nigeria received in the 1970s were directed to export crops and infrastructure to support an export economy.

7 Of course, both the colonial state and its successor had plenty of experience dealing with populations who posed existential risks to the state itself. For an exemplary colonial example, see Caroline Ifeka-Moller's (1975) study on the women's war in eastern Nigeria, in which a women's army rose up against the British colonizing force. The most noteworthy example in the postcolonial moment is the 1967–70 civil war. When the eastern part of the country seceded, calling itself Biafra, it threatened the Nigerian state's existence since the new international boundary cut it off from all oil supplies.

8 For how this period of militarism differs from early postcolonialism, see Richard Sklar (1998).

9 In the Pidgin English used in Nigeria, "now" at the end of the sentence is used to emphasize a point.

10  In the transcript, my question was: "So you just came to see or to buy?"

11  I was incorrect: it was twenty-one naira to the U.S. dollar. But the black-market (and thus real-life) exchange rate at the time of our conversation was about 145 naira to the dollar, which was a great difference.

12  The first two coups in large part were signs of the conflict and resistance to the IMF within the government, enhanced by a great deal of pressure and reaction from the public. The coup in 1983 was orchestrated by Major General Muhammed Buhari, who emerged as the leader of the Supreme Military Council, the country's new ruling body. Buhari had replaced a civilian president, Shehu Shagari, whose administration had been marred by claims of widespread corruption and public discontent. But one thing that Shagari did was refuse a key IMF condition, currency devaluation. The Buhari government, which also resisted some key points of IMF-imposed austerity such as devaluation, was overthrown by the Supreme Military Council's third-ranking member, General Babangida, in August 1985.

13  Importantly, Babangida decided to float the naira instead of imposing a 40 percent devaluation (Olukoshi 1993), as requested by the IMF. Within a year, devaluation climbed to 60 percent (Olukoshi 1993). By 2010, the U.S. dollar was worth 150 times more than the naira.

14  The peak of Babangida's regime was marked by the infamous events of June 12, 1993, when he annulled the national election results that would have made Chief Mosood Abiola president. The country exploded into several days of riots. After Abiola insisted that he had a public mandate to take office, the military imprisoned him. The aborted Third Republic ended with Abacha's sudden death in 1998.

15  Mbembe writes: "I examine those trajectories by which the state of exception and the relation of enmity have become the normative basis of the right to kill. In such instances, power (and not necessarily state power) continuously refers and appeals to exception, emergency, and a fictionalized notion of the enemy. It also labors to produce that same exception, emergency, and fictionalized enemy. In other words, the question is: What is the relationship between politics and death in those systems that can function only in a state of emergency?" (2003, 16).

16  Foucault characterized biopolitics as a dichotomy between make live and let die, in which population management tends to create excluded populations. João Biehl's work (2007) on AIDS in Brazil examines the let die side of things, where systems enumerating people with health problems fail to count those who fall through the treatment cracks, which counteracts the purpose of such enumerations. But following Megan Vaughan (1991) I also draw on Foucault quite cautiously. There were great differences between the liberal European state and the African colony. Foucault argued that repressive power gave way to productive power by the eighteenth century Europe. Vaughan rightly states that colonial states drew upon repressive power and that Foucault's medical power/knowledge complex was far more germane to European states. Indeed, a medicalized Other in the colonies was already racialized and made group classifications far more important than individualization. These differences were not simply germane to the colony but traces of such power still exist in the modern African state (Vaughan 1991, 8–12).

17 The new schools were established at the University of Nigeria, Nsukka; the University of Benin; and the University of Lagos. Few students enrolled during a time when there was one pharmacist to 40,000 people (Efob, 1982, 22).

18 Citing pharmaceutical industry reports, Sunder Rajan states that "to reach even a 10 percent growth rate requires three to five new chemical entities to be approved each year, which is difficult to achieve. If only one in five drug candidates entering clinical trials makes it to market, then in order to generate three to five new chemical entities a year, a pharmaceutical company would need a large pipeline of drugs entering clinical trials" (2012, 323).

19 In his work on the genomics company DeCode, Michael Fortun describes the rise and fall of the company's public offerings on the stock market. Much of the volatility was because investors' notions of the marketplace were in a constant state of flux—and the reason for that was the company's unfounded speculative promises of future earnings. Capturing the volatility of the 1990s pharmaceutical and genomics stocks, Fortun asks what value is: "How do you tell a real genomics company from a counterfeit one?" (2008, 11). Moreover, Sunder Rajan (2006) points out, speculating on new start-up companies was highly attractive to investors because the start-ups had cheaper share prices and greater expected profits.

20 A cost in this case could be pollution that is detrimental to health or other industries; a benefit could be something that results in research and development.

21 In his work on social costs, Ronald Coase (1960) argued that there are times when two parties could work out the problem of unintended externalities and other times when government should do this work. Economists in the Austrian school argued that there is no such thing as market failure because the market itself is working out inefficiencies, which cannot be equated to failure. For example, Israel Kirzner (1963) makes actors more accountable for their choices than is imagined in the case of Pareto efficiency. Kirzner argues that inefficiency arises only when actors make decisions that contradict their real interests.

22 By 1965 Pfizer was selling products in 100 countries, and its foreign sales amounted to $175 million; in 1989 it was doing business in 140 countries (Corporate Watch n.d.).

23 The takeover of Warner-Lambert reportedly cost Pfizer $84 billion (Reference for Business n.d.).

24 See Julie Livingston's (2012) remarkable book about Botswana's only oncology ward—one example of the neglect throughout Africa of cancer, a disease that is seen as relevant only to North American and European societies.

25 As Susan O. Oremule, managing director of the Nigerian drug firm Associated Manufacturing Company, stated in an interview at the time, "Small scale manufacturing requires assistance of the government because it augments the services of the MNCs [multinational corporations] thereby forming a vital link to the entire pharmaceutical industry. So free markets work against the interests of MNC pharma. Moreover, it works against the interest of public health because drugs that are

needed are neglected. Only the cheap ones get produced" ("Mrs. Oremule Pleads for Small Scale Producers" 1991, 1).

26  These included Norvasc (amlodipine besylate, used to treat blood pressure and angina), Zithromax (azithromycin, an antibiotic), Zoloft (sertraline hydrochloride, used to treat depression, obsessive-compulsive disorder, panic attacks, and post-traumatic stress disorder), Viagra (sildenafil citrate, used to treat erectile dysfunction), Aricept (donepezil hydrochloride, used to treat dementia), Celebrex (celecoxib, used to treat arthritis), Lipitor (atorvastatin calcium, a statin used to treat high cholesterol), and Diflucan (used to treat antifungal infections).

27  Pfizer sold its Medical Technology Group in different transactions: Valleylab was sold to U.S. Surgical Corporation for $425 million; AMS to E. M. Warburg, Pincus and Company for $130 million; Schneider to Boston Scientific Corporation for $2.1 billion; and Howmedica to Stryker Corporation for $1.65 billion (Pfizer 2000).

28  According to Reference for Business (n.d.), Pfizer "spends $4.5 billion a year shepherding candidates through the product pipeline, which at any one time can include more than 130 possible new products. R&D efforts also are aided by the 250 alliances that Pfizer has formed with academia and industry."

29  G. D. Lahan explains that in real terms this meant that within three years of SAP, manufacturers had to import over 90 percent of raw materials, 30 percent of packaging materials, and all equipment and spare parts. The declining exchange rate meant that drug costs completely skyrocketed. "It calls for at least eight times the original capital base to operate at the same level as [before SAP]" (Lahan 1989, 15). These policy issues combined with increased competition with parallel imports, which undercut marketers working for the manufacturers. And as the purchasing power of society dramatically decreased, industry garnered industry stockpiles, slowed down manufacturing momentum, and increased labor layoffs (Lahan 1989).

*Chapter 3: Regulation as a Problem of Discernment*

1  Niara Sudarkasa (1973) has pointed out that markets in rural parts of Yorubaland have long taken root at the intersections of roads connecting communities and capturing both local and long-haul trading traffic. See also Falola (1984) and Fourchard and Olukoju (2007), who document the histories of markets in Ibadan and Lagos.

2  Smaller drug markets in Lagos have popped up as well, in Agege, Ikotun or Egbe, Mushin, Alaba Rago, and other places.

3  Of course, this meant that until the multinational manufacturers of brand-name drugs abandoned the markets that they had created, they had the de facto role of regulators of the products they themselves produced and marketed.

4  The regulatory laws adopted in 1990 and 1993 were meant to curb the importation of potentially dangerous drugs and regulate the quality of drugs manufactured in Nigeria. The Poisons and Pharmacy Act, Cap 366 of 1990, regulates the compounding, sale, distribution, supply, and dispensing of drugs and provides different levels

of control for different categories of drugs and poisons. The Food and Drugs Act, Cap 150 of 1990, prohibits the sale of certain foods, drugs, cosmetics, and devices to treat certain diseases. It also prohibits the importation, exportation, distribution, and sale of specified drugs as well as practices such as the use of misleading packaging, labeling, and advertising and the manufacturing of food and drugs in unsanitary conditions. The Counterfeit and Fake Drugs Act, Cap 73 of 1990, prohibits the production, importation, manufacture, sale, and distribution of any counterfeit, adulterated, banned, or fake drugs. It also bars people from selling any drug in an open market without permission from the proper authority. The Drugs and Related Products (Registration) Decree No. 19 of 1993 prohibits the manufacture, importation, exportation, advertisement, sale, or distribution of drugs, drug products, cosmetics, or medical devices unless they have been registered in accordance with the provisions of the decree. It also stipulates the procedure for applying for registration of a drug product (Erhun, Babalola, and Erhun 2001: 24–25).

5   This divide between the formal and informal has been debated by scholars, some of whom have convincingly argued that these categories do not always map onto the reality of social relations and economic exchange (Roitman 2005; Hart 2006). As Kate Meagher (2010) points out, it would be inaccurate to suggest that the blurring of these boundaries in the context of liberalization means that the state no longer regulates anything (Portes and Haller 2005) or that it is difficult to actually discern what is happening at formal-informal interfaces or at the level of the law and economy. Several scholars (Tranberg and Vaa 2004; Hart 2006; Chalfin 2010) have stressed that it is not that regulation has ceased to exist with the onset of liberalization but rather that new kinds of regulatory practices have formed— from social networks to international trading bodies—that may exist outside of the state.

6   Keith Hart (1973) first coined the term *informal economy* to describe the growing economic exchanges largely taking place in the absence of formal institutions. But later Hart (2006) asserted that the downfall of state institutions after liberalization meant that entire economies had become informal. He stressed the need to understand the social forms organizing the informal economy. See also Elyachar (2005).

7   The "triangle" contains four countries in Southeast Asia (Burma, Vietnam, Laos, and Thailand) and the Golden Crescent, which in turn contains Afghanistan and Pakistan. It is the most extensive opium-producing area in the world.

8   Gernot Klantschnig (2013) found the same pattern in his research on drug trafficking in Nigeria.

9   Writing in the late 2000s, Stephen Ellis (2009) asserts that one of the striker's jobs is to make sure there is a distance between the courier and the actual drug baron.

10  Of course, there are variations on this pattern. In 2011 the National Drug Law Enforcement Agency arrested nearly 9,000 drug trafficking suspects and confiscated 31 billion naira in illegal drugs. Nigeria is a major transit point between grower and consumer continents (Akpor 2012; Bayart, Ellis, and Hibou 1999).

11  There are two kinds of bans on pharmaceutical products in Nigeria. One pertains to imports that are banned because the same products are produced in the country. That

ban is meant to support local industries. The other pertains to products that are known to be toxic and dangerous to human health. While they have been banned in North American or European markets, for example, they can still be manufactured and sold in difficult-to-regulate markets such as Nigeria.

12 It should be noted that the World Trade Organization (1998) makes no mention of the problem of product dumping—a side effect of deregulated trade—in Nigeria.

13 For a thorough analysis of the Nigerian banking sector during this and other historical periods that traces Nigerian bank crashes and liquidity problems, see Howard Stein, Olu Ajakaiye, and Peter Lewis (2002). For a remarkable study of the relationship between liberalization, currency markets, and cross-border trade, see Yahaya Hashim and Kate Meagher (1999).

14 Changing money this way avoids falling prey to armed robbers, who either position themselves near money changers or even inside banks, watching out for large transactions.

15 Cori Hayden (2003) in her work on bioprospecting at the side of the road has analyzed the making of multiple public spaces that slip through various legal and regulatory cracks.

16 Felix Ugbojiaku & 2 Ors v Attorney General of the Federation & 4 Ors.

17 Pharmacists Council of Nigeria 2005, B48–B49.

18 The well-known pharmacist Fred Adenika had this to say on the matter: "There are . . . today's burning issues: how pharmacists will regain control of pharmacy; problems with pharmacy ownership, patent medicine vending and elimination of illegal drug peddlers, dupes, fakes, charlatans and many others who have seized the initiative from the professionals. Then, there are issues of the environment of practices—drug distribution maladministration, professional supervision and control, the health team—or lack of it—among health care professionals, and the working conditions of pharmacists, including their remuneration, job-satisfaction and professional stature in public and private employment. One of the theses [here] is that pharmacy's professional advancement and cohesion have suffered a significant downturn over the past decade" (1998, 9).

### Chapter 4: Derivative Life

1 The methods of turning other words into nouns include derivational morphology, in which a noun is derived directly from a verb (for example, *applicability* is derived from *apply*, and *failure* is derived from *fail*), and zero derivation, where a verb expression is converted into a noun phrase (as when *I will change* is converted into *I need a change*).

2 Phillips describes *nominalization* in two registers: the social and the economic. At the economic level, there is a drive to move investments away from more costly production and into less expensive activities like trading and importing goods that have been manufactured elsewhere. Under structural adjustment, the Nigerian economy was never actually reformed to produce diversified economic growth, as

the World Bank had promised would be the case. Rather, the petroleum industry became more consolidated and grew even larger, while job loss proliferated and the productive sector either tanked or could not meet its "capacity utilization," a term used in Nigeria to refer to a situation in which although infrastructure is in place, the cost to put it to work is too high; thus, production remains low.

3  Other authors have shown how new social formations have developed in the aftermath of devaluation (see especially Roitman 2005; Larkin 2008; Simone 2004; Guyer 2002; Chalfin 2010; Bayart, Ellis, and Hibou 1999; Ferguson 1999 and 2006; MacGaffey and Bazenguissa-Ganga 2000).

4  I acknowledge that there are many different kinds of informal credit institutions in Nigeria, including private moneylenders, savings and credit associations, savings and credit cooperatives, savings and loan companies, and credit unions. Esusu and Isusu are respectively Yoruba and Igbo associations (found in both rural and urban areas) in which members make regular contributions of money and the total is distributed to each member in turn (see Soyibo 1997; Bascom 1952). But I do not examine here how these associations are directly connected to the way traders in Idumota may access credit, especially if they are just starting out in business for themselves after an apprenticeship.

5  *Amala* is derived from yams and is eaten mostly in Yorubaland; *ewedu* is mallow in English, a vegetable; and a typical stew is made from a tomato base with onions, garlic, and plenty of hot peppers.

6  See Edward La Puma and Benjamin Lee (2004), who stress how the derivative in finance has the capacity to sever the fundamentals of the economy from the state and the livelihoods of citizens.

7  In many ways, I extend the analysis of flexibility in late capitalism that accounted for post-Fordist capitalist activity. Emily Martin (1994), for instance, discusses flexibility among both companies and individuals who must adapt to changing and risky conditions. But these kinds of adaptations, which form neoliberal subjects, are very different from the flexibility found in the context of massive dispossession, in which these kinds of corporate organizational structures do not exist on a massive scale, if they are present at all. Derivative life is situated in the absence of such structures, although it uses techniques of speculation that hedge daily survival strategies.

8  In 2006 Nigeria agreed to completely privatize its national energy sector and reorganize its banking sector as well as making other concessions in exchange for a massive debt cancellation. The deal included forgiving all but $12 billion that Nigeria owed to Paris Club members. It also included Nigeria's promise to adhere to the controversial Support Policy Instrument of the International Monetary Fund, which is extended to countries that do not need loans from the Fund but that nonetheless seek its endorsement, which makes multilateral donors and banks more willing to loan money to the countries. This mechanism extends older forms of legitimacy-making in the context of worthiness for debt (not necessarily credit). In return, countries must adhere to the usual privatization schemes for export and extraction economies.

9 Stein (2008, 57–60) focuses on the Polak as well as the Swan-Salter models. The Polak model was based on stabilizing the balance of payments, initially intended for use in the fixed-exchange regime of the Bretton Woods era, prior to the delinking of gold from the dollar. If a country achieves balance of payments for all its transactions with the rest of the world—including imported and exported goods and services—then these transactions produce no surplus or deficit. The World Bank held that balance of payments was key to international economic stabilization. The Swan-Salter model focused on the impact of devaluations on tradable commodities.

10 The classical economist Adam Smith famously presented dominant notions of liberalism through his theory of the "invisible hand," which was imagined to regulate people's natural and innate tendency to barter and exchange goods. Key was supply and demand dynamics, where sellers and buyers come to agreements that are satisfactory to both parties. For Smith, this meant that the right or natural price was a sign of a self-equilibrating market.

11 Schultz, who was the first to articulate human capital theory, states that "laborers have become capitalists not from a diffusion of the ownership of corporation stocks, as folklore would have it, but from the acquisition of knowledge and skill that have economic value" (1961, 3).

12 Foucault (2008, 239–66) thought of this economy as made up of what he called "enterprise-units," for which the image of the work force disappears. Instead the body, genetics, and education are responsible for creating an entrepreneur whose fitness is molded for entrepreneurial activity. This individual transformation is linked to the transformation of society and the economy as one that suitably accommodates new forms and trajectories of entrepreneurial capital.

13 Fortune was communally determined in traditional Igbo society, and individual gains and achievements were directed back into the family. Both the Igbo and Yoruba paradigms contrast with the Weberian notion of reinvestment in the market, which is characteristic of rational European liberal enterprise.

14 For example, in some parts of Igboland, children were named for the market days that corresponded to their birth dates (this tradition is dying out today). These names are derived from deities who are considered owners of the market days (Onukawa 1998). Professor of English Afam Ebogu asserts that "the Igbo naming system establishes the identity and sex of a child the moment it is born, which asserts the child's place in the cosmology of Igbo people. The oneness of the four corners of the universe is expressed in the union between the four market-days of the week each forming the diurnal unit for computing the people's calendar" (qtd. in Onukawa 1998, 75).

15 See, for example, Marilyn Strathern (1990), Jonathan Parry and Maurice Block (1989), and Nancy Munn (1986), who argue that cultural and social processes such as personhood, moral evaluation, and gender relations get tied to value within exchange systems.

16 Tom Forrest (1994) discusses the socialization of apprenticeship that fosters virtues of discipline and perseverance in the face of hardship, which are seen as critical to commercial success (they are also traditional Protestant virtues).

17　Wealthy traders often send their own children to college at home or abroad rather than apprenticing them. Biko Agozino and Ike Anyanike (2007) document various types of conflicts that emerge between apprentices and their ogas, or bosses. For example, ogas may stake claims in fraud or may accuse apprentices of siphoning off money in accounting practices. Apprentices may complain that they did not get an adequate settlement after the end of the apprenticeship, that their apprenticeship was ended prematurely, or that they were not taught everything they needed to know because their boss feared their competition after the apprenticeship ended. Some apprentices pay for their training up front to avoid some of these problems or future tensions. See also Allen (1982).

18　In 2000 Kate Meagher found that less than 10 percent of apprentices in the garment and shoe-making industries had actually been settled in their own businesses (2010, 65) and that there was a lot of pressure from families to shorten the length of the apprenticeship—general signs of breakdown in the apprenticeship system.

19　Polly Hill (1970, 139–40) documented the numerous trading terms used in Hausa, including *baranda*. In the case she documents, farmers sold groundnuts to local consumers, which were in turn resold to the Marketing Board (or other consumers) for export crops. For a short period of time this practices was forbidden, which caused great hardships to many farmers who had trouble waiting for a long period of time for the marketing season to open.

20　Claudia Zaslavsky (1973) cites Marion Johnson (1970) and Paul Einzig (1966), who document how profit is built into the numeration systems of accounting and transaction. Guyer asserts that "in accounting, one needs the balance to be (or appear to be) explicit and precise, neither dramatized nor masked. Exigencies or ambitions to which tropic logic lent itself could include collective adjustment to turbulent economic circumstances as well as exploitation of ignorant and powerless individual buyers or sellers. Both processes employed the same transaction frameworks" (2004, 58–59).

21　Classical economists such as Adam Smith ([1776] 1991) worked with several theories of relative prices and argued that price is determined by the total cost of the resources that go into making a good (capital, labor, rent, and so forth), supply and demand, and value in exchange; price, to these thinkers, was an indicator of an assumed market equilibrium. David Ricardo elaborated a labor theory of value, according to which the relative price of two goods is determined by how much labor is required to produce each of them ([1817] 1996). Karl Marx ([1867] 1992) showed how labor power forms the crux of value; he particularly emphasized the point that surplus value is possible only because the price of commodity production is not identical with that commodity's value. The point here in political economic theory is that from Smith to Marx, value has been attached to the productive process.

22　Compare with the neighboring country, the Republic of Benin, where both wholesaling and price are regulated. Benin obtains a large percentage of drugs from Nigeria as well as from Ghana (Baxerres and Le Hesran 2011).

23  As Guyer argues, price, money, and value are outcomes of various sorts of clas-
    sifications and valuations that have to do with product origins and product quality
    (2004, 83–96). She describes regularly used categories of grading products in
    Nigeria (such as original versus fake), which are common anchors of discernment
    in determining pricing scales (89–92).
24  The $10,000 figure predates the SAP and was a common minimum figure during the oil
    boom. The drug companies managed to make it stick in spite of massive devaluation.


*Chapter 5: Chemical Arbitrage*
Lyrics reprinted courtesy of Mr. Bongo Music. My translation from Yoruba and
Pidgin English follows (*shit* in this song can refer to a range of things: economic
policy, Nigerian politics, foreign dumped products, and foreign aid):

> We've seen plenty of shit dumped in Africa
> We have held this burden for such a long time,
> We've seen plenty of shit dumped in Africa
> We've held this burden for such a long time
> We've held this burden for such a long time
> We lived, lived, lived it; we got tired of it
> We ate, ate, ate it; we got tired of it
> Political shit [referring to the quality of Nigerian leadership], economic shit
>     [referring to liberalization policies]
> We lived, lived, lived it; we got tired of it
> We ate, ate, ate it; we got tired of it
> We drank, drank, drank it; we got tired of it
> We lived, lived, lived it; we got tired of it
> White people dump shit on Africa
> Africans take the bullshit dumped on Africa
> The shit caused trouble in Africa
> This shit caused trouble, oh!
> Don't bring that shit to me—my brothers and sisters
> Don't bring that shit to Africa—you hear?

1  In 2011, an industry report estimated that contract manufacturing organizations
   grossed over $31 billion (Sahoo 2012).
2  The U.S. Food and Drug Administration defines bioequivalence as "the absence of
   a significant difference in the rate and extent to which the active ingredient or active moiety in pharmaceutical equivalents or pharmaceutical alternatives becomes
   available at the site of drug action when administered at the same molar dose under
   similar conditions in an appropriately designed study" (Center for Drug Evaluation and Research 2003, 4).
3  Arjun Appadurai (1990) thinks of objects as being in motion and having actual dynamic lives. A commodity's value or status, for example, can change over time from
   being something exchangeable to something sacred. He states, "[to understand

these changes] we have to follow the things themselves, for their meanings are in-scribed in their forms, their uses, their trajectories. It is only through the analysis of these trajectories that we can interpret the human transactions and calculations that enliven things" (Appadurai 1986, 5).

4 These included amoxicillin-clavulanic acid, ampicillin, cefepime, ceftriaxone, chloramphenicol, ciprofloxacin, gentamicin, nalidixic acid, streptomycin, sulpha-methoxazole, tetracycline, and trimethoprim.

5 See also Paul Farmer's (1999) work on multidrug resistant tuberculosis.

6 Nadia Nikroo, David Liu, and I counted and categorized these figures from the Na-tional Agency for Food and Drug Administration and Control (2011) Registered Products Catalog, which lists all registered pharmaceuticals in Nigeria.

7 There are 104 registered anthelmintics in Nigeria, and in the average year there are millions of cases of worm infections: thirty-eight million cases of hookworm infections, twenty-nine million for schistosomiasis, fifty-five million for arcariasis, and thirty-four million for trichuriasis, to name only a few (Hotez et al. 2012, 2). Although there are some good registered anthelmintics, and 104 different prod-ucts more than adequate, these drugs are not widely available, especially in the rural areas where helminth infections are high. Moreover, there is no national policy to address worm infections, with the exception of scattered free drug programs that are administered more often by state governments and non-governmental organizations (Hotez 2009; Ekundayo et al. 2007). This is in con-trast to antibiotics, which are easily available without prescription throughout the rural and urban areas of the country. Perhaps the greatest problem, though, is that newer and desperately needed drugs to treat worm infections are not pri-oritized by drug developers. In fact, infections such as these are commonly called "neglected tropical diseases." International aid agendas have focused on HIV/AIDS, malaria, and tuberculosis, leaving little money for worm infections and other ne-glected diseases, including cancer in Nigeria (Abdulkareen 2009).

8 Regarding the literature on product surpluses, companies exported drugs to na-tional markets in the global South for a number of reasons—for instance, they were about to expire, a contract to sell them elsewhere had fallen through, unexpected surpluses had been manufactured, or an unintentionally substandard batch of drugs had been produced that could not be marketed in the United States but could be in other countries where regulatory systems were weak (Braithwaite 1984). Braithwaite (1984, 261) reported that company officials he interviewed admitted that substan-dard drugs that were unsellable in the United States were pushed not only onto the global South's national markets but also onto global black markets. In this case, com-panies can hide their involvement in such practices by blaming counterfeiters, be-cause once pharmaceuticals hit the black market, they cannot be traced back to the firms that dumped them there in the first place. Another practice reported in this literature was the fact that drug package inserts that list uses approved by the U.S. Food and Drug Administration are often radically altered to include unauthorized statements on the use of drugs outside of U.S. markets (Kanji et al. 1992; Silverman and Lee 1992). Regarding dangerous drug products, Depo-Provera, an injectable

contraceptive, was banned in the United States because it caused malignant tumors in beagles and monkeys. It was sold by Upjohn in seventy other countries, where it was widely used in population-control programs sponsored by the U.S. government (Bunkle 1993; Ehrenreich et al. 1979).

9  I leave out contraceptive, tuberculosis, and HIV medications because they are entirely confined to what pharmacists refer to as a social market in Nigeria. This means that they are not sold on the private market; instead, they enter the country through international donation programs. The largest is the U.S. President's Emergency Program for AIDS Relief, initiated during the administration of President George W. Bush (see Peterson 2012a).

10  Other sites of outsourced manufacturing include Eastern European countries in the former Soviet bloc. More recently, U.S. drug manufacturing has been relocated to the Caribbean, Mexico, and other countries in Latin America, mostly because these places are close to the United States (Virk 2008).

11  As of 2011, the market size for outsourcing to China, for example, stood at $2 billion, and according to industry reports, is growing at well over 20 percent per year (KPMG 2011, 35).

12  For example, Pfizer shut down manufacturing plants in the United States and England between 2007 and 2012 and at the same time increased its representatives in China—many of them trained doctors—to 3,200 in 252 cities in 2012 (KPMG 2011, 20–21); it also doubled its investments in India during the same period (Pore et al. 2008). Others such as Roche, Merck, Bayer, and GlaxoSmithKline, among others, are following suit (KPMG 2011, 21–26; Pole et al. 2008, 107–8).

13  The Committee on the Offshoring of Engineering (Pore et al. 2008, 108) states that "GlaxoSmithKline (GSK) . . . cooperated with Shanghai Institute of Material Medica (SIMM) in evaluating approximately 10,000 herbal medicines and undertook collaborative projects worth $7 million. Since the merger, GlaxoSmithKline has invested more than $10 million in R&D projects in China. . . . Roche invested more than $10 million in a new R&D center in Shanghai's Zhangjiang High-Tech Park at the end of 2004. . . . Twenty percent of Lilly's chemistry work is being done in China, where costs are one-quarter of what they are in the United States or Western Europe. . . . In addition, Lilly does about 50 percent of its clinical research outside the United States, mostly in Western Europe. However, it has been predicted that Lilly will do 20 to 30 percent of its testing in China and India in the next few years. . . . AstraZeneca was one of the first MNPCs [multinational pharmaceutical corporations] to set up clinical trials in China in 2002. . . . Pfizer, one of the largest foreign pharmaceutical enterprises in China, has more than 1,500 employees in four state-of-the-art plants throughout the country, as well as a management center and a trade company. Pfizer China located an R&D center in Shanghai, following the lead of AstraZeneca and Roche."

14  As of 2010, China's pharmaceutical sector was valued at $46.5 billion and growing at about 17 percent per year since the country's ascension to the World Trade Organization (WTO) in 2001; this is in contrast to the average global rate of pharmaceutical growth, which is 7 percent (Chan and Diam 2011, 172).

15  New drug regulation was enacted in 1985 to match expansive market growth and then later in 2001 to accompany China's compliance with the World Trade Organization's Trade Related Aspects of Intellectual Property Agreement (WTO TRIPS), as well as significant foreign direct investment in this sector (Deng and Kaitin 2004). As of 2011, there were more than 5,000 domestic pharmaceutical manufacturers in China (KPMG 2011, 26). Only one thousand of these companies had good manufacturing practice certificates required by the WTO and issued by the regulatory authority; and sixty companies produced 70 percent of the industry profits (KPMG 2011, 37). In India compliance with WTO TRIPS has also led to drug-industry consolidation. India's 1970 Patent Act allowed drug manufacturing processes to be patented, but not drug products. This gave rise to a prolific low-cost generic drug industry, one that exports pharmaceuticals to African countries. Compliance with the WTO in 2005 has meant that Indian drug companies can no longer manufacture generics as they have in the past, and it has encouraged rapid industry consolidation via mergers and acquisitions. It has also encouraged smaller firms to become contract manufacturers for the global brand-name drug industry (Chadha 2006).

16  In 2010, there were 1,200 API manufacturers in China making 15,000 different categories of API (KPMG 2011, 26). API manufacturing consumes 44 percent of the global pharmaceutical workforce (Pore et al. 2008, 104).

17  China is not unique in this regulatory scenario. Donald deKieffer has shown that in the United States, "at the Federal level, at least three government agencies [the Federal Trade Commission, the Food and Drug Administration, and the Drug Enforcement Administration], have nominal jurisdiction over great swaths of the pharmaceutical industry and its components. . . . In all, more than twenty federal agencies have developed controls of one sort or another over pharmaceutical products" (2006, 329–30). See also Chen 2011.

18  Although in the United States prescription drug prices are largely unregulated, other high-income countries on which the drug research and development companies rely, especially in Europe, regulate multiple aspects of price. For example, they control prices at the time of a product launch, control reimbursement prices under national insurance schemes, and limit overall profits (Vernon 2003).

19  As deKieffer (2006, 333) points out: "Arbitrage is a respected mechanism for setting world prices for commodities such as oil and cotton. It is easily adaptable, however, and can be as readily applied to dog food or pharmaceuticals as it is to iron ore. 'Arbs' look for price disparities around the world for the same product, buy that item in a low-cost country and resell it where it can command a higher price. The Arbs take a bit of the spread for themselves, of course. When significant price disparities exist, as they do with pharmaceuticals, Arbs become ravenous. They aggressively seek supplies of low-cost merchandise for resale at just below wholesale prices in higher-cost markets. The spreads in these cases can be enormous—often topping 100%. This can be a bonanza for Arbs familiar with working commodities where spreads are in the 4–9% range."

20  These include the Cotonou Declaration (Chirac Foundation 2009), which was spearheaded by the former French president Jacques Chirac as well as the Montreux

Resolution of October 2010 (Heads of State and Government of the Organisation Internationale de la Fracophonie 2010)—also a declaration against fake drugs—signed by French-speaking countries. There also is the controversial Anti-Counterfeiting Trade Agreement (Government of Japan 2011), which uses intellectual property law to conflate generic drugs with fake ones.

21 *Bioavailability* is defined by the U.S. Food and Drug Administration as "the rate and extent to which the active ingredient or active moiety is absorbed from a drug product and becomes available at the site of action. For drug products that are not intended to be absorbed into the bloodstream, bioavailability may be assessed by measurements intended to reflect the rate and extent to which the active ingredient or active moiety becomes available at the site of action" (Center for Drug Evaluation and Research 2003, 3). Bioavailability establishes a benchmark in order to standardize dosing whereas bioequivalence specifically formalizes chemically equivalent comparisons.

22 For an analysis of Seers' work, see Guyer (2004, 116–22), who explains that over time, there have been numerous debates about the nature of these influences. For example, there have been questions about how to solve problems involved in falling prices and how to cushion the inevitable blows of external market trends on domestic markets that could move beyond various forms of economic dependence (see Hopkins 1973). Although Anthony G. Hopkins demonstrated that African markets had their own internal logics that developed over time to cope, Frederick Cooper (1981) argued that neoclassical economic, dependency, and Marxist explanations could not explain the mismatch between representations of macroeconomic dynamics and those of internal, local dynamics. More recently, as Jane Guyer points out, financial dependence and primary commodity production are more or less taken for granted, as are the shocks and volatility that accompanied the end of the Bretton Woods regime and structural adjustment (2004).

### Chapter 6: Marketing Indefinite Monopolies

Quoted in *Power, Inc.: The Epic Rivalry Between Big Business and Government—and the Reckoning That Lies Ahead*, by David Rothkopf (New York: Macmillan, 2012), 210.

1 According to the U.S. Department of Commerce's International Trade Administration, "the world pharmaceutical market in 2009 was estimated at $837 billion. . . . The U.S. accounts for about 36 percent of global pharmaceutical sales, and the U.S., Europe and Japan collectively account for over three-quarters of global expenditures" (International Trade Administration 2010, 8).

2 The top seven U.S. firms account for about 40 percent of the world's drug sales. These, ranked by revenue, are as follows: Pfizer, Merck, Johnson and Johnson, Eli Lilly, Bristol-Myers Squibb, Abbott Labs, and Amgen (International Trade Administration 2010, 7).

3 The TRIPS Agreement was negotiated at the 1986 Uruguay Round of the General Agreement on Tariffs and Trade. At the same time, the United States removed laws

governing monopolies from antitrust scrutiny (Sell 2004). The combination of relaxed antitrust regulation and stronger IP protections led to corporate concentration, reduced competition, and more consolidated monopoly power. The right to monopoly was rationalized and brought to the Uruguay Round as a matter of negotiation (Drahos 1995; Drahos and Braithwaite 2002; Sell 1997; Raghavan 1990).

4 Several key changes accompanied the expanding definitions of IP. In addition to the drug industry's new connection to the speculative marketplace, U.S. regulations became more stringent, especially after drug controversies such as the thalidomide scandal. Moreover, with new molecular technologies and IP laws, research and development began to shift away from organic chemistry and toward more complex biological molecules. Research universities also played a large role in these developments. The partial deregulation of the Food and Drug Administration that facilitated fast approval timelines not just for orphan drugs but for all pharmaceuticals and the launch of direct-to-consumer advertising by pharmaceutical companies converged to facilitate the necessity for new IP laws governing the circulation of pharmaceuticals.

5 For anthropological works analyzing these changes within intellectual property law, see Coombe 1998; Fortun 2008; Reardon 2004; Strathern 1999; and Verran 1998.

6 See Mario Biagioli (2011, 25–39) on the evolution of patent criteria.

7 The *Diamond v. Chakrabarty* decision led to global debates, new convergences in the market and the law, and new analytical conundrums (Anderson 2009; Boateng 2011; Coombe 2003; Correa 2008; Hayden 2003; Jasanoff 1995; Juma 1989; K. Nnadozie et al. 2003; Peterson 2001).

8 Technology is very important in shaping the way new property forms can be made, but it is not the focus here. Marilyn Strathern (1999) describes how IP, articulated via technology, creates divisions between people and things as well as between people. These divisions set the terms of negotiations and debates on the dispersal of benefits rising up from inventions. See also Peterson 2001; Ekpere 2003; Hayden 2003; and Van Rinsum and Tangwa 2004.

9 Although it is certainly true that much genomic research takes place in universities and government research institutions, the actual commercial development of such research is often licensed out to the private drug industry.

10 Although this understanding constitutes the legal rationale for a patent, Biagioli (2006) has discussed the convoluted nature of patent description. Michael Carolan (2010) argues that the purpose of patents and what they produce in terms of material effects can vary.

11 See especially P. Sean Brotherton 2012; Kaushik Sunder Rajan 2011; João Biehl 2007; and João Biehl and Adriana Petryna 2013.

12 There are several avenues through which the drug monopoly becomes "indefinite." Two examples involve data exclusivity and are entirely linked to the patent. The first, "evergreening," entails several legal and business strategies that attempt to extend the life of the patent, which ultimately establishes very long delays for generic producers to materialize new drug applications and enter new products on the

market. Strategies can include extensions to patents that do not always pertain to the active pharmaceutical ingredients but to chemical delivery systems, new pharmaceutical mixtures, new dosages, new packaging, and so on. The second example is more directly linked to data exclusivity, through invocation of the Bolar Exception. To secure a patent, an inventor must disclose how an invention is made. The Bolar Exception allows the inventor to keep the data secret until the expiration date of the patent. Drug companies that make generic versions of patented products usually acquire the data that allow them to reverse engineer a product prior to patent expiration so that its generic version can be launched as soon as the patent expires. Keeping data secret until expiration effectively reduces the generic drug industry's capacity to quickly manufacture generics coming off patent and extends the life of the patent (Peterson 2012b).

13  As Sachs and Huizinga (1987, 3) describe, "The exposure of the top 9 [U.S.] banks in just the top 4 [indebted] countries (Argentina, Brazil, Mexico, and Venezuela) accounts for $41 billion, or 45 percent of total U.S. exposure in the developing countries . . . The top 9 banks account for a remarkable 65 percent of total exposure of U.S. banks in Latin America . . . Sovereign loans (i.e., loans to foreign public sector borrowers) account for about two thirds of U.S. bank lending to the LDCs." The top nine banks at this juncture included Citicorp, Bank of America, Chase Manhattan, Manufacturer's Hanover, J. P. Morgan, Chemical NY, Security Pacific, First Interstate, and Bankers Trust.

14  This entailed a number of situations. One example is that bank accounting records allowed bad debts to be turned into unallocated provisions such that they were not tied to particular loans or countries, which does not affect the cash flow of the banks. This meant that "they do not involve a write down in value of particular assets. (A fortiori, they do not involve any forgiveness by the banks of any part of the debts owed by the developing countries.) On the balance sheet, the increased provisioning is a transfer from shareholder's equity to loan loss reserves . . . This shift does not affect measured primary capital of the bank. In that sense it is a cosmetic move only. In the future, if the banks write off some portion of their LDC exposure (e.g., by selling the assets at a discount, or by settling with the countries at below market terms), they will be able to charge the losses to the loan reserves without any effect on reported income at the future date. At that point the capital base of the bank would shrink, and the taxable earnings of the bank would fall in line with the writeoff. Thus, by accepting large reported losses now, the banks will be better placed to report positive earnings in the future, even if the LDC loans go sour" (Sachs and Huizinga 1987, 15–17).

15  I did not record this conversation but jotted down notes both during and after our lunch.

16  K. Bala and Kirin Sagoo (2000) found that prices for brand-name drugs in countries in the Organisation for Economic Co-operation and Development were often higher than in Africa or Latin America.

17  Similar legal pursuits initiated by the pharmaceutical industry can be found in other middle-income countries with strong generic competition. For example,

in 1998, forty brand-name manufacturers jointly sued the South African government, asserting that the country's medicines policy violated the TRIPs Agreement (t'Hoen 2003). After much bad press, they withdrew the suit. After being propped up as a good example of compliance with the WTO, Brazil faced trade sanctions over quibbles the United States had with compulsory licensing policies in its Industrial Property Act (Biehl 2009; Shankar 2007), which were later resolved via negotiations over drug prices.

# BIBLIOGRAPHY

Abani, Chris. 2003. *Daphne's Lot*. Los Angeles: Red Hen.

Abdulkareem, Fatimah. 2009. "Epidemiology and Incidence of Common Cancers in Nigeria." Cancer Registry and Epidemiology Workshop, Lagos, December 7. http://ihvnigeria.org/ihvnweb/webnew/rokdownloads/Cancer%20Registration%20Training%20lectures/Epidemiology%20of%20common%20Cancers%20in%20Nigeria.pdf.

Aboderin, A. Oladipo, Abdul-Rasheed Abdu, Babatunde W. Odetoyin, and Adebayo Lamikanra. 2009. "Antimicrobial Resistance in Escherichia Coli Strains from Urinary Tract Infections." *Journal of the National Medical Association* 101, no. 12 (December): 1268–73.

Aboderin, A. Oladipo, Olufemi Adefehinti, Babatunde W. Odetoyin, Amadin A. Olotu, Iruka N. Okeke, and Olugbenga Adeodu. 2012. "Prolonged Febrile Illness Due to CTX-M-15 Extendedspectrum β-Lactamase-Producing Klebsiella Pneumoniae Infection in Nigeria." *African Journal of Laboratory Medicine* 1, no. 1. doi:10.4102/ajlm.v1i1.16.

"Absence of Quality Assurance Aids Faking." 1988. *Pharmanews* 10, no. 8: 1.

Achebe, Chinua. 2010. *Girls at War and Other Stories*. New York: Penguin Classics.

Adagu, I. S., D. C. Warhurst, W. N. Ogala, I. Abdu-Aguye, L. I. Audu, F. O. Bamgbola, and U. B. Ovwigho. 1995. "Antimalarial Drug Response of Plasmodium Falciparum from Zaria, Nigeria." *Transaction of the Royal Society of Tropical Medicine and Hygiene* 89: 422–25.

Adebanjo, Tokunbo. 1987. "SFEM Worsened Drug Faking." *Pharmanews* 9, no. 9 (September): 1.

Adeleye, I. A. 1992. "Conjugal Transferability of Multiple Antibiotic Resistance in Three Generations of Enterobacteriaceae in Nigeria." *Journal of Diarrhoeal Diseases Research* 10, no. 2 (June): 93–96.

Adelusi-Adeluyi, Julius. 1982. "Pharmacy: Past, Present, and Future." *Nigerian Journal of Pharmacy* 13, no. 5 (September–October): 123–26.

Ademoyega, Adewale. 1981. *Why We Struck*. Ibadan, Nigeria: Evans.

Adenika, Fred. 1982. "Prospects for Pharmacists in the Nigerian Pharmaceutical Industry—The Next Twenty Years." *Nigerian Journal of Pharmacy* 13, no. 1: 7–11.

Adenika, Fred. 1998. *Pharmacy in Nigeria*. Lagos, Nigeria: Panpharm Limited.

Adenika, Fred. 2000. "Poor Distribution Practices Create Problems in the Industry." *Pharmanews* 22, no. 4 (April): 12.

Adichie, Chimamanda Ngozi. 2007. *Half of a Yellow Sun.* New York: Anchor Books.

Adikibi, Owen. 1988. "The Multinational Corporation and the Monopoly of Patents in Nigeria." *World Development* 16, no. 4: 511–26.

Aduloju, Kayode. 2000. "Pharmaceutical Services in Nigeria—Which Way Forward?" *Pharmanews* 22, no. 2 (February): 10–11.

Afigbo, Adiele. 1981. *Ropes of Sand: Studies in Igbo History and Culture.* Ibadan, Nigeria: University Press Limited.

Agozino, Biko, and Ike Anyanike. 2007. "Imu Ahia: Traditional Igbo Business School and Global Commerce Culture." *Dialectical Anthropology* 31, nos. 1–3: 233–52.

Ake, Claude. 1996. *Democracy and Development in Africa.* Washington, DC: Brookings Institution.

Akinyemi, K. O., A. O. Coker, D. K. Olukoya, A. O. Oyefolu, and E. P. Amorighoye. 2000. "Prevalence of Multi-drug Resistant Salmonella Typhi among Clinically Diagnosed Typhoid Fever Patients in Lagos, Nigeria." *Zeitschrift für Naturforschung, Journal of Biosciences* 55, nos. 5–6 (May–June): 489–93.

Akoria, O. A., and A. O. Isah. 2009. "An Evaluation of Doctors' Prescribing Performance in Nigeria." *Pakistan Journal of Medical Science* 25, no. 4: 533–38.

Akpor, Albert. 2012. "N31b Drug Wars: The Suspects, Their Cargo and NDLEA's Pains." *Vanguard News.* April 1. http://www.gbooza.com/group/narcotic/forum/topics/n31b -drug-wars-the-suspects-their-cargo-and-ndlea-s-pains#ixzz2TyB4S5Q 5.

Allen, Rob. 1982. "Capitalist Development and the Educational Role of Nigerian Apprenticeship." *Comparative Education* 18, no. 2: 123–37.

Alubo, S. Ogoh. 1990. "Debt Crisis, Health, and Health Services in Africa." *Social Science and Medicine* 31, no. 6: 639–48.

Alubo, S. Ogoh. 1994. "Death for Sale: A Study of Drug Poisoning and Deaths in Nigeria." *Social Science and Medicine* 38, no. 1: 97–103.

Anderson, Jane. 2009. *Law, Knowledge, Culture: The Production of Indigenous Knowledge in Intellectual Property Law.* Cheltenham, UK: Edward Elgar Publications.

Anyanwu, Geoffrey. 2007. "17 Lorry-Load of Banned Drugs Recovered from Onitsha Market." *The Daily Sun,* March 16. www.sunnewsonline.com/webpages/news/national /2007/mar/16/national-16-03-2007-09.htm.

Appadurai, Arjun, ed. 1986. *The Social Life of Things: Commodities in Cultural Perspective.* Cambridge: Cambridge University Press.

Appadurai, Arjun. 1996. *Modernity at Large: Cultural Dimensions of Globalization.* Minneapolis: University of Minnesota Press.

Apter, Andrew. 2005. *The Pan-African Nation: Oil and the Spectacle of Culture in Nigeria.* Chicago: University of Chicago Press.

Arrighi, Giovanni. 2002. "The African Crisis: World Systemic and Regional Aspects." *New Left Review* 15 (May–June): 5–36.

Arrighi, Giovanni. 2003. "The Social and Political Economy of Global Turbulence." *New Left Review* 20 (March–April): 5–71.

Atueyi, Ifeanyi. 1985. "Good Riddance, 1984." *Pharmanews* 7, no. 1 (January): 3.

Atueyi, Ifeanyi. 1988. "Sources of Fake Drugs." *Pharmanews* 10, no. 4 (April): 17–18.

Atueyi, Ifeanyi. 2004. *Fake Drugs in Nigeria: Topical Issues and Facts You Need to Know.* Lagos, Nigeria: Pharmanews.

Austen, Gareth. 1993. "Indigenous Credit Institutions in West Africa, c.1750–1960." In *Local Suppliers of Credit in the Third World, 1750–1960,* 93–159, ed. Gareth Austin and Kaoru Sugihara. New York: St. Martin's Press.

Awolowo, Obafemi. 1966. *Path to Nigerian Freedom.* London: Faber and Faber.

Baker, Raymond W. 2012. "Plundering a Continent." *Association of Concerned Africa Scholars Bulletin* 87 (fall): 59–62.

Bala, K., and Kirin Sagoo. 2000. "Patents and Prices." HAI News, 112. http://www.haiweb .org/pubs/hainews/Patents%20and%20Prices.html.

Bangura, Yusuf. 1994. "Economic Restructuring, Coping Strategies, and Social Change: Implications for Institutional Development in Africa." *Development and Change* 25, no. 4: 785–827.

Bangura, Yusuf, and Bjorn Beckman. 1993. "African Workers and Structural Adjustment: A Nigerian Case Study." In *The Politics of Structural Adjustment,* ed. Adebayo Olukoshi, 75–96. London: James Currey.

Barboza, David, and Walt Bogdanich. 2008. "Twists in Chain of Raw Supplies for Blood Drug." *New York Times,* February 28, A1.

Barry, Andrew. 2005. "Pharmaceutical Matters: The Invention of Informed Materials," *Theory, Culture, and Society* 22, no. 1: 51–69.

Bascom, William R. 1952. "The Esusu: A Credit Institution of the Yoruba." *Journal of the Royal Anthropological Institute of Great Britain and Ireland* 82, no. 1 (January–June): 63–69.

Bate, Roger. 2012. *Phake: The Deadly World of Falsified and Substandard Medicines.* Washington, DC: AEI.

Baxerres, Carine, and Jean-Yves Le Hesran. 2011. "Where Do Pharmaceuticals on the Market Originate? An Analysis of the Informal Drug Supply in Cotonou, Benin." *Social Science and Medicine* 73: 1249–56.

Bayart, Jean-François. [1993] 2009. *The State in Africa: Politics of the Belly.* Translated by Mary Harper, Christopher Harrison, and Elizabeth Harrison. London: Longman.

Bayart, Jean-François, Stephen Ellis, and Beatrice Hibou. 1999. *The Criminalization of the State in Africa.* Translated by Stephen Ellis. Bloomington: Indiana University Press.

Beck, Ulrich. 1992. *Risk Society: Towards a New Modernity.* London: Sage.

Becker, Gary. 1994. *Human Capital: A Theoretical and Empirical Analysis, with Special Reference to Education.* Chicago: University of Chicago Press.

Beckman, Bjorn. 1982. "Whose State? State and Capitalist Development in Nigeria." *Review of African Political Economy* 23, Scandinavian Perspectives on Africa (January–April): 37–51.

Belasco, Bernard I. 1980. *The Entrepreneur as Culture Hero: Preadaptations in Nigerian Economic Development.* New York: Praeger.

Bensaude-Vincent, Bernadette, and Isabelle Stengers. 1996. *A History of Chemistry.* Cambridge, MA: Harvard University Press.

Berry, Sara. 1985. *Fathers Work for Their Sons: Accumulation, Mobility, and Class Formation in an Extended Yoruba Community.* Berkeley: University of California Press.

Biagioli, Mario. 2006. "Patent Republic: Representing Inventions, Constructing Rights and Authors." *Social Research* 73, no. 4: 1129–72.

Biagioli, Mario. 2011. "Patent Specification and Political Representation: How Patents Became Rights." In *Making and Unmaking Intellectual Property: Creative Production in Legal and Cultural Perspective,* ed. Mario Biagioli, Peter Jaszi, and Martha Woodmansee, 25–40. Chicago: University of Chicago Press.

Biehl, João. 2007. *Will to Live: AIDS Therapies and the Politics of Survival.* Princeton, NJ: Princeton University Press.

Biehl, João, and Adriana Petryna, eds. 2013. *When People Come First: Critical Studies in Global Health.* Princeton, NJ: Princeton University Press.

Boateng, Boatema. 2011. *The Copyright Thing Doesn't Work Here: Adinkra and Kente Cloth and Intellectual Property in Ghana.* Minneapolis: University of Minnesota Press.

Bogdanich, Walt, Jake Hooker, and Andrew W. Lehren. 2007. "Chinese Chemicals Flow Unchecked to Market." *New York Times,* October 31, A1.

Bogdanich, Walt, and Jake Hooker. 2008. "China Didn't Check Drug Supplier, Files Show." *New York Times,* February 16, A1.

Borger, Julian. 2001. "Industry That Stalks the US Corridors of Power." *Guardian,* February 13. http://www.guardian.co.uk/world/2001/feb/13/usa.julianborger#history-link-box.

Braithwaite, John. 1984. *Corporate Crime in the Pharmaceutical Industry.* London: Routledge and Kegan Paul.

Bräutigam, Deborah. 2003. "Close Encounters: Chinese Business Networks as Industrial Catalyst in Sub-Saharan Africa." *African Affair* 102, no. 408: 447–67.

Brotherton, P. Sean. 2012. *Revolutionary Medicine: Health and the Body in Post-Soviet Cuba.* Durham, NC: Duke University Press.

Bryan, Dick, Randy Martin, and Michael Rafferty. 2009. "Financialization: Giving Labour and Capital a Financial Makeover." *Review of Radical Political Economy* 41, no. 3: 458–72.

Bunkle, Phillida. 1993. "Calling the Shots? The International Politics of Depo-Provera." In *The "Racial" Economy of Science: Toward a Democratic Future,* ed. Sandra Harding, 287–302. Bloomington: Indiana University Press.

Business Monitor International. 2007. *Nigeria Pharmaceuticals & Healthcare Report Q4 2010.* London: Business Monitor International.

Cabral, Amilcar. 1979. *Unity and Struggle: Speeches and Writings of Amilcar Cabral.* Edited by African Party for the Independence of Guinea and Cape Verde. Translated by Michael Wolfers. New York: Monthly Review.

Caffentzis, George Constantine. 2004. "Academic Freedom, the Crisis of Neoliberalism and the Epistemology of Torture and Espiorage: Some Cautions." Paper delivered at the African Studies Association meeting. New Orleans, November 12.

Callon, Michel. 1998. *The Laws of Markets*. Hoboken, NJ: Wiley-Blackwell.

Carlson, Dennis G. 1982. "Drug Supply Systems in West Africa: A Historical Overview with Particular Reference to Nigeria." *Pharmacy in History* 24, no. 2: 73–82.

Carolan, Michael S. 2010. "The Mutability of Biotechnology Patents: From Unwieldy Products of Nature to Independent 'Object/s.'" *Theory, Culture and Society* 27, no. 1: 110–29.

Carpenter, Daniel. 2010. *Reputation and Power: Organizational Image and Pharmaceutical Regulation at the* FDA. Princeton, NJ: Princeton University Press.

Carpenter, Daniel, and Dominique Tobbell. 2011. "Bioequivalence: The Regulatory Career of a Pharmaceutical Concept." *Bulletin of the History of Medicine* 85, no. 1: 93–131.

Cazdyn, Eric. 2012. *The Already Dead: The New Time of Politics, Culture, and Illness*. Durham, NC: Duke University Press.

Center for Drug Evaluation and Research (CDER). 2003. *Guidance for Industry Bioavailability and Bioequivalence Studies for Orally Administered Drug Products—General Considerations*. Washington, DC: U.S. Department of Health and Human Services, Food and Drug Administration. http://www.fda.gov/downloads/Drugs/ . . . /Guidances/ucm070124.pdf

Chadha, Alka. 2006. "Destination India for the Pharmaceutical Industry." *The Delhi Business Review* 7, no. 1 (January–June): 1–8.

Chalfin, Brenda. 2010. *Neoliberal Frontiers: An Ethnography of Sovereignty in West Africa*. Chicago: University of Chicago Press.

Chan, Leong, and Tugrul U. Daim. 2011. "Multi-Perspective Analysis of the Chinese Pharmaceutical Sector: Policy, Enterprise and Technology." *Journal of Technology Management in China* 6, no. 2: 171–90.

Chen, Shaoyu. 2011. *The Regulatory Approval for New Drugs & Devices in China*. Beijing: Covington and Burling LLP.

Chigor, Vincent. N., Veronica J. Umoh, Stella I. Smith, Etinosa O. Igbinosa, and Anthony I. Okoh. 2010. "Multidrug Resistance and Plasmid Patterns of *Escherichia coli* O157 and other *E. coli* Isolated from Diarrhoeal Stools and Surface Waters from Some Selected Sources in Zaria, Nigeria." *International Journal of Environmental Research and Public Health* 7, no. 10: 3831–41.

Chirac Foundation. 2009. *Cotonou Declaration*. http://www.fondationchirac.eu/wp -content/uploads/2009/12/appel-anglais.pdf

Choy, Timothy. 2011. *Ecologies of Comparison: An Ethnography of Endangerment in Hong Kong*. Durham, NC: Duke University Press.

Chukwuezi, Barth. 2001. "Through Thick and Thin: Igbo Rural-Urban Circularity, Identity and Investment." *Journal of Contemporary African Studies* 19, no. 1: 55–66.

Clarke, Kamari. 2004. *Mapping Yoruba Networks: Power and Agency in the Making of Transnational Communities*. Durham, NC: Duke University Press.

Coase, Ronald H. 1960. "The Problem of Social Cost." *Journal of Law and Economics* 3, no. 1: 1–44.

Collier, Stephen, and Andrew Lakoff. 2005. "On Regimes of Living." In *Global Assemblages: Technology, Politics, and Ethics as Anthropological Problems*, 22–39. Hoboken, NJ: Wiley-Blackwell.

Comaroff, Jean, and John Comaroff. 2001. *Millennial Capitalism and the Culture of Neoliberalism*. Durham, NC: Duke University Press.

Comaroff, Jean, and John Comaroff. 2011. *Theory from the South: Or, How Euro-America is Evolving Toward Africa*. Boulder, CO: Paradigm Publishers.

Coombe, Rosemary. 1998. *The Cultural Life of Intellectual Properties*. Durham, NC: Duke University Press.

Coombe, Rosemary. 2003. "Fear, Hope and Longing for the Future of Authorship and a Revitalized Public Domain in Global Regimes of Intellectual Property." *DePaul Law Review* 52, no. 4: 1171–93.

Cooper, Frederick. 1981. "Africa and the World Economy." *African Studies Review* 24, nos. 2/3 (June–September): 1–86.

Cooper, Frederick. 2001. "What Is the Concept of Globalization Good For? An African Historian's Perspective." *African Affairs* 100: 189–213.

Cooper, Melinda. 2008. *Life as Surplus: Biotechnology and Capitalism in the Neoliberal Era*. Seattle: University of Washington Press.

Cooper, Melinda. 2011. "Complexity Theory after the Financial Crisis: The Death of Neoliberalism or the Triumph of Hayek?" *Journal of Cultural Economy* 4, no. 4: 371–85.

Corporate Watch. n.d. "Pfizer Inc." Accessed August 25, 2013. http://www.corporatewatch.org/?lid=327.

Correa, Carlos. 2008. "Patent Rights." In *Intellectual Property and International Trade: The TRIPS Agreement*, 2nd ed., ed. Carlos M. Correa and Abdulqawi A. Yusuf, 227–58. Austin: Wolfers Kluwer Law and Business.

da Cunha, Manuella, and Marianno Carneiro da Cunha. 1985. *From Slave Quarters to Town Houses: Brazilian Architecture in Nigeria and the People's Republic of Benin*. São Paulo, Brazil: Nobel.

Dada-Adegbola, Hannah O., and Kamaldeen A. Muili. 2010. "Antibiotic Susceptibility Pattern of Urinary Tract Pathogens in Ibadan, Nigeria." *African Journal of Medicine and Medical Sciences* 39, no. 3 (September): 173–79.

Daini, Oluwole A., David O. Ogbolu, and Afolabi Ogunledun. 2006. "Plasmid Determined Resistance to Quinolones in Clinical Isolates of Gram-negative Bacilli." *African Journal of Medicine and Medical Sciences* 35, no. 4 (December): 437–41.

Dalil, Abubakar. 1987. "The Role of Financial Institutions in the Debt-Equity Swap." *Central Bank Bullion* 11, no. 3: 15–22.

de Boeck, Filip 2013. "Challenges of Urban Growth: Toward an Anthropology of Urban Infrastructure in Africa." In *Afritecture: Building Social Change*, ed. Andres Lepik, 92–102. Ostfildern, Germany: Hatje Cantz.

de Boeck, Filip, and Marie-Françoise Plissart. 2004. *Kinshasa: Tales of the Invisible City*. Ghent, Belgium: Ludion.

deKieffer, Donald. 2006. "Trojan Drugs: Counterfeit and Mislabeled Pharmaceuticals in the Legitimate Market." *American Journal of Law & Medicine* 32, nos. 2/3: 325–49.

de la Torre, Nathalie. 2001. "Survey on Access to Essential Medicines in the Lagos Area, Nigeria." Lagos, Nigeria: Access Campaign for Essential Medicines, Médecins Sans Frontières.

Deng, Rongling, and Kenneth I. Kaitin. (2004). "The Regulation and Approval of New Drugs in China." *Drug Information Journal* 38, no. 1: 29–39.

Diawara, Manthia. 1998. "Toward a Regional Imaginary in Africa." In *The Cultures of Globalization*, ed. Fredric Jameson and Masoa Miyoshi, 103–24. Durham, NC: Duke University Press.

Dike, Kenneth Onwuka. [1956] 1981. *Trade Politics in the Niger Delta, 1830–1885: An Introduction to the Economic and Political History of Nigeria.* Westport, CT: Greenwood.

Drahos, Peter. 1995. "Global Property Rights in Information: The Story of TRIPs at the GATT." *Prometheus* 13, no. 1: 6–19.

Drahos, Peter, and John Braithwaite. 2002. *Information Feudalism: Who Owns the Knowledge Economy?* New York: New Press.

Dumit, Joseph. 2012a. *Drugs for Life: How Pharmaceuticals Define Our Health.* Durham, NC: Duke University Press.

Dumit, Joseph. 2012b. "Prescription Maximization and the Accumulation of Surplus Health in the Pharmaceutical Industry: The 'Biomarx' Experiment." In *Lively Capital: Biotechnologies, Ethics and Governance in Global Markets*, ed. Kaushik Sunder Rajan, 45–92. Durham, NC: Duke University Press.

Eban, Katherine. 2005. *Dangerous Doses: How Counterfeiters Are Contaminating America's Drug Supply.* Orlando, FL: Harcourt.

Ecks, Stefan. 2008. "Global Pharmaceutical Markets and Corporate Citizenship: The Case of Novartis' Anti-cancer Drug Glivec." *BioSocieties* 3, no. 2, 165–81.

Edelman, Mark, and Angelique Haugerud, eds. 2005. *The Anthropology of Development and Globalization: From Classical Political Economy to Contemporary Neoliberalism.* Malden, MA: Blackwell Publishers.

Edozie, Rita Kiki. 2002. *People Power and Democracy: The Popular Movement against Military Despotism in Nigeria, 1989–1999.* Trenton, NJ: Africa World Press.

Efobi, C. U. 1982. "Manpower Development for General Practice Pharmacy." *Nigerian Journal of Pharmacy* 13, no. 1 (January–February): 22–23.

Egboh, Andrew A. 1971. *History of Pharmacy in Nigeria: A Guide and Survey of the Past and Present, 1887–1971.* 4th ed. Lagos, Nigeria: Pharma-Chemical Services.

Egbue, Ngozi G. 2006. "Gender Constraints in the Training of Women Traders in South Eastern Nigeria: A Case Study of Onitsha Main Market." *Journal of Social Science* 12, no. 3: 163–70.

Egbuonu, Douglas Nnamdi. 2000. "The Endangered Pharmacy Profession—How Much of Our Woes Are Self-Inflicted—How Does It Survive?" *Pharmanews* 22, no. 5 (May): 10–11.

Ehianeta, Teddy, Bidemi Williams, Jadesola Surakat, Nura Mohammed, and Chimezie Anyakora. 2012. "Quality Survey of Some Brands of Artesunate-Amodiaquine in Lagos Drug Market." *African Journal of Pharmacy and Pharmacology* 6, no. 9: 636–42.

Ehrenreich, Barbara, Steven Minkin, and Mark Dowie. 1979. "The Charge: Gynocide, The Accused: The U.S. Government." *Mother Jones*, November 1, 26–28. http://www.motherjones.com/print/15298.

Einzig, Paul. 1966. *Primitive Money.* 2nd ed. Oxford: Pergamon.

Eko, F. O., and S. J. Utsalo. 1991. "Antimicrobial Resistance Trends of Shigellae Isolates from Calabar, Nigeria." *Journal of Tropical Medicine and Hygiene* 94, no. 6 (December): 407–10.

Ekpere, Johnson. 2003. "African Model Law on the Rights of Local Communities, Farmers and Breeders, and for the Regulation of Access to Biological Resources." In *African Perspectives on Genetic Resources: A Handbook on Laws, Policies, and Institutions*, ed. Kent Nnadozie, Robert Lettington, Carl Bruch, Susan Bass, and Sarah King, 275–86. Washington, DC: Environmental Law Institute.

Ekundayo, Olaniyi J., Muktar H. Aliyu, and Pauline E. Jolly. 2007. "A Review of Intestinal Helminthiasis in Nigeria and the Need for School-Based Intervention." *Journal of Rural and Tropical Public Health* 6: 33–39.

Ellis, Stephen. 2009. "West Africa's International Drug Trade." *African Affairs* 108 (431): 171–96.

Elyachar, Julia. 2005. *Markets of Dispossession: NGOS, Economic Development, and the State in Cairo*. Durham, NC: Duke University Press.

Emeagwali, Gloria. 2011. "The Neoliberal Agenda and the IMF/World Bank Structural Adjustment Programs with Reference to Africa." In *Critical Perspectives on Neoliberal Globalization, Development, and Education in Africa and Asia*, ed. Dip Kapoor, 3–13. Boston: Sense.

Emeto, Charles. 1986. "Pharmacy Services Toward 'Health for All by the Year 2000.'" *Pharmanews* 8, no. 6:10–11.

Erhun, Wilson O., Oladipo O. Babalola, and Mercy O. Erhun. 2001. "Drug Regulation and Control in Nigeria: The Challenge of Counterfeit Drugs." *Journal of Health and Population in Developing Countries* 4, no. 2: 23–34.

Ewald, François. 1993. "Two Infinities of Risk." In *The Politics of Everyday Fear*, ed. Brian Massumi, 221–28. Minneapolis: University of Minnesota Press.

Ezeanya, Chike Chukwubuikem. 2000. "Drug Distribution Channels in Nigeria." *Pharmanews* 22, no. 3 (March): 11.

Fadahunsi, Akin. 1993. "Devaluation: Implications for Employment, Inflation, Growth and Development." In *The Politics of Structural Adjustment in Nigeria*, ed. Adebayo O. Olukoshi, 33–53. London: James Curry.

Falola, Toyin. 1984. *The Political Economy of a Pre-Colonial State: Ibadan, 1830–1900*. Ile-Ife, Nigeria: Ile-Ife Press.

Falola, Toyin. 1992. "'An Ounce Is Enough': The Gold Industry and the Politics of Control in Colonial Western Nigeria." *African Economic History* 20: 27–50.

Falola, Toyin, and Akanmu Gafari Adebayo. 2000. *Culture, Politics and Money among the Yoruba*. New Brunswick, NJ: Transaction.

Fanon, Frantz. 2005. *The Wretched of the Earth*. Translated by Richard Philcox. New York: Grove Press.

Farmer, Paul. 1999. *Infection and Inequalities: The Modern Plaques*. Berkeley: University of California Press.

Fassin, Didier. 1988. "Illicit Sale of Pharmaceuticals in Africa: Sellers and Clients in the Suburbs of Dakar." *Tropical and Geographical Medicine* 40, no. 2: 166–70.

Feierman, Steven, and John Janzen. 1992. *The Social Basis of Health and Healing in Africa.* Berkeley: University of California Press.

Felix Ugbojiaku & 2 Ors v Attorney General of the Federation & 4 Ors. 2001. Federal High Court, Ikeja, Lagos. Suit No. FHC/LCS/423/95.

Ferguson, Anne. 1981. "Commercial Pharmaceutical Medicine and Medicalization: A Case Study from El Salvador." *Culture, Medicine and Psychiatry* 5, no. 2: 105–34.

Ferguson, James. 1999. *Expectations of Modernity: Myths and Meanings of Urban Life on the Zambian Copperbelt.* Berkeley: University of California Press.

Ferguson, James. 2006. *Global Shadows: Africa in the Neoliberal World Order.* Durham, NC: Duke University Press.

Fischer, Michael M. J. 2003. *Emergent Forms of Life and the Anthropological Voice.* Durham, NC: Duke University Press.

Forrest, Tom. 1994. *The Advance of African Capital: The Growth of Nigerian Private Enterprise.* Charlottesville: University of Virginia Press.

Forrest, Tom. 1995. *The Makers and Making of Nigerian Private Enterprise.* Ibadan, Nigeria: Spectrum Books.

Forsyth, Frederick. 1969. *The Biafran Story.* London: Hutchinson.

Fortun, Kim. 2001. *Advocacy after Bhopal: Environmentalism, Disaster, New Global Orders.* Chicago: University of Chicago Press.

Fortun, Mike. 2008. *Promising Genomics: Iceland and deCODE: Genetics in a World of Speculation.* Berkeley: University of California Press.

Foucault, Michel. 1990. *History of Sexuality. Vol. 1: An Introduction.* Translated by Robert Hurley. New York: Vintage.

Foucault, Michel. 2008. *The Birth of Biopolitics: Lectures at the Collège de France, 1978–1979.* Edited by François Ewald and Alessandro Fontana. Translated by Graham Burchell. New York: Palgrave Macmillian.

Fourchard, Laurent, and Ayodeji Olukoju. 2007. "State, Local Governments and the Management of Markets in Lagos and Ibadan since the 1950s." In *Gouverner Les Villes D'Afrique: État, Gouvernement Local Et Acteurs Privés,* ed. Laurent Fourchard, 107–24. Paris: Karthala.

Freund, Bill. 1978. "Oil Boom and Crisis in Contemporary Nigeria." *Review of African Political Economy* 5, no. 13 (September–December): 91–100.

Friedman, Milton. 1953. *Essays in Positive Economics.* Chicago: University of Chicago Press.

Funding Universe. n.d. "The Upjohn Company History." Accessed November 1, 2011. http://www.fundinguniverse.com/company-histories/the-upjohn-company-history/.

Government of Japan. 2011. *Anti-Counterfeiting Trade Agreement.* Tokyo, October 1. Accessed August 14, 2012. http://www.mofa.go.jp/policy/economy/i_property/pdfs/acta1105_en.pdf

Greene, Jeremy. 2007. *Prescribing by Numbers: Drugs and the Definition of Disease.* Baltimore: The Johns Hopkins University Press.

Greene, Jeremy. 2011. "Making Medicines Essential: The Evolving Role of Pharmaceuticals in Global Health." *BioSocieties* 6: 10–33.

Greene, Jeremy. Forthcoming. *The Same but Not the Same: A History of Generics*. Baltimore: The Johns Hopkins University Press.

Greenhouse, Carol, ed. 2010. *Ethnographies of Neoliberalism*. Philadelphia: University of Pennsylvania Press.

Guyer, Jane. 1994. *Money Matters: Instability, Values, and Social Payments in the Modern History of West African Communities*. Portsmouth, NH: Heinemann.

Guyer, Jane. 2002. *Money Struggles and Daily Life: Devaluation in Ibadan and Other Urban Centers in Southern Nigeria, 1986–1996*. Portsmouth, NH: Heinemann.

Guyer, Jane. 2004. *Marginal Gains: Monetary Transactions in Atlantic Africa*. Chicago: University of Chicago Press.

Habib, A. G., E. E. Nwokedi, U. I. Ihesiulor, A. Mohammed, and Z. G. Habib. 2003. "Widespread Antibiotic Resistance in Savannah Nigeria." *African Journal of Medicine and Medical Sciences* 32, no. 3 (September): 303–5.

Hacking, Ian. 1990. *The Taming of Chance*. Cambridge: Cambridge University Press.

Harris, Gardiner. 2008. "U.S. Identifies Tainted Heparin in 11 Countries." *New York Times*, April 22. http://www.nytimes.com/2008/04/22/health/policy/22fda.html?_r=0.

Harris, Gardiner, and Walt Bogdanich. 2008. "F.D.A. Broke Its Rules by Not Inspecting Chinese Plant With Problem Drug." *New York Times*, February 15, A15.

Hart, Keith. 1973. "Informal Income Opportunities and Urban Employment in Ghana." *Journal of Modern African Studies* 11, no. 1: 61–89.

Hart, Keith. 2006. "Bureaucratic Reform and the Informal Economy." In *Linking the Formal and Informal Economy: Concepts and Politics*, ed. B. Guha-Khasnobis, K. Kahbur, and E. Ostrom, 21–35. Oxford: Oxford University Press.

Harvey, David. 1991. *The Condition of Postmodernity: An Enquiry into the Origins of Cultural Change*. Oxford: Wiley-Blackwell.

Harvey, David. 2001. *Spaces of Capital: Towards a Critical Geography*. New York: Routledge.

Harvey, David. 2007. *A Brief History of Neoliberalism*. Oxford: Oxford University Press.

Hashim, Yahaya, and Kate Meagher. 1999. *Cross-Border Trade and the Parallel Currency Market—Trade and Finance in the Context of Structural Adjustment: A Case Study from Kano*. Uppsala, Sweden: Nordiska Afrikainstitutet.

Hayden, Cori. 2003. "From Market to Market: Bioprospecting's Idioms of Inclusion." *American Ethnologist* 30, no. 3: 359–71.

Hayden, Cori. 2010. "The Proper Copy." *Journal of Cultural Economy* 3, no. 1: 85–102.

Hayden, Cori. 2012. "Population." In *Inventive Methods: The Happening of the Social*, ed. Celia Lury and Nina Wakefield, 172–84. London: Routledge.

Hayek, Friedrich August von. [1941] 2007. *The Pure Theory of Capital*, ed. Lawrence H. White. Chicago: University of Chicago Press.

Hayek, Friedrich August von. 1967. "The Theory of Complex Phenomena." In *Studies in Philosophy, Politics and Economics*, 22–42. London: Routledge and Kegan Paul.

Hayek, Friedrich August von. 1974. "The Pretence of Knowledge." Accessed August 1, 2013. http://www.nobelprize.org/nobel_prizes/economic-sciences/laureates/1974/hayek-lecture.html.

Hayek, Friedrich August von. 1988. *The Fatal Conceit: The Errors of Socialism: Collected Works of F. A. Hayek. Vol. 1.* Edited by W. W. Bartley III. London: Routledge.

Heads of State and Government of the Organisation Internationale de la Fracophonie. 2010. *Montreux Resolution of 2010.* Accessed November 30, 2011. http://www.fondationchirac.eu/wp-content/uploads/Montreux-Resolution1.pdf

Healy, David. 2004. *Let Them Eat Prozac: The Unhealthy Relationship Between the Pharmaceutical Industry and Depression.* New York: New York University Press.

Hill, Polly. 1970. *Studies in Rural Capitalism in West Africa.* Cambridge: Cambridge University Press.

Ho, Karen. 2009. *Liquidated: An Ethnography of Wall Street.* Durham, NC: Duke University Press.

Hodgson, Geoffrey M. 1994. "Hayek, Evolution and Spontaneous Order." In *Natural Images in Economic Thought: "Markets Read in Tooth and Claw,"* ed. Philip Mirowski, 408–47. Cambridge: Cambridge University Press.

Hopkins, Anthony G. 1973. *An Economic History of West Africa.* London: Longman.

Hotez, Peter J. 2009. "Mass Drug Administration and Integrated Control for the World's High-Prevalence Neglected Tropical Diseases." *Clinical Pharmacology and Therapeutics* 85 (June): 659–64.

Hotez, Peter J., Oluwatoyin A. Asojo, Adekunle M. Adesina. 2012. "Nigeria: 'Ground Zero' for the High Prevalence Neglected Tropical Diseases." *PLoS Neglected Tropical Disease* 6, no. 7: e1600. doi:10.1371/journal.pntd.0001600.

Hudson, Michael. 2003. *Super Imperialism: The Origin and Fundamentals of U.S. World Dominance.* Ann Arbor, MI: Pluto Press

Hudson, Michael. 2005. *Global Fracture: The New International Economic Order.* Ann Arbor, MI: Pluto Press.

Hunt, Nancy. 1999. *A Colonial Lexicon of Birth Ritual, Medicalization, and Mobility in The Congo.* Durham, NC: Duke University Press.

Idia, Umolu P., O. Omigie, Y. Tatfeng, F. I. Omorogbe, F. Aisabokhale, and O. Ugbodagah. 2006. "Antimicrobial Susceptibility and Plasmid Profiles of *Escherichia coli* Isolates Obtained from Different Human Clinical Specimens in Lagos, Nigeria." *Journal of American Science* 2, no. 4: 70–75.

Idigbe, E. O., J. P. Duque, E. K. John, and O. Annan. 1992. "Resistance to Antituberculosis Drugs in Treated Patients in Lagos, Nigeria." *The Journal of Tropical Medicine and Hygiene* 95, no. 3 (June): 186–91.

Ifeka-Moller, Caroline. 1975. "Female Militancy and Colonial Revolt: The Women's War of 1929, Eastern Nigeria." In *Perceiving Women,* ed. Shirley Ardener, 127–57. New York: John Wiley and Sons.

Igué, O. J. 2003. *Les Yoruba en Afrique de l'Ouest francophone, 1910e1980: Essai sur une diaspora.* Paris: Présence Africaine.

Ikioda, Faith Ossy. 2013. "Urban Markets in Lagos, Nigeria." *Geography Compass* 7, no. 7: 517–26. doi:10.1111/gec3.12057.

International Monetary Fund. 2005. *Global Financial Stability Report.* Washington, DC: International Monetary Fund. http://www.imf.org/External/Pubs/FT/GFSR/2005/02/.

International Monetary Fund. 2012. *Global Financial Stability Report*. Washington, DC: International Monetary Fund. http://www.imf.org/external/pubs/ft/gfsr/2012 /01/.

International Trade Administration. 2010. *Pharmaceutical Industry Profile*. Washington, DC: U.S. Department of Commerce. http://www.trade.gov/td/health/Pharmaceu-ticalIndustryProfile2010.pdf.

Isichei, Elizabeth. 1973. *The Ibo People and the Europeans: The Genesis of a Relationship—to 1906*. London: Faber and Faber.

Isichei, Elizabeth. 1978. *Igbo Worlds: An Anthology of Oral Histories and Historical Descriptions*. Philadelphia: Institute for the Study of Human Issues.

"Issue Import Licenses Now." 1985. *Pharmanews* 7, no. 3: 4.

Isute, Dominic. 1989. "West Africa Shuns Nigeria Drugs." *Pharmanews* 11, no. 1: 1.

Janzen, John. 1978. *The Quest for Therapy in Lower Zaire*. Berkeley: University of California Press.

Jasanoff, Sheila. 1995. *Science at the Bar: Law, Science, and Technology in America*. Cambridge, MA: Harvard University Press.

Jega, Attahiru. 2000. *Identity Transformation and Identity Politics under Structural Adjustment in Nigeria*. Uppsala, Sweden: Nordiska Afrikainstitutet.

Johnson, Marion. 1970. "The Cowrie Currencies of West Africa, Part II." *Journal of African History* 11, no. 3: 331–53.

Juma, Calestous. 1989. *The Gene Hunters: Biotechnology and the Scramble for Seeds*. Princeton, NJ: Princeton University Press.

Kalu, Abieye. 1984a. "Locally Produced Drugs May Cost More." *Pharmanews* 6, no. 7 (July): 1.

Kalu, Abieye. 1984b. "The Pharmaceutical Wholesaler." *Pharmanews* 6, no. 4 (July): 10.

Kalu, Abieye. 1985. "PTG Advises FMG on Import License." *Pharmanews* 7, no. 1 : 1.

Kanji, Najmi, Anita Hardon, Jan Willem Harnmeijer, Masuma Mamdani, Gill Walt. 1992. *Drug Policies in Developing Countries*. London: Zed.

Kehinde, Prince Shofoyeke. 1993. "Pharmacists and Depressed Economy." *Pharmanews* 15, no. 12: 8–10.

Kilby, Peter. 1969. *Industrialization in an Open Economy: 1946–1966*. Cambridge: Cambridge University Press.

Kirzner, Israel. 1963. *Market Theory and the Price System*. Princeton, NJ: D. Van Nostrand.

Klantschnig, Gernot. 2013. *Crime, Drugs and the State in Africa: The Nigerian Connection*. Dordrecht; Leiden, The Netherlands: Brill.

Klein, Axel. 1999. "Nigeria and the Drugs War." *Review of African Political Economy* 26, no. 79: 51–73.

KPMG. 2011. "China's Pharmaceutical Industry—Poised for the Giant Leap." Accessed May 16, 2013. http://www.swissnexchina.org/foryou/kpmg-china-pharmaceutical -201106.pdf.

Krugman, Paul. 2009. *The Return of Depression Economics and the Crisis of 2008*. New York: W. W. Norton.

Lahan, G. D. 1989. "Drug Production in the Present Economic Situation." *Nigerian Journal of Pharmacy* 20, no. 1: 15–17.

Lakoff, Andrew. 2005. *Pharmaceutical Reason: Knowledge and Value in Global Psychiatry.* Cambridge: Cambridge University Press.

Lamikanra, Adebayo, Jennifer Crowe, Rebeccah Lijek, Babatunde Odetoyin, John Wain, A. Oladipo Aboderin, and Iruka Okeke. 2011. "Rapid Evolution of Fluoroquinolone-Resistant Escherichia coli in Nigeria Is Temporally Associated with Fluoroquinolone Use." BMC *Infectious Diseases* 11: 312.

Landecker, Hannah. 2013. "Biofallibility Today: From Antibiotic Resistance to Epigenetic Regulation." Paper delivered at Medicine at the Edge Conference. University of California, Santa Cruz, May 3.

Langwick, Stacey. 2011. *Bodies, Politics, and African Healing: The Matter of Maladies in Tanzania.* Bloomington: Indiana University Press.

La Puma, Edward, and Benjamin Lee. 2004. *Derivatives and the Globalization of Risk.* Durham, NC: Duke University Press.

Larkin, Brian. 2008. *Signal and Noise: Media, Infrastructure, and Urban Culture in Nigeria.* Durham, NC: Duke University Press.

Lave, Jean. 1986. "The Values of Quantification." In *Power, Action, and Belief: A New Sociology of Knowledge,* ed. John Law. Sociological Review Monograph 32, 88–111. London: Routledge and Kegan Paul.

Lave, Jean. 2011. *Apprenticeship in Critical Ethnographic Practice.* Chicago: University of Chicago Press.

Lawson, L., A. G. Habib, M. I. Okobi, D. Idiong, I. Olajide, N. Emenyonu, N. Onuoha, L. E. Cuevas, and S. O. Oriri. 2010. "Pilot Study on Multidrug Resistant Tuberculosis in Nigeria." *African Annals of Medicine* 9, no. 3 (July–September): 184–87.

Lefebvre, Henri. 1991. *The Production of Space.* Translated by Donald Nicholson-Smith. Cambridge, MA: Blackwell.

Leslie, Charles. 1976. *Asian Medical Systems: A Comparative Study.* Berkeley: University of California Press.

Lin, Yi-Chieh Jessica. 2011. *Fake Stuff: China and the Rise of Counterfeit Goods.* New York: Routledge.

Livingston, Julie. 2012. *Improvising Medicine: An African Oncology Ward in an Emerging Cancer Epidemic.* Durham, NC: Duke University Press.

Lock, Margaret. 1995. *Encounters with Aging: Mythologies of Menopause in Japan and North America.* Berkeley: University of California Press.

Lock, Margaret, and Vinh-Kim Nguyen. 2010. *An Anthropology of Biomedicine.* Malden, MA: Wiley-Blackwell.

Loewy, Matías. 2007. "Deadly Imitations." *Perspectives in Health (Pan American Health Organization)* 11, no. 1. Accessed April 16, 2010. http://www.paho.org/English/DD/PIN/Number23_article3.htm.

Luhmann, Niklas. 2005. *Risk: A Sociological Theory.* Translated by Rhodes Barrett. New Brunswick, NJ: Aldine Transaction.

Lupton, Deborah. 1999. *Risk.* London: Routledge.

Mabogunje, Akin L. 1964. "The Evolution and Analysis of the Retail Structure of Lagos, Nigeria." *Economic Geography* 40, no. 4: 304–23.

MacGaffey, Janet, and Rémy Bazenguissa-Ganga. 2000. *Congo-Paris: Transnational Traders on the Margins of the Law*. Oxford: James Currey.

MacKenzie, Donald. 2006. *An Engine, Not a Camera: How Financial Models Shape Markets*. Cambridge, MA: MIT Press.

Mackenzie, Donald. 2009. *Material Markets: How Economic Agents Are Constructed*. Oxford: Oxford University Press.

Mamdani, Mahmood. 1996. *Citizen and Subject: Contemporary Africa and the Legacy of Late Colonialism*. Princeton, NJ: Princeton University Press.

Mann, Kristin. 2007. *Slavery and the Birth of an African City: Lagos, 1760–1900*. Bloomington: Indiana University Press.

Marcus, George. 1995. "Ethnography in/of the World System: The Emergence of Multi-sited Ethnography." *Annual Review of Anthropology* 24: 95–117.

Marcus, George, and Michael M. J. Fischer. 1986. *Anthropology as Cultural Critique: An Experimental Moment in the Human Sciences*. Chicago: University of Chicago Press.

Martin, Emily. 1994. *Flexible Bodies: Tracking Immunity in American Culture from the Days of Polio to the Age of AIDS*. Boston: Beacon Press.

Marx, Karl. [1857–58]. 1973. *Grundrisse: Foundations of the Critique of Political Economy*. Translated by Martin Nicolaus. London: Penguin.

Marx, Karl. [1867] 1992. *Capital: A Critique of Political Economy. Vol. 1*. London: Penguin Classics.

Marx, Karl. [1894] 1974. *Capital: A Critique of Political Economy. Vol. 3*. Edited by Frederich Engels. Moscow: Progress.

Maskus, Keith E., and Matthias Ganslandt. 1999. *Parallel Imports of Pharmaceutical Products in the European Union*. Washington, DC: The World Bank.

Matory, J. Lorand. 2005. *Black Atlantic Religion: Tradition, Transnationalism, and Matriarchy in the Afro-Brazilian Candomblé*. Princeton, NJ: Princeton University Press.

Maurer, Bill. 2005. *Mutual Life, Limited: Islamic Banking, Alternative Currencies, Lateral Reason*. Princeton, NJ: Princeton University Press.

Maurer, Bill. 2007. "Incalculable Payments: Money, Scale, and the South African Offshore Grey Money Amnesty." *African Studies Review* 50, no. 2: 125–38.

May and Baker. 2007. *Annual Report and Accounts*. Lagos, Nigeria: May and Baker Nigeria PLC.

Mbembe, Achille. 2001. *On the Postcolony*. Berkeley: University of California Press.

Mbembe, Achille. 2003. "Necropolitics." *Public Culture* 15, no. 1: 11–40.

Mbembe, Achille, and Janet Roitman. 1995. "Figures of the Subject in Times of Crisis." *Public Culture* 7, no. 2: 323–52.

Meagher, Kate. 2007. "Manufacturing Disorder: Liberalization, Informal Enterprise and Economic 'Ungovernance' in African Small Firm Clusters." *Development and Change* 38, no. 3: 473–503.

Meagher, Kate. 2009. "The Informalization of Belonging: Igbo Informal Enterprise and National Cohesion from Below." *Africa Development* 34, no. 1: 31–46.

Meagher, Kate. 2010. *Identity Economics: Social Networks and the Informal Economy in Nigeria*. Woodbridge, UK: James Currey.

Médecins Sans Frontières. n.d. *Access Campaign*. Accessed November 19, 2013. http://www.msfaccess.org/the-access-campaign.

Mgbokwere, N. 1984. "The Pharmaceutical Wholesaler and His Supplier." *Pharmanews* 6, no. 4: 10–13.

"The Minister of Health and Fake Drugs." 1988. *Pharmanews* 10, no. 8:3.

Mirowski, Philip, and Dieter Plehwe. 2009. *The Road from Mont Pelerin: The Making of the Neoliberal Thought Collective*. Cambridge, MA: Harvard University Press.

Mises, Ludwig von. [1957] 1985. *Theory and History*. Auburn, AL: Mises Institute.

Miyazaki, Hirokazu. 2013. *Arbitraging Japan: Dreams of Capitalism at the End of Finance*. Berkeley: University of California Press.

Mkandawire, Thandika, and Charles Soludo. 1998. *Our Continent, Our Future: African Perspectives on Structural Adjustment*. Dakar: Council for the Development of Social Science Research in Africa (CODESRIA).

Monteagudo, Manuel. 1994. "The Debt Problem: The Baker Plan and the Brady Initiative: A Latin American Perspective." *International Lawyer* 28, no. 1: 59–81.

Montefiore, D., V. O. Rotimi, and F. A. Adeyemi-Doro. 1989. "The Problem of Bacterial Resistance to Antibiotics among Strains Isolated from Hospital Patients in Lagos and Ibadan, Nigeria." *Journal of Antimicrobial Chemotherapy* 23, no. 4 (April): 641–51.

"Mrs. Okoli Pleads for Indigenous Producers." 1990. *Pharmanews* 12, no. 9: 1.

"Mrs. Oremule Pleads for Small Scale Producers." 1991. *Pharmanews* 13, no. 5: 1.

Mueller, Oliver, and Clifford Mintz. 2012. "CMOS and Final Dosage Manufacturing in China: The Far East Market Evolves." *Contract Pharma*, May 30. Accessed October 24, 2013. http://www.contractpharma.com/issues/2012-06/view_features/cmos-and-final-dosage-manufacturing-in-china/.

Munn, Nancy. 1986. *The Fame of Gawa: A Symbolic Study of Value Transformation in a Massim Society*. Durham, NC: Duke University Press.

Murphy, Michelle. 2006. *Sick Building Syndrome and the Problem of Uncertainty: Environmental Politics, Technoscience, and Women Workers*. Durham, NC: Duke University Press.

National Agency for Food and Drug Administration and Control. 2011. *Registered Products Catalog*. Abuja, Nigeria: NAFDAC.

Nguyen, Vinh-Kim. 2010. *The Republic of Therapy: Triage and Sovereignty in West Africa's Time of AIDS*. Durham, NC: Duke University Press.

Nichter, Mark. 1980. "The Layperson's Perception of Medicine as Perspective into the Utilization of Multiple Therapy Systems in the Indian Context." *Social Science and Medicine. Part B: Medical Anthropology* 14, no. 4: 225–33.

Nkrumah, Kwame. 1970. *Consciencism: Philosophy and Ideology for De-Colonisation*. New York: Monthly Review.

Nnadozie, Emmanuel. 2002. "African Indigenous Entrepreneurship Determinants of Resurgence and Growth of Igbo Entrepreneurship during the Post-Biafra Period." *Journal of African Business* 3, no. 1: 49–80.

Nnadozie, Kent, Robert Lettington, Carl Bruch, and Susan Bass, eds. 2003. *African Perspectives on Genetic Resources: A Handbook on Laws, Policies and Institutions*. Washington, DC: Environmental Law Institute.

Nordstrom, Carolyn. 2004. *Shadows of War: Violence, Power, and International Profiteering in the Twenty-First Century*. Berkeley: University of California Press.

Northrup, David. 1978. *Trade without Rulers: Pre-Colonial Economic Development in South-Eastern Nigeria*. Oxford: Clarendon Press.

Nuhu, Shem Z. 2002. "The Future of Pharmacy." *Pharmanews* 24, no. 11 (November): 45–47.

Nyerere, Julius. 1974. UJAMAA: *Essays on Socialism*. Oxford: Oxford University Press.

Nyang'oro, Julius E., and Timothy Shaw, eds. 1992. *Beyond Structural Adjustment in Africa: The Political Economy of Sustainable and Democratic Development*. New York: Praeger.

Obaseiki-Ebor, E. E., S. M. Oyaide, and E. E. Okpere. 1985. "Incidence of Penicillinase Producing Neisseria Gonorrhoeae (PPNG) Strains and Susceptibility of Gonococcal Isolates to Antibiotics in Benin City, Nigeria." *Genitourin Medicine* 61, no. 6: 367–70.

Obi, Ben, Abu Nurudeen, and Obida Gobna Wafure. 2010. "Determinants of Exchange Rate in Nigeria, 1970–2007: An Empirical Analysis." *Indian Journal of Economics and Business*. http://www.thefreelibrary.com/Determinants+of+exchange+rate+in+Nigeria,+1970-2007%3A+an+empirical . . . -a0225073258.

Obinwanne, Odimgbe. 1986. "Coping with the Challenges of Drug Distribution Today: A Survey of the Nigerian Drug Industry." *Nigerian Journal of Pharmacy* 17, 3 (May–June): 25–26.

Oboho, K. O. 1984. "Problems of Venereal Disease in Nigeria. 1. Gonococcal Resistance to Antibiotics and Treatment of Gonorrhoea." *Family Practice* 1: 219–21.

Ofeimun, Odia. 2008. "A Kind of Lovemaking." In *I Will Ask Questions with Stones If They Take My Voice*, 22–24. Lagos, Nigeria: Hornbill.

Ogbuagu, Chibuzo S. A. 1983. "The Nigerian Indigenization Policy: Nationalism or Pragmatism?" *African Affairs* 82, no. 327: 241–66.

Ohaeri, Roland. 2002. "Impoverished Pharmacists." *Pharmanews* 24, no. 2 (February): 15.

Ohaju-Obobo, J. O., A. O. Isah, and A. F. B. Mabadeje. 1998. "Prescribing Pattern of Clinicians in Private Health Institutions in Edo and Delta States of Nigeria." *Nigerian Quarterly Journal of Hospital Medicine* 8, no. 2 (April–June): 91–94.

Okeke, Iruka. 2011. *Divining Without Seeds: The Case for Strengthening Laboratory Medicine in Africa*. Ithaca, NY: Cornell University Press.

Okeke, Iruka N., Susan T. Fayinka, and Adebayo Lamikanra. 2000. "Antibiotic Resistance in Escherichia coli from Nigerian Students, 1986–1998." *Emerging Infectious Diseases* 6, no. 4 (July–August). doi:10.3201/eid0604.009913.

Okelola, Kunle. 2009. *Pharmaceutical Manufacturers Group of the Manufacturers Association of Nigeria: An Overview of the Pharmaceutical Sector*. Abuja, Nigeria: PMG-MAN.

Okereke, S. E. 1987. "With and Without Conditionality in Selling Some Pharmaceuticals in Nigeria: What Can Go Wrong." *Pharmanews* 9, no. 7 (November): 12.

Okereke, S. E. 1988. "Pharmacy Profession in Nigeria: Image on the Line." *Pharmanews* 10, no. 1 (January): 12–14.

Okesola, A. O., and T. I. Aroundegbe. 2011. "Antibiotic Resistance Pattern of Uropathogenic *Escherichia coli* in South West Nigeria." *African Journal of Medicine and Medical Sciences* 40, no. 3 (September): 235–38.

Okoli, Stella. n.d. *The Pharmaceutical Industry in Nigeria: Historical Review, Problems and Expectations*. Lagos: PGM-MAN.

Okoli, Stella C., and Emma Ebere. 2001. "Dangers Posed to Life and the Economy by Drugs and Medicines from Illegal Sources: A Presentation to the Public Hearing of the Health and Social Services Committee." Federal House of Representatives, National Assembly. Lagos: PGM-MAN.

Okome, Mojubaolu Olufunke. 1998. *A Sapped Democracy: The Political Economy of the Structural Adjustment Program and the Political Transition in Nigeria*. Lanham, MD: University Press of America.

Okonjo-Iweala, Ngozi, Charles C. Soludo, and Mansur Muhtar. 2003. *The Debt Trap in Nigeria: Towards a Sustainable Debt Strategy*. Trenton, NJ: Africa World Press.

Olaniyan, R. Omotayo, and Chibuzo Nwoke, eds. 1990. *Structural Adjustment in Nigeria: The Impact of SFEM on the Economy*. Lagos, Nigeria: Nigerian Institute of International Affairs.

Olaoye, Ben. 1991. "Flaws in Dispensing." *Pharmanews* 13, no. 1: 10.

Olowe, O., B. Okanlawon, R. Olowe, and A. Olayemi. 2008. "Antimicrobial Resistant Pattern of *Escherichia Coli* from Human Clinical Samples in Osogbo, South Western Nigeria." *African Journal of Microbiology Research* 2, no. 1 (January): 8–11.

Olugbenga, Ebenezer Olatunji. 2013. "The Politics of Pharmaceutical Regulation in Nigeria: Policy Options for Third World Countries." *Public Policy and Administration Research* 3, no. 8: 80–101.

Olukoshi, Adebayo, ed. 1993. *The Politics of Structural Adjustment in Nigeria*. London: James Currey.

Olukoshi, Adebayo, ed. 1996. *Economic Crisis, Structural Adjustment and the Coping Strategies of Manufacturers in Kano, Nigeria*. Geneva: United Nations Research Institute for Social Development.

Olutayo, Olanrewaju Akinpelu. 1999. "The Igbo Entrepreneur in the Political Economy of Nigeria." *African Study Monographs* 20, no. 3 (September): 147–74.

Omoregie, R., and N. O. Eghafona. 2009. "Urinary Tract Infection among Asymptomatic HIV Patients in Benin City, Nigeria." *British Journal of Biomedical Science* 66, no. 4: 190–93.

Ong, Aiwha. 1999. *Flexible Citizenship: The Cultural Logics of Transnationality*. Durham, NC: Duke University Press.

Ong, Aiwha. 2006. *Neoliberalism as Exception: Mutations in Citizenship and Sovereignty*. Durham, NC: Duke University Press.

"Only 30% Drugs in Nigeria Are Genuine." 1987. *Pharmanews* 9, no. 7 (July): 1.

Onukawa, M. C. 1998. "An Anthropolinguistic Study of Igbo Market-Day Anthroponyms." *Journal of African Cultural Studies* 11, no. 1: 73–83.

Onwuejeogwu, M. Angulu. 1981. *An Igbo Civilization: Nri Kingdom and Hegemony*. Ibadan, Nigeria: Tabansi Press.

Oparah, O. Victor. 2005. "NAFDAC: Sustaining the Grip on the Campaign Against the Production, Importation, Exportation, Advertisement, and Distribution of Fake and Adulterated Food and Drug Products in Nigeria." Presented at the National

Workshop on Regulation of ARV/OI Drugs and Related Biological Products. May 26, Lagos, Nigeria.

Oyelese, A. O., and E. A. Oyewo. 1995. "The Menace of Beta-Lactamase Production on Antibiotic Prescription in Community Acquired-Infections in Nigeria." *African Journal of Medicine and Medical Sciences* 24, no. 2 (June): 125–30.

Ozumba, Uchenna C. 2007. "Bacteriology of Wound Infections in the Surgical Wards of a Teaching Hospital in Enugu, Nigeria." *African Journal of Medicine and Medical Sciences* 36, no. 4 (December): 341–44.

Pang, Laikwan. 2008. "'China Who Makes and Fakes': A Semiotics of the Counterfeit." *Theory, Culture and Society* 25, no. 6: 117–40.

Parry, Jonathan, and Maurice Block. 1989. *Money and the Morality of Exchange.* Cambridge: Cambridge University Press.

Peel, John D. Y. 2000. *Religious Encounter and the Making of the Yoruba.* Bloomington: Indiana University Press.

"Percentages of Locally Produced Drugs." 1979. *Nigerian Journal of Pharmacy* 9, no. 6: 3–6.

Peterson, Kristin. 2001. "Benefit Sharing for All? Bioprospecting NGOs, Intellectual Property Rights, New Governmentalities." *Political and Legal Anthropology Review* 24, no. 1 (May): 78–91.

Peterson, Kristin. 2009. "Phantom Epistemologies." In *Fieldwork Is Not What It Used to Be: Learning Anthropology's Method in a Time of Transition,* ed. James D. Faubion and George E. Marcus, 37–51. Ithaca, NY: Cornell University Press.

Peterson, Kristin. 2012a. "AIDS Policies for Markets and Warriors: Dispossession, Capital, and Pharmaceuticals in Nigeria." In *Lively Capital: Biotechnologies, Ethics and Governance in Global Markets,* ed. Kaushik Sunder Rajan, 228–43. Durham, NC: Duke University Press.

Peterson, Kristin. 2012b. "Intellectual Property Designs: Drugs, Governance, and Nigerian (Non) Compliance with the World Trade Organization." In *Rethinking Biomedicine and Governance in Africa: Contributions from Anthropology,* ed. Richard Rottenberg, Julia Zenker, and Wenzel Geissler, 141–60. Bielefeld, Germany: Transcript [Verlag für Kommunikation, Kultur und Soziale Praxis].

Petryna, Adriana. 2002. *Life Exposed: Biological Citizens After Chernobyl.* Princeton, NJ: Princeton University Press.

Petryna, Adriana, Andrew Lakoff, and Arthur Kleinman, eds. 2006. *Global Pharmaceuticals: Ethics, Markets, Practices.* Durham, NC: Duke University Press.

Pfizer. 2000. "The 2000 Annual Report." Accessed October 11, 2011. http://www.sec .gov/Archives/edgar/data/78003/000095012301002716/y46668ex13-a.htm.

"Pfizer Divests, Neimeth Is Born." 1997. *Pharmanews* 19, no. 4: 1.

"Pfizer Products PLC." 1992. *Pharmanews* 14, no. 6: 12.

Pharmacists Council of Nigeria. 1992. "Pharmacists Council of Nigeria Decree 1992." *Official Gazette Extraordinary* 7, no. 9 (December 31): Part A—A1065.

Pharmacists Council of Nigeria. 2005. "Pharmacists Council of Nigeria Act (1992 No. 91) Inspection, Location and Structure of Pharmaceutical Premises Regulation." *Federal Republic of Nigeria Official Gazette* 92, no. 152 (August 10): 147–51.

Phillips, Adedotun. 1992. *The Nominalization of the Nigerian Economy*. Ibadan, Nigeria: Niser Institute for Social and Economic Research.

Phillips, Kevin. 2008. *Bad Money: Reckless Finance, Failed Politics, and the Global Crisis of American Capitalism*. New York: Viking.

Pigou, Arthur C. [1920] 2012. *The Economics of Welfare*. Oxford: Oxford University Press.

Pore, Mridula, Yu Pu, Lakshman Pernenkil, and Charles Cooney. 2008. "Offshoring in the Pharmaceutical Industry." In *The Offshoring of Engineering: Facts, Unknowns, and Potential Implications*, Committee of the Offshoring of Engineering, 103–24. Washington, DC: National Academy of Engineering.

Portes, Alejandro, and William Haller. 2005. "The Informal Economy." In *Handbook of Economic Sociology*, ed. Neal J. Smelser and Richard Swedberg. 2nd ed. New York: Russell Sage Foundation.

"PSN Wades in Import License Crisis." 1984. *Pharmanews* 6, no. 8: 1.

Rabinow, Paul. 1992. "Artificiality and Enlightenment: From Sociobiology to Biosociality." In *Incorporations*, ed. Jonathan Crary and Sanford Kwinter, 190–201. New York: Zone.

Raghavan, Chakravarthi. 1990. *Recolonization: GATT, The Uruguay Round, and the Third World*. London: Zed.

Reardon, Jenny. 2004. *Race to the Finish: Identity and Governance in the Age of Genomics*. Princeton, NJ: Princeton University Press.

Redfield, Peter. 2013. *Life in Crisis: The Ethical Journey of Doctors without Borders*. Berkeley: University of California Press.

Reed, Carol, dir. and prod. 1949. *The Third Man*. London: British Lion Film Corporation.

Reference for Business. n.d. "Pfizer Inc." Accessed November 10, 2010. http://www .referenceforbusiness.com/history2/42/Pfizer-Inc.html.

Ricardo, David. [1817] 1996. *On the Principles of Political Economy and Taxation*. Amherst, NY: Prometheus.

Roitman, Janet. 2005. *Fiscal Disobedience: An Anthropology of Economic Regulation in Central Africa*. Princeton, NJ: Princeton University Press.

Rothkopf, David. 2012. *Power, Inc.: The Epic Rivalry Between Big Business and Government—and the Reckoning That Lies Ahead*. New York: Macmillan.

Sachs, Jeffrey D., and Henry Huizinga. 1987. "US Commercial Banks and the Developing Country Debt Crisis." NBER Working Paper Series, Working Paper No. 2455. Cambridge, MA: National Bureau of Economic Research. Accessed July 21, 2012. http://www.nber.org/papers/w2455.

Sahoo, Alison. 2012. *The CMO Market Outlook to 2017: Emerging Markets, Key Players and Future Trends*. Zug, Switzerland: Informa.

Salako, Lateef. 1997. "Health for All Nigerians—So Far, So What?" *Nigerian Quarterly Journal of Hospital Medicine* 7, no. 3: 199–206.

Samba, Ebrahim Malick. 2004. "African Health Care Systems: What Went Wrong?" *News Medical*. December 8. Accessed August 25, 2013. http://www.news-medical.net /?id=6770.

Sankara, Thomas. 2007. *Thomas Sankara Speaks: The Burkina Faso Revolution 1983–87.* Atlanta: Pathfinder Press.

Sanusi, Joseph O. 1987. "Nigeria's External Debt: Genesis, Structure, and Management." *The Central Bank Bullion* 11, no. 3: 6–14.

Saro Wiwa, Ken. 1989. *On a Darkling Plain: An Account of the Nigerian Civil War.* Epson, UK: Saros.

Savage, G. M. 1973. "Spectinomycin Related to the Chemotherapy of Gonorrhea." *Infection* 1, no. 4: 227–33.

Schoepf, Brooke G., Claude Schoepf, and Joyce V. Millen. 2000. "Theoretical Therapies, Remote Remedies: SAPs and the Political Ecology of Poverty and Health in Africa." In *Dying for Growth: Global Inequality and the Health of the Poor,* ed. J. Y. Kim et al., 91–125. Monroe, ME: Common Courage Press.

Schultz, Theodore. 1961. "Investment in Human Capital." *American Economic Review* 51, no. 1: 1–17.

Schumpeter, Joseph A. 2008. *Capitalism, Socialism, and Democracy.* New York: HarperCollins.

Seers, Dudley. [1963] 1970. "The Stages of Economic Development of a Primary Producer in the Middle of the Twentieth Century." In *Imperialism and Underdevelopment: A Reader,* ed. Robert I. Rhodes, 163–80. New York: Monthly Review Press.

Sell, Susan. 1997. *Power and Ideas: North-South Politics of Intellectual Property and Antitrust.* Albany: State University of New York Press.

Sell, Susan. 2004. "What Role for Humanitarian Intellectual Property? The Globalization of Intellectual Property Rights." *Minnesota Journal of Legal Science and Technology Studies* 6, no. 1: 191–211.

Shankar, Daya. 2002. "Brazil, the Pharmaceutical Industry, and the WTO." *Journal of World Intellectual Property* 5, no. 1: 53–104.

"Shortfall in Drug Import Caused by Fake Companies." 1985. *Pharmanews* 7, no. 4: 1.

Silverman, Milton, and Philip Randolph Lee. 1992. *Bad Medicine: The Prescription Drug Industry in the Third World.* Palo Alto, CA: Stanford University Press.

Simone, AbdouMaliq. 2001. "Straddling the Divides: Remaking Associational Life in the Informal African City." *International Journal of Urban and Regional Research* 25, no. 1: 102–17.

Simone, AbdouMaliq. 2004. "People as Infrastructure: Intersecting Fragments in Johannesburg." *Public Culture* 16, no. 3: 407–29.

Simone, AbdouMaliq. 2011. "Deals with Imaginaries and Perspectives: Reworking Urban Economics in Kinshasa." *Social Dynamics* 37, no. 1 (March): 111–24.

Sklar, Richard. 1998. *African Politics in Postimperial Times: The Essays of Richard L. Sklar,* ed. Toyin Falola. New Brunswick, NJ: Africa World Press.

Smith, Adam. [1776] 1991. *An Inquiry into the Nature and Causes of the Wealth of Nations.* General eds. R. H. Campbell and A. S. Skinner; textual ed. W. B. Todd. Oxford: Clarendon Press.

Smith, Daniel. 2008. *A Culture of Corruption: Everyday Deception and Popular Discontent in Nigeria.* Princeton, NJ: Princeton University Press.

Sowunmi, Idowa, and Steve Dada. 2007. "Nigeria: Akunyili—Onitsha Drug Market, Den of Criminals." *This Day*. Accessed May 18, 2010. http://allafrica.com/stories /200703200218.html

Soyibo, Adedoyin. 1997. "The Informal Financial Sector in Nigeria: Characteristics and Relationship with the Formal Sector." *Development Policy Review* 15, no. 1: 5–22.

Stein, Howard. 2008. *Beyond the World Bank Agenda: An Institutional Approach to Development.* Chicago: University of Chicago Press.

Stein, Howard, Olu Ajakaiye, and Peter Lewis, eds. 2002. *Deregulation and the Banking Crisis in Nigeria: A Comparative Study.* New York: Palgrave Macmillan.

Strathern, Marilyn. 1990. *The Gender of the Gift: Problems with Women and Problems with Society in Melanesia.* Berkeley: University of California Press.

Strathern, Marilyn. 1999. *Property, Substance, and Effect: Anthropological Essays on Persons and Things.* New Brunswick, NJ: Athlone Press.

Sudarkasa, Niara. 1973. *Where Women Work: A Study of Yoruba Women in the Marketplace and in the Home.* Ann Arbor: University of Michigan Press.

Sunder Rajan, Kaushik. 2006. *Biocapital: The Constitution of Postgenomic Life.* Durham, NC: Duke University Press.

Sunder Rajan, Kaushik. 2011. "Property, Rights, and the Constitution of Contemporary Indian Biomedicine: Notes from the Gleevec Case." *Social Research* 78, no. 3: 975–98.

Sunder Rajan, Kaushik. 2012. "Pharmaceutical Crises and Questions of Value: Terrains and Logics of Global Therapeutic Politics." *South Atlantic Quarterly* 111, no. 2 (spring): 321–46.

Taylor, R. B., O. Shakoor, R. H. Behrens, M. Everard, A. S. Low, J. Wangboonskul, R. G. Reid, and J. A. Kolawole. 2001. "Pharmacopoeial Quality of Drugs Supplied by Nigerian Pharmacies." *Lancet* 357, no. 9272: 1933–36.

t'Hoen, Ellen F. M. 2003. "TRIPS, Pharmaceutical Patents and Access to Essential Medicines: Seattle, Doha and Beyond." In *Economics of AIDS and Access to HIV/AIDS Care in Developing Countries: Issues and Challenges,* ed. Jean-Paul Moatti, Benjamin Coriat, Yves Souteyrand, Tony Barnett, Jérôme Dumoulin, and Yves-Antoine Flori, 39–68. Paris: Agence Nationale de Researches sur la Sida (ANRS).

Thomas-Emeagwali, Gloria. 1995. *Women Pay the Price: Structural Adjustment in Africa and the Caribbean.* New Brunswick, NJ: Africa World Press.

Tobin-West, Charles I., and Foluke O. Adeniji. 2012. "Knowledge and Practices of Patent Medicine Vendors in Rivers State, Nigeria: Implications for Malaria Control in Rural and Sub-Urban Communities." *Indian Journal of Pharmacy Practice* 5, no. 1 (January–March): 34–39.

Tranberg, Karen, and Mariken Vaa, eds. 2004. *Informality Reconsidered: Perspectives from Urban Africa.* Uppsala, Sweden: Nordic Africa Institute.

Tsing, Anna Lowenhaupt. 2005. *Friction: An Ethnography of Global Connection.* Princeton, NJ: Princeton University Press.

Turshen, Meredeth. 1976. "An Analysis of the Medical Supply Industry." *International Journal of Health Services* 6, no. 2: 271–94.

Turshen, Meredeth. 1999. *Privatizing Health Services in Africa.* New Brunswick, NJ: Rutgers University Press.

Uche, Chibuike. 2004. "Ethics in Nigerian Banking." *Journal of Money Laundering Control* 8, no. 1 (September): 66–74.

Uchendu, Victor. 2007. "Ezi Na Ulo: The Extended Family in Igbo Civilization." *Dialectical Anthropology* 31, nos. 1–3: 167–219.

Uchendu, Victor C., George Spindler, and Louise Spindler, eds. 1965. *The Igbo of Southeast Nigeria.* New York: Holt, Rinehart and Winston.

Ugbodaga, Kazeem. 2010. "Lagos Shuts Down 1,253 Illegal Pharmaceutical Shops." *PM News,* Lagos, October 22.

Ujumadu, Vin. 1986. "Drug Importation and Import License." *Pharmanews* 8, no. 10 (October): 6.

United States Food and Drug Administration. 2011. *Pathway to Global Product Safety and Quality.* Accessed April 5, 2013. http://www.fda.gov/AboutFDA/CentersOffices /OfficeofGlobalRegulatoryOperationsandPolicy/GlobalProductPathway/default .htm.

United States Food and Drug Administration. 2013. *Global Engagement.* Accessed April 5, 2013. http://www.fda.gov/downloads/AboutFDA/ReportsManualsForms/Reports /UCM298578.pdf.

UN Office on Drugs and Crime. 2009. *Transnational Trafficking and the Rule of Law in West Africa: A Threat Assessment.* Vienna: UN Office on Drugs and Crime.

Uwaezuoke, Emmanuel. 1991. "Adulterated Drugs: Pharmacists Take Census." *Guardian Financial Weekly,* April 15, 20.

Van der Geest, Sjaak. 1988. "The Articulation of Formal and Informal Medicine Distribution in South Cameroon." In *The Context of Medicines in Developing Countries: Studies in Pharmaceutical Anthropology,* ed. Sjaak van der Geest and Susan Reynolds Whyte, 131–48. Dordrecht, The Netherlands: Kluwer Academic Publishers.

Van der Geest, Sjaak, Susan Reynolds Whyte, and Anita Hardon. 1996. "The Anthropology of Pharmaceuticals: A Biographical Approach." *Annual Review of Anthropology* 25: 153–78.

Van Rinsum, Henk J., and Godfrey B. Tangwa. 2004. "Colony of Genes, Genes of the Colony: Diversity, Difference and Divide." *Third World Quarterly* 25, no. 6: 1031–43.

Vasuvendan, Parvathi. 2010. "The Changing Nature of Nigeria–India Relations." London: Chatham House. Accessed November 17, 2011. http://www.chathamhouse.org /publications/papers/view/109543.

Vaughan, Megan. 1991. *Curing Their Ills: Colonial Power and African Illness.* Palo Alto, CA: Stanford University Press.

Verger, Pierre. 1976. *Trade Relations between the Bight of Benin and Bahia from the 17th to 19th Century.* Translated by Evelyn Crawford. Ibadan: Ibadan University Press.

Vernon, John. 2003. "The Relationship between Price Regulation and Pharmaceutical Profit Margins." *Applied Economics Letters* 10, no. 8: 467–70.

Verran, Helen. 1998. "Re-imagining Land Ownership in Australia." *Postcolonial Studies* 1, no. 2: 237–54.

Verran, Helen. 2001. *Science and African Logic*. Chicago: University of Chicago Press.

Virk, Karen Politis. 2008. "Biopharmaceutical Manufacturing and Offshoring in Puerto Rico—Linguistic and Cultural Challenges." Language Connections, June, Boston. Accessed June 15, 2012. www.languageconnections.com/portal/descargas/White Paper_BiopharmaManufacturing_PuertoRico.pdf.

Wambebe, Charles, and Nelson Ochekpe. 2011. *Pharmaceutical Sector Profile: Nigeria*. Vienna: United Nations Industrial Development Organization. Accessed January 13, 2012. http://www.unido.org/fileadmin/user_media/Services/PSD/BEP/Nigeria _Pharma%20Sector%20Profile_032011_Ebook.pdf.

Watts, Michael. 1984. "State, Oil, and Accumulation: From Boom to Bust." *Society and Space* 2: 402–28.

West African Health Organization. 2011. *Roundtable: A Joint Action against Fake Medicine in West Africa*. Bobo-Dioulasso, Burkina Faso: WAHO. Accessed December 15, 2011. http://www.diplomatie.gouv.fr/fr/IMG/pdf/General_Report_Ouagadougou _Round_Table-En_cle4746d9.pdf.

Whitehead, Alfred N. 1978. *Process and Reality*. New York: Free Press.

Whyte, Susan Reynolds, Sjaak van der Geest, and Anita Hardon, eds. 2003. *Social Lives of Medicines*. Cambridge: Cambridge University Press.

Williams, Gavin. 1985. "Marketing without and with Marketing Boards: The Origins of State Marketing Boards in Nigeria." *Review of African Political Economy* 12, no. 34 (December): 4–15.

Wiseberg, Laurie Sheila. 1973. "The International Politics of Relief: A Case Study of the Relief Operations Mounted During the Nigerian Civil War, 1967–1970." PhD diss., University of California, Los Angeles.

World Bank. 1981. *Accelerated Development in Sub-Saharan Africa: An Agenda for Action*. Washington, DC: World Bank.

World Bank. 2005. "Household Final Consumption Expenditure per Capita (constant 2005 US$)." Accessed July 16, 2013. http://data.worldbank.org/indicator/NE.CON .PRVT.PC.KD.

World Intellectual Property Organization. 2013. "Statistical Country Profiles: Nigeria." Accessed November 16. http://www.wipo.int/ipstats/en/statistics/countryprofile /countries/ng.html.

World Trade Organization. 1998. "Structural Reforms and Increased Transparency Needed to Generate Trade and Growth in Nigeria." Trade Policy Reviews: First Press Release, Secretariat and Government Summaries. Geneva: World Trade Organization. Accessed December 12, 2004. http://www.wto.org/english/tratop_e/tpr_e/tp75_e .htm

Yai, Olabiyi Babalola. 2001. "The Identity, Contributions, and Ideology of the Aguda (Afro-Brazilians) of the Gulf of Benin: A Reinterpretation." *Slavery and Abolition* 22, no. 1: 61–71.

Yankus, Wyatt. 2006. "Counterfeit Drugs: Coming to a Pharmacy Near You." *American Council on Science and Health*. August 24. Accessed April 15, 2011. http://www.acsh .org/publications/pubID.1379/pub_detail.asp.

Yeboah, Sybil Ossei Agyeman. 2013. "The Illicit Trafficking of Counterfeit Medicines." Presentation made at the Technical Conference of Experts on the Trafficking in Fraudulent Medicines. UN Office of Drugs and Crime (UNODC), Vienna, Austria, February 14–15.

Zaslavsky, Claudia. 1973. *Africa Counts: Number and Pattern in African Culture*. Boston: Prindle, Weber, and Schmidt.

# INDEX

Eban, Katherine, 143
Ebogu, Afam, 199n14
Ecks, Stefan, 175
economics and economic theory, 73, 104,
     120; Austrian School, 111, 194n21; Bretton
     Woods system, 168, 199n9, 205n22;
     Chicago School, 113; Igbo Market theory,
     113–15; informal/formal economy, 83, 90–94,
     125, 188n1, 196n6; Keynesian economics,
     111; nationalization, 44; nominalization,
     104, 197–98n2; open economies, 153;
     popular economy, 26, 38, 81, 83, 89, 91–93,
     107, 117, 124; post-Fordist capitalism,
     192n4, 198n7; Yoruba Market theory,
     112–13, 199n13
Edelman, Mark, and Angelique Haugerud,
     187n17
Ehianeta, Teddy, 10
Ellis, Stephen, 196n9
Emeagwali, Gloria, 170
ethnography, x, 181
extended-spectrum beta-lactamases (ESBL),
     131–33

Falola, Toyin, 195n1
Fanon, Franz, 65
*Felix Ugbojiaku & 2 Ors v Attorney General of
     the Federation & 4 Ors*, 84, 95–101
Ferguson, James, 187n17
financialization, 180
Food and Drugs Act, 196n4
"foreign exchange scarcity," 47
Forrest, Tom, 199n16
Fortun, Kim, 152
Fortun, Mike, 194n19
Foucault, Michel, 63, 113–14, 193n16,
     199n12
Fourchard, Laurent, and Ayodeji Olukoju,
     195n1
free-trade zones, 144, 146
Freund, Bill, 41, 190n15, 191n23

genomics, 194n19
globalization, 181–82, 187n17
Golden Crescent, 196n7
Guyer, Jane, 92, 93, 117, 188n1, 200n20, 201n23,
     205n22

Hart, Keith, 196n6
Harvey, David, 191n22, 192n4
Hashim, Yahaya, and Kate Meagher, 92,
     197n13
Hayden, Cori, 152, 153, 197n15
Hill, Polly, 200n19
HIV/AIDS, ix, 8, 156, 161–62, 174, 193n16
Ho, Karen, 72
Hopkins, Anthony, 205n22
Hudson, Michael, 168
human capital theory, 113–15, 199n11

Idumota Drug Market, 7, 9, 39, 57, 101–2, 105;
     and PCN, 95–100; and drug task force,
     148; as main market, 16–17, 81–82; as open
     market, 95–96; description, 15–17, 25–33,
     189n10; history of, 33, 35–40; market
     volume, 42, 189n6
Ifeka-Moller, Caroline, 192n7
Igbos, 27, 35, 103, 113, 189n8, 189nn10–13, 198n4,
     199nn13–14; civil war, 35, 37; credit as-
     sociations, 198n4; diaspora, 36–37;
     entrepreneurialism, 36–38; market liberal-
     ism, 22, 105, 113–15; traders, 21, 34, 50–51, 79,
     81, 105, 120, 139 (*see also* apprenticeship)
import substitution policies, 66, 180, 190n16
India, 137, 154, 175, 183, 203n12, 204n15; and
     fake drugs, 145–46, 148; and intellectual
     property, 175–76; and offshore drug manu-
     facturing, 127, 140–41; acquiring American
     and European drug firms, 141; generic drug
     manufacturers, 21; exported drugs to Nige-
     ria, 43, 88–89, 106, 119, 128; overseas inspec-
     tion, 12; trading partner with China, 141
indigenization, 44, 49, 68; decree (1972), 66,
     190n19
intellectual property (IP), 156, 163, 164, 206n5;
     law, 23, 31, 141, 164, 179, 205n20; "fair ex-
     change" as legal fiction, 165, 167–68
—patent, 206; Bolar exception, 207n12;
     secure monopoly, 167; patent law, 165, 182;
     patent rights, 164–65
International Monetary Fund (IMF), 4, 54,
     62, 66, 109, 111–12, 170, 192n2, 193nn12–13;
     Support Policy Instrument, 198n8
Interpol, 148
Isah, Ambrose O., 161